DARKLIGHT™

KULTGEN   KOWALSKI

Published by
ARCHAIA™

Published by **Archaia**
A Division of **Boom Entertainment, Inc.**
WWW.ARCHAIA.COM

BOOM! Studios
5670 Wilshire Boulevard, Suite 450
Los Angeles, California 90036-5679

ROSS RICHIE CEO & Founder · **JACK CUMMINS** COO & President · **MARK SMYLIE** Chief Creative Officer · **MATT GAGNON** Editor-in-Chief · **FILIP SABLIK** VP of Publishing & Marketing
STEPHEN CHRISTY VP of Development · **LANCE KREITER** VP of Licensing & Merchandising · **PHIL BARBARO** VP of Finance · **BRYCE CARLSON** Managing Editor · **MEL CAYLO** Marketing Manager
SCOTT NEWMAN Production Design Manager · **IRENE BRADISH** Operations Manager · **DAFNA PLEBAN** Editor · **SHANNON WATTERS** Editor · **ERIC HARBURN** Editor · **REBECCA TAYLOR** Editor
IAN BRILL Editor · **CHRIS ROSA** Assistant Editor · **ALEX GALER** Assistant Editor · **WHITNEY LEOPARD** Assistant Editor · **JASMINE AMIRI** Assistant Editor · **CAMERON CHITTOCK** Assistant Editor
HANNAH NANCE PARTLOW Production Designer · **KELSEY DIETERICH** Production Designer · **DEVIN FUNCHES** E-Commerce & Inventory Coordinator · **ANDY LIEGL** Event Coordinator
BRIANNA HART Executive Assistant · **AARON FERRARA** Operations Assistant · **JOSÉ MEZA** Sales Assistant · **ELIZABETH LOUGHRIDGE** Accounting Assistant

DARKLIGHT, Original Graphic Novel Hardcover, April 2014.

FIRST PRINTING   10 9 8 7 6 5 4 3 2 1   ISBN: 978-1-60886-294-8   eISBN: 978-1-61398-173-3

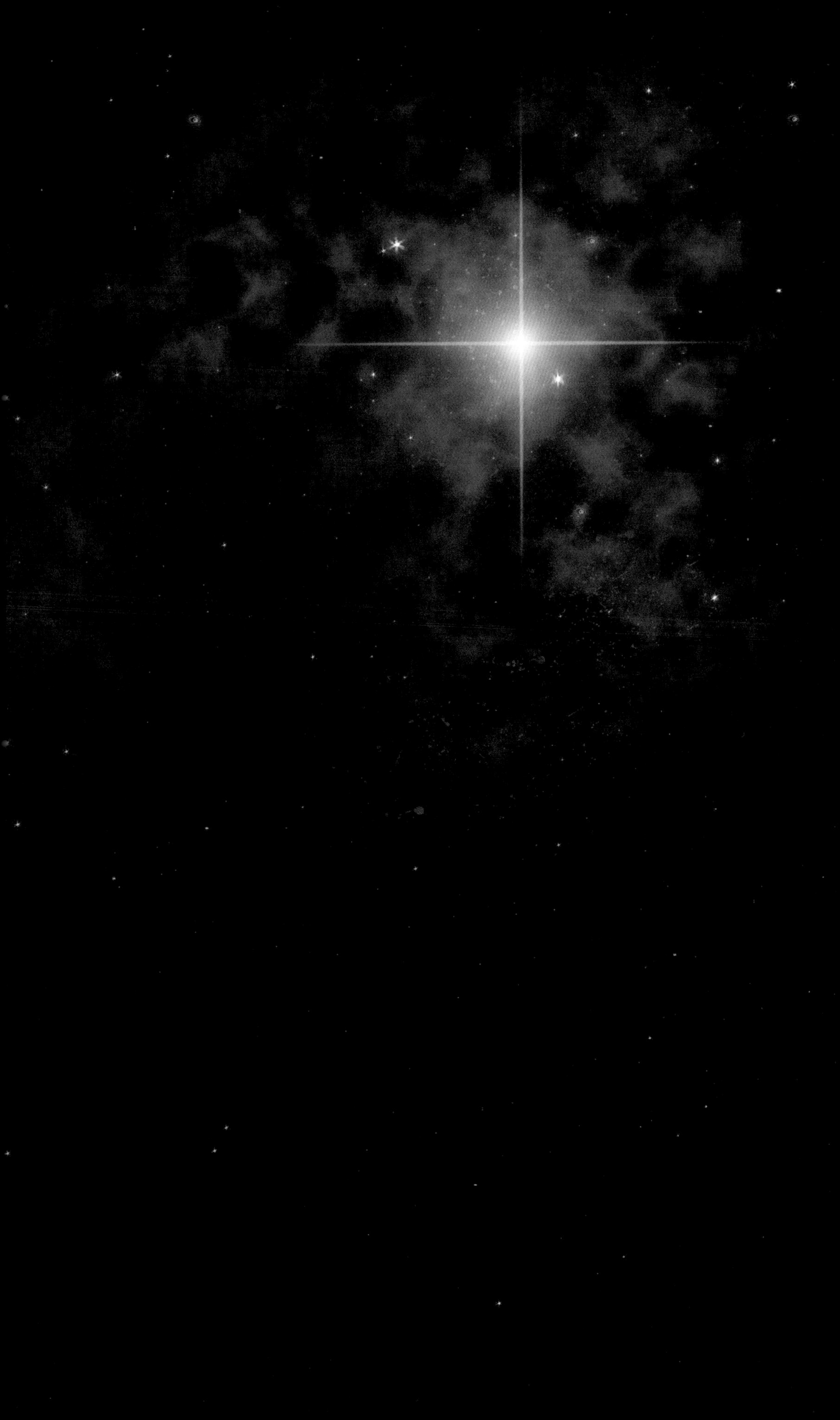

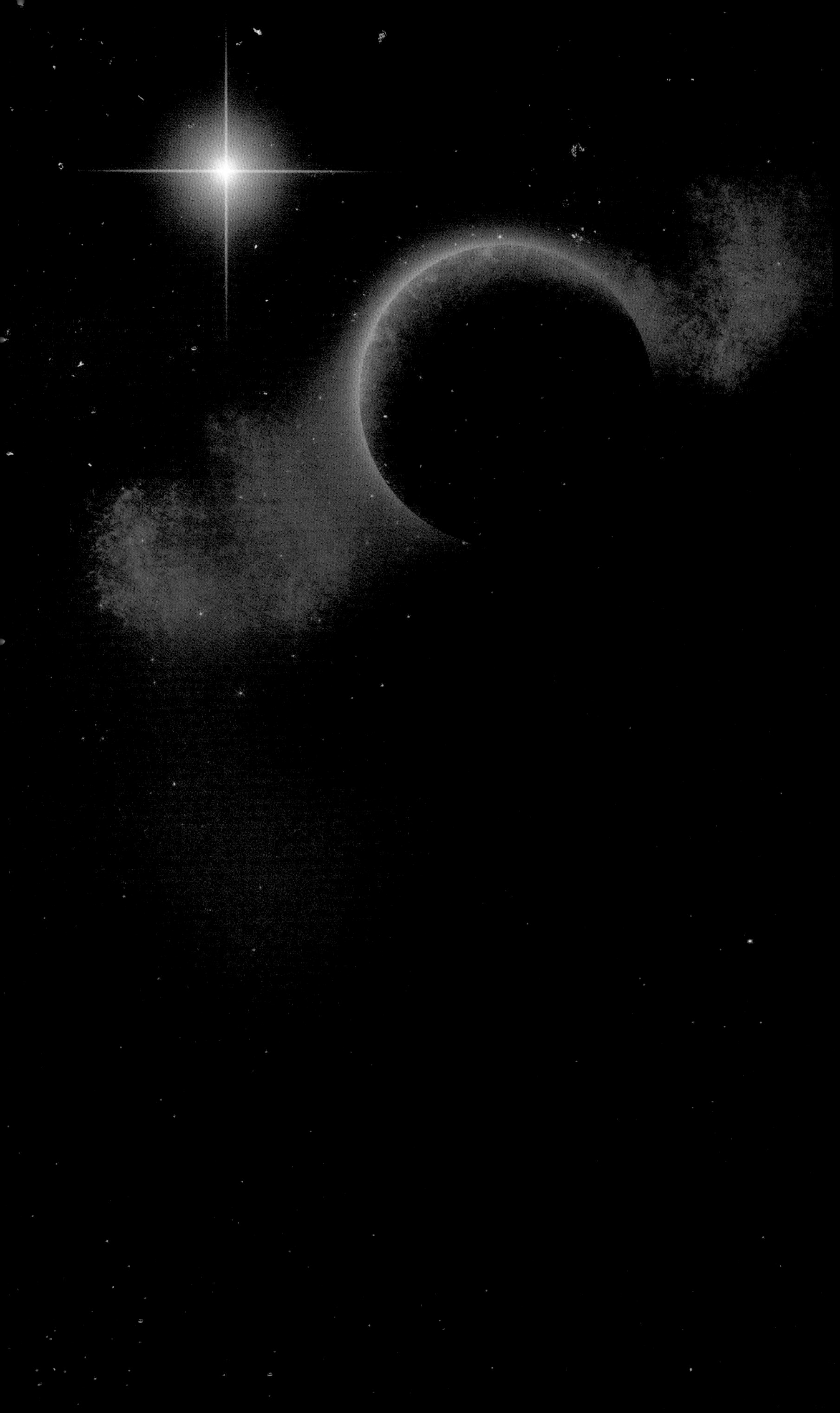

DARKLIGHT™

CREATED AND WRITTEN BY
CHAD KULTGEN

ART BY
PIOTR KOWALSKI

COLORS BY
VLADIMIR POPOV

LETTERS BY
DERON BENNETT

COVER BY
FRAZER IRVING

CHARACTER DESIGNS BY
ALEX MASSACCI AND **PIOTR KOWALSKI**

ASSISTANT EDITOR
ALEX GALER

EDITOR
ERIC HARBURN

DESIGN BY
SCOTT NEWMAN

SPECIAL THANKS
REBECCA TAYLOR

PROLOGUE //

Before we could leave our planet, we poisoned it. We depleted it of every resource we could find a use for. We killed countless trillions in the name of gods that never existed and imaginary lines that were erased and redrawn more times than anyone could remember. We were on the threshold of extinction by our own hand time and time again... but we survived.

When the time eventually came that our Sun threatened to destroy us, we were forced to seek refuge in the stars, and we prepared for the first time to survive threats that were not of our own making.

The first generations living on ships, space stations, and asteroids were hard. Like the steel of a sword folded a thousand times to build strength, being confined to Earth for so long forged a race that could not only survive but could flourish in the deep reaches of space.

We explored everything we could, and we found life. Most was simple and unintelligent, but it was everywhere. Single-celled life was found in asteroids, in seas of ammonia on distant planets, in the cores of ice moons. Multi-cellular life was found on a multitude of planets, and even sentient life existing in tribal, pre-industrial societies was found to exist on hundreds of thousands of worlds across the cosmos. The Human Empire grew as it catalogued all of these things, and in that growth our technology blossomed.

We learned to extend the basic human lifespan to near infinite with cybernetic and genetic enhancements, but were careful to never go so far as to lose what it was that made us human. We harnessed the power of stars to fuel our expansion, and it seemed there was no place in the universe that was out of our reach. And once we had seen so much, we began to wonder if we would ever find another species that was as advanced as we were, that wondered, as we did, if they were alone.

Eventually, we encountered two alien civilizations on the far side of the universe from the place we originally called home. They were locked in a war that had been raging in this isolated corner of the cosmos for millions of years.

One of the two races, the Luminids, had developed a technology entirely based on machines, far more advanced than anything we had ever created. Ultimately, the Luminids created an ever-flowing datastream into which all members of the entire race uploaded their consciousness. This gave them a type of immortality, but not without a price. Luminids very quickly realized the value in making decisions as a group over individual thought. And once every Luminid consciousness had awareness of all others in the datastream, it was immediately apparent that very few of them were unique in their thought patterns and contributions to Luminid society. The rest were redundant, creating unnecessary noise for those who shaped the datastream with unique thought.

A decision was made to erase almost all of the identities swimming through their datastream, leaving only a few thousand. These few thousand, without the burden of interacting with the rest of the billions upon billions of other voices in the datastream, were able to

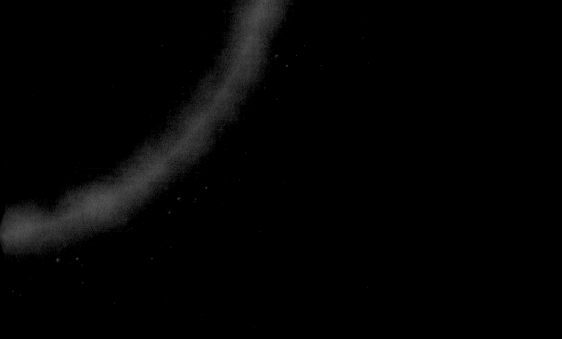

expand their technology even further, and even more rapidly than they already had.

They created technologies that allowed them to inhabit any piece of machinery they constructed and to move from machine to machine at will if they so desired – as if they were ghosts.

They abandoned their home planets in favor of a constructed cluster of intricately linked machines that could house them all and keep the datastream flowing forever.

The other race, the Duron, excelled in medical genetic technology very early in their evolution. They discovered and perfected methods to cure diseases, to repair virtually any injury, and to extend their lives indefinitely. Once the threat of death was eliminated, they expanded knowledge of their own genome exponentially and quickly discovered that living material could be manipulated to suit any purpose they collectively needed. New life forms were created for every possible function in Duron society, and a thousand-tiered caste system developed.

At the top, Duron engineered to have superior cognitive capabilities make all of the decisions for their entire race. Below them, each Duron was created to perform a specific function. Eventually, no life was thought of as sacred or valuable in any way to the Duron except the ruling tier. The Duron culture eventually embraced the expendable nature of the individual.

As we watched the war and strategized about the best way to make first contact, we became aware of something far worse than the war. Long after the last star had burned out, as we floated through the endless black of space, we came to discover that our universe was dying.

At the very edges of the fabric of space-time, things were starting to unravel. The universe's endless expansion had finally started to take its toll, and we faced the inevitable end of existence itself. We developed a plan to stop the collapse of our universe, but we would need the help of both the Luminids and the Duron.

With no more time to decide the best strategy of first contact, we sent a delegation to each civilization to introduce ourselves as Human and to share with each race the information we had about the approaching catastrophe and our plan for a possible way to stop it. It would require them both to end the war they had been fighting for longer than either of them could remember.

They were hesitant, but ultimately both the Luminids and the Duron understood what was at stake. A treaty was agreed upon by both sides, and humanity was understood to be a thoughtful and helpful race.

Humanity offered the solution to the problem – a device that would serve as a super-dense anchor at the core of the universe that, once enabled, would halt its expansion. While our abstract reasoning was our expertise, we needed the other two alien races' technologies to make the device a reality. And beyond that, we needed something dense enough, something with enough mass to allow the device to operate. We needed… a new star.

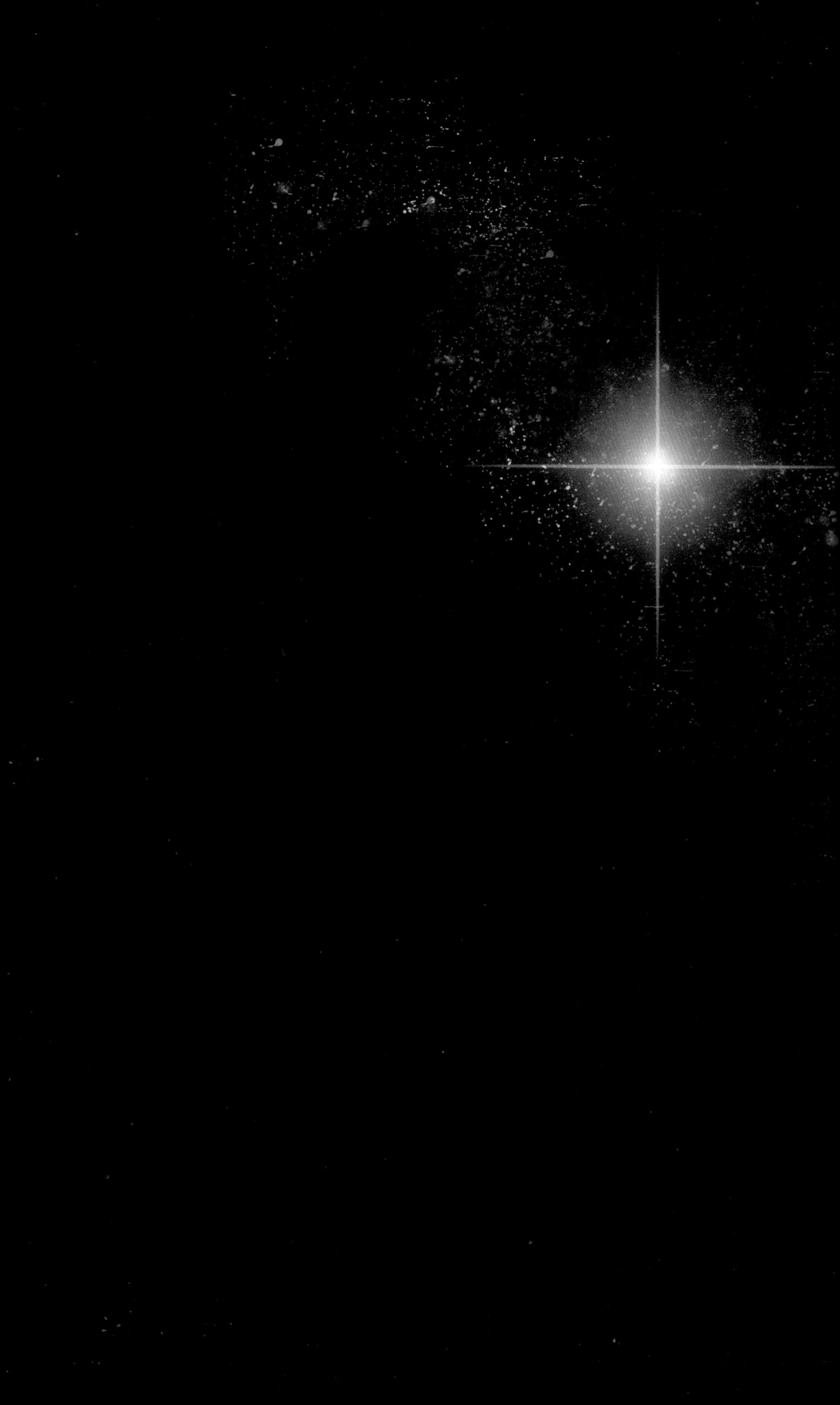

CHAPTER ONE//

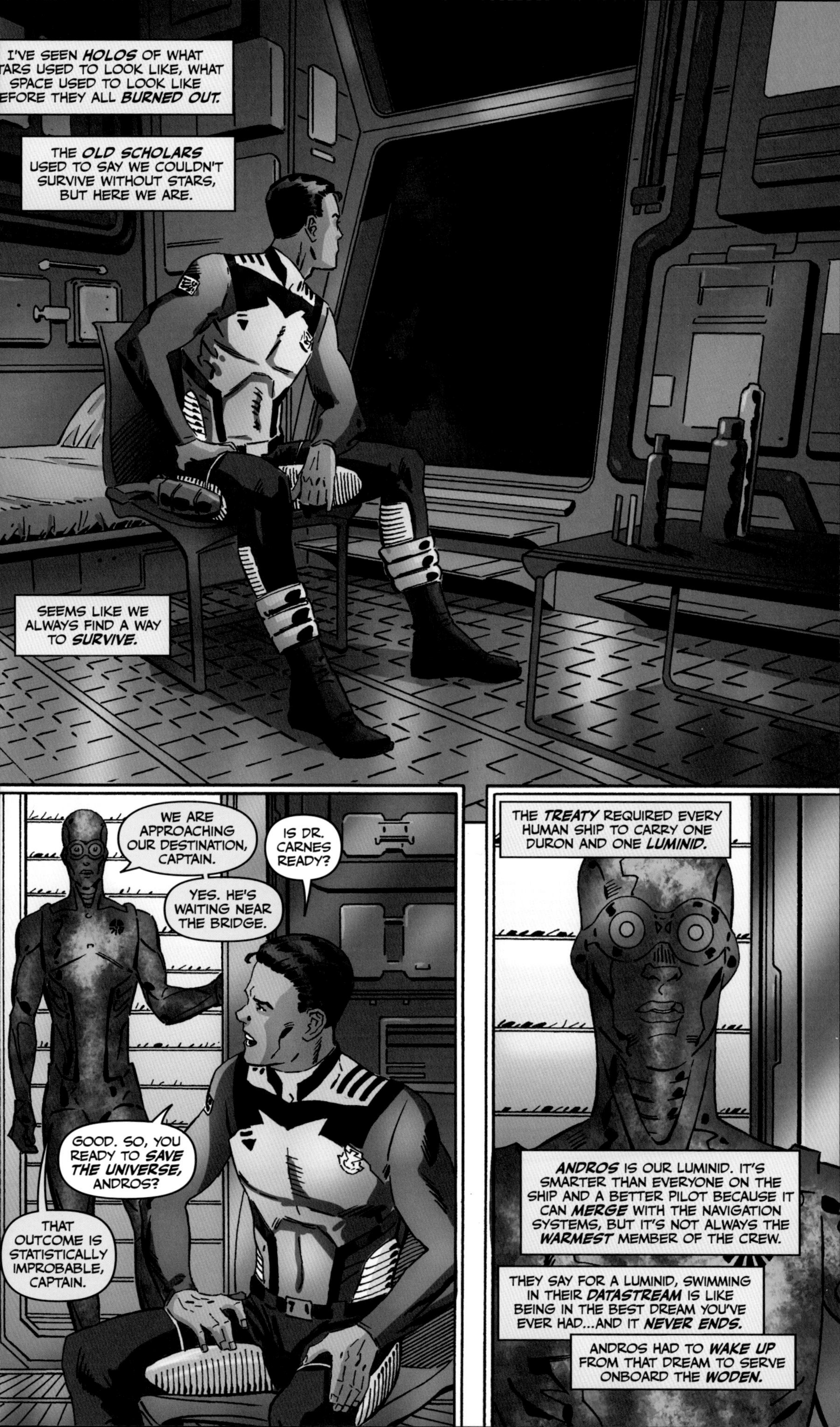
I'VE SEEN HOLOS OF WHAT TARS USED TO LOOK LIKE, WHAT SPACE USED TO LOOK LIKE EFORE THEY ALL BURNED OUT.
THE OLD SCHOLARS USED TO SAY WE COULDN'T SURVIVE WITHOUT STARS, BUT HERE WE ARE.
SEEMS LIKE WE ALWAYS FIND A WAY TO SURVIVE.
WE ARE APPROACHING OUR DESTINATION, CAPTAIN.
IS DR. CARNES READY?
YES. HE'S WAITING NEAR THE BRIDGE.
GOOD. SO, YOU READY TO SAVE THE UNIVERSE, ANDROS?
THAT OUTCOME IS STATISTICALLY IMPROBABLE, CAPTAIN.
THE TREATY REQUIRED EVERY HUMAN SHIP TO CARRY ONE DURON AND ONE LUMINID.
ANDROS IS OUR LUMINID. IT'S SMARTER THAN EVERYONE ON THE SHIP AND A BETTER PILOT BECAUSE IT CAN MERGE WITH THE NAVIGATION SYSTEMS, BUT IT'S NOT ALWAYS THE WARMEST MEMBER OF THE CREW.
THEY SAY FOR A LUMINID, SWIMMING IN THEIR DATASTREAM IS LIKE BEING IN THE BEST DREAM YOU'VE EVER HAD...AND IT NEVER ENDS.
ANDROS HAD TO WAKE UP FROM THAT DREAM TO SERVE ONBOARD THE WODEN.

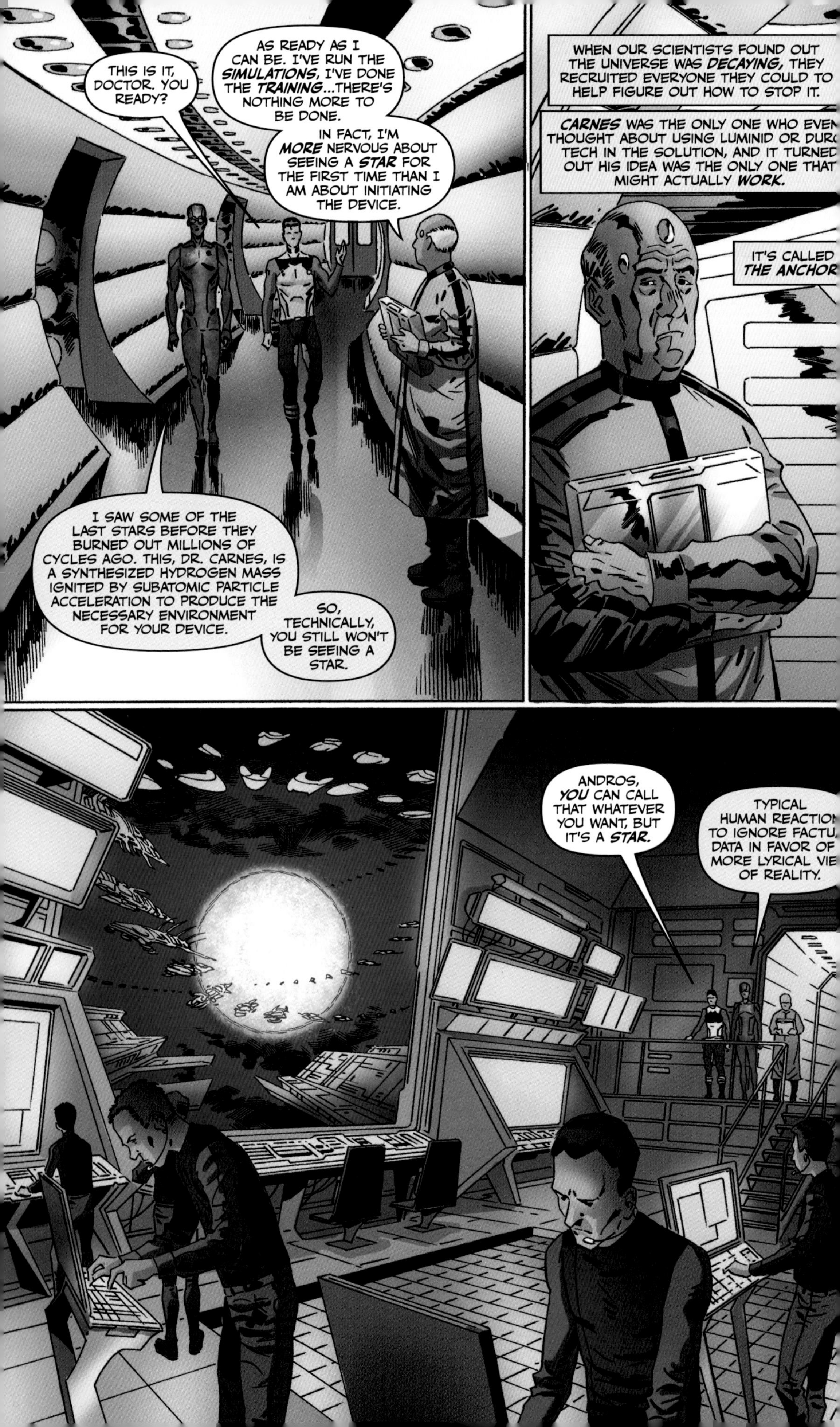
THIS IS IT, DOCTOR. YOU READY?
AS READY AS I CAN BE. I'VE RUN THE SIMULATIONS, I'VE DONE THE TRAINING...THERE'S NOTHING MORE TO BE DONE.
IN FACT, I'M MORE NERVOUS ABOUT SEEING A STAR FOR THE FIRST TIME THAN I AM ABOUT INITIATING THE DEVICE.
I SAW SOME OF THE LAST STARS BEFORE THEY BURNED OUT MILLIONS OF CYCLES AGO. THIS, DR. CARNES, IS A SYNTHESIZED HYDROGEN MASS IGNITED BY SUBATOMIC PARTICLE ACCELERATION TO PRODUCE THE NECESSARY ENVIRONMENT FOR YOUR DEVICE.
SO, TECHNICALLY, YOU STILL WON'T BE SEEING A STAR.
WHEN OUR SCIENTISTS FOUND OUT THE UNIVERSE WAS DECAYING, THEY RECRUITED EVERYONE THEY COULD TO HELP FIGURE OUT HOW TO STOP IT.
CARNES WAS THE ONLY ONE WHO EVEN THOUGHT ABOUT USING LUMINID OR DURO TECH IN THE SOLUTION, AND IT TURNED OUT HIS IDEA WAS THE ONLY ONE THAT MIGHT ACTUALLY WORK.
IT'S CALLED THE ANCHOR
ANDROS, YOU CAN CALL THAT WHATEVER YOU WANT, BUT IT'S A STAR.
TYPICAL HUMAN REACTION TO IGNORE FACTU DATA IN FAVOR OF MORE LYRICAL VIE OF REALITY.

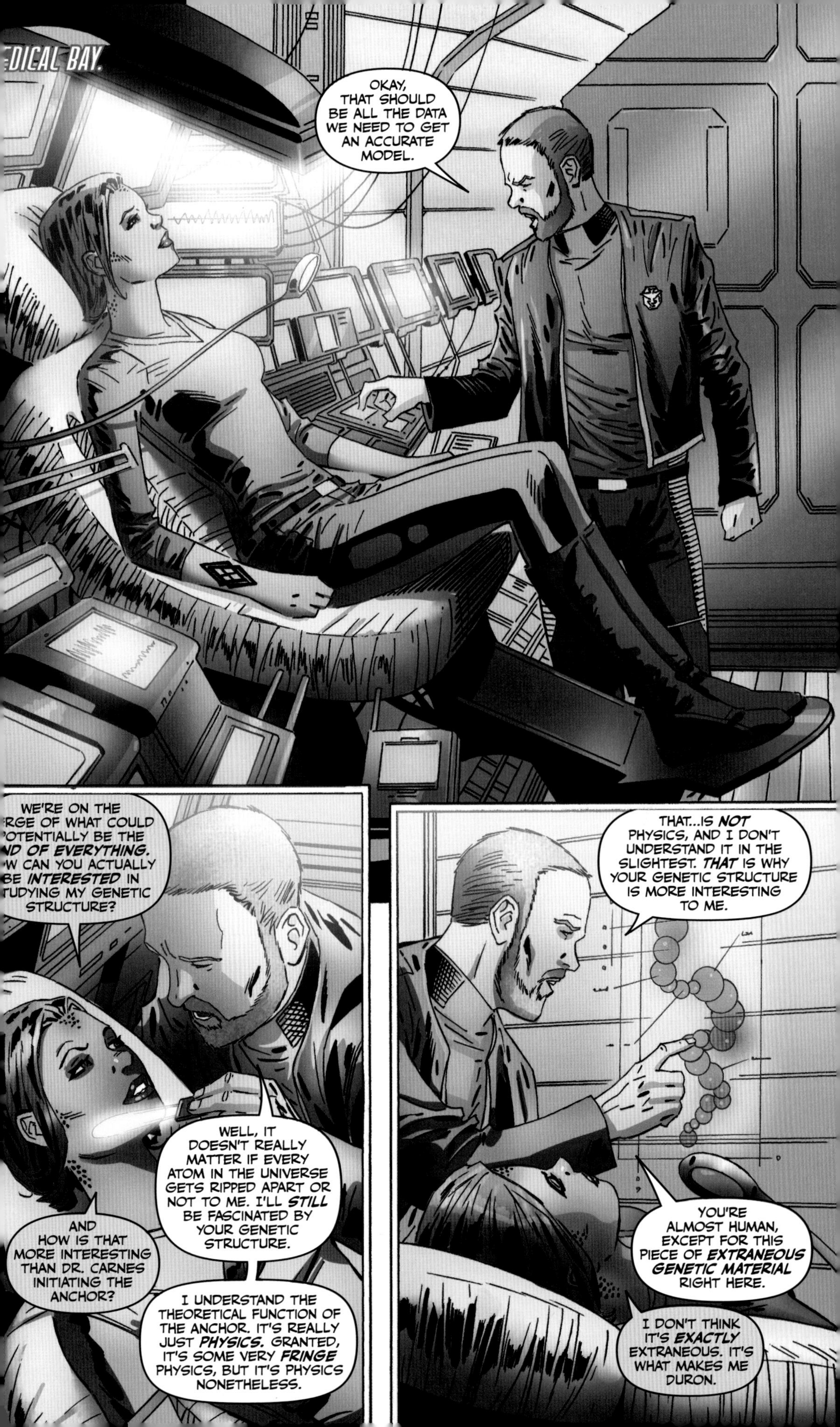
EDICAL BAY.
OKAY, THAT SHOULD BE ALL THE DATA WE NEED TO GET AN ACCURATE MODEL.
WE'RE ON THE ERGE OF WHAT COULD POTENTIALLY BE THE ND OF EVERYTHING. W CAN YOU ACTUALLY BE INTERESTED IN TUDYING MY GENETIC STRUCTURE?
WELL, IT DOESN'T REALLY MATTER IF EVERY ATOM IN THE UNIVERSE GETS RIPPED APART OR NOT TO ME. I'LL STILL BE FASCINATED BY YOUR GENETIC STRUCTURE.
AND HOW IS THAT MORE INTERESTING THAN DR. CARNES INITIATING THE ANCHOR?
I UNDERSTAND THE THEORETICAL FUNCTION OF THE ANCHOR. IT'S REALLY JUST PHYSICS. GRANTED, IT'S SOME VERY FRINGE PHYSICS, BUT IT'S PHYSICS NONETHELESS.
THAT...IS NOT PHYSICS, AND I DON'T UNDERSTAND IT IN THE SLIGHTEST. THAT IS WHY YOUR GENETIC STRUCTURE IS MORE INTERESTING TO ME.
YOU'RE ALMOST HUMAN, EXCEPT FOR THIS PIECE OF EXTRANEOUS GENETIC MATERIAL RIGHT HERE.
I DON'T THINK IT'S EXACTLY EXTRANEOUS. IT'S WHAT MAKES ME DURON.

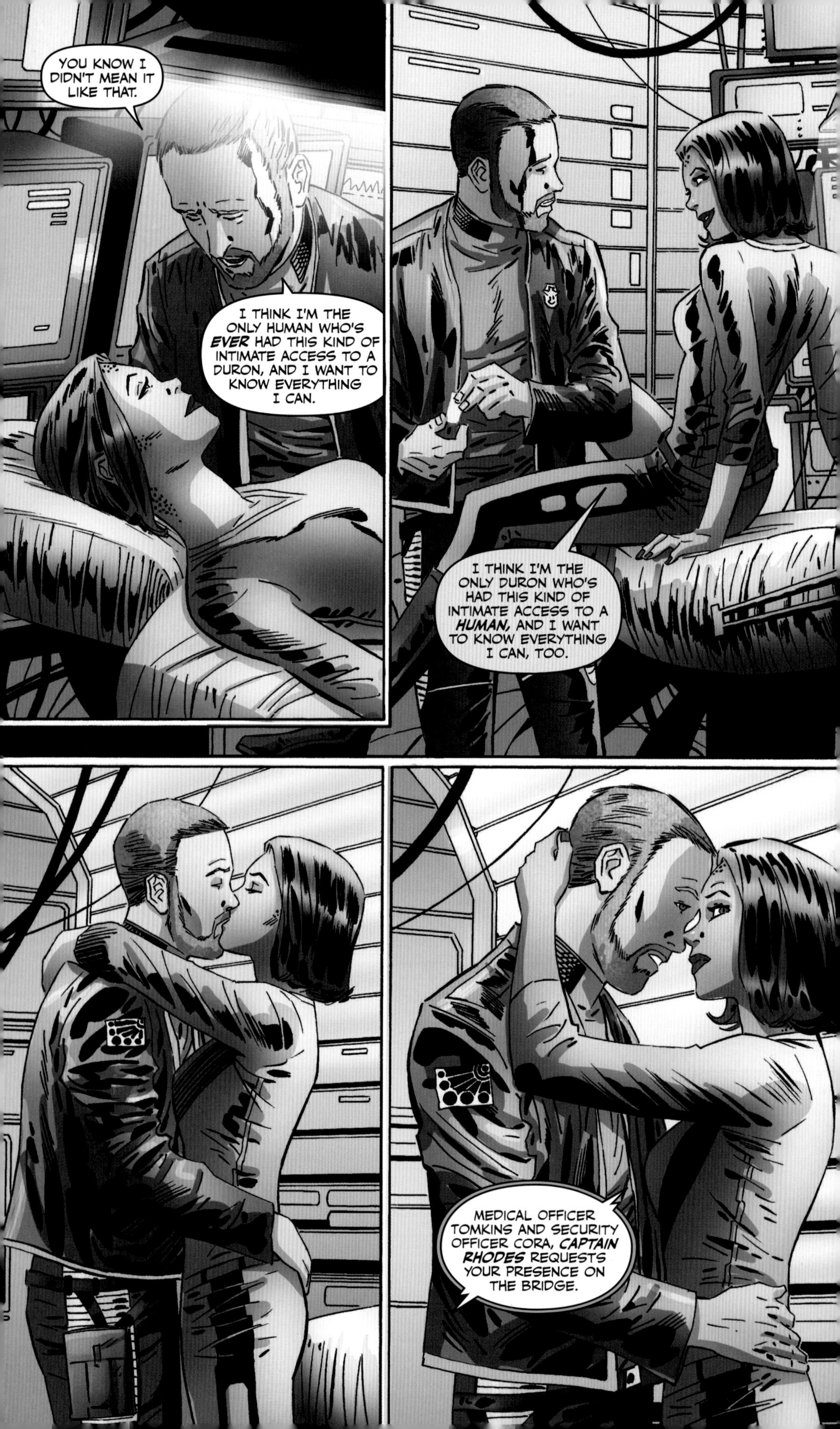

YOU KNOW I DIDN'T MEAN IT LIKE THAT.
I THINK I'M THE ONLY HUMAN WHO'S *EVER* HAD THIS KIND OF INTIMATE ACCESS TO A DURON, AND I WANT TO KNOW EVERYTHING I CAN.
I THINK I'M THE ONLY DURON WHO'S HAD THIS KIND OF INTIMATE ACCESS TO A *HUMAN,* AND I WANT TO KNOW EVERYTHING I CAN, TOO.
MEDICAL OFFICER TOMKINS AND SECURITY OFFICER CORA, *CAPTAIN RHODES* REQUESTS YOUR PRESENCE ON THE BRIDGE.

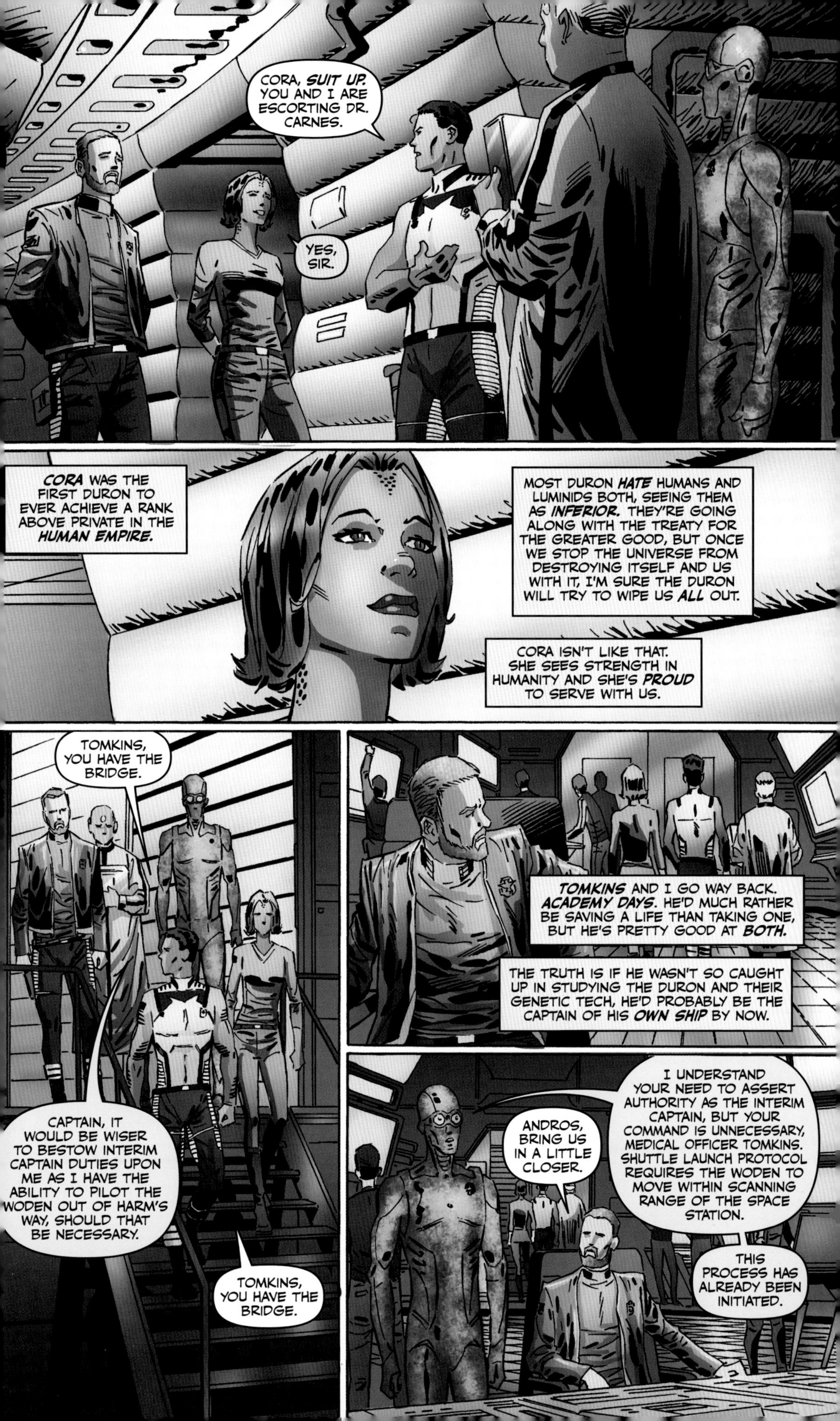
CORA, SUIT UP. YOU AND I ARE ESCORTING DR. CARNES.
YES, SIR.
CORA WAS THE FIRST DURON TO EVER ACHIEVE A RANK ABOVE PRIVATE IN THE HUMAN EMPIRE.
MOST DURON HATE HUMANS AND LUMINIDS BOTH, SEEING THEM AS INFERIOR. THEY'RE GOING ALONG WITH THE TREATY FOR THE GREATER GOOD, BUT ONCE WE STOP THE UNIVERSE FROM DESTROYING ITSELF AND US WITH IT, I'M SURE THE DURON WILL TRY TO WIPE US ALL OUT.
CORA ISN'T LIKE THAT. SHE SEES STRENGTH IN HUMANITY AND SHE'S PROUD TO SERVE WITH US.
TOMKINS, YOU HAVE THE BRIDGE.
CAPTAIN, IT WOULD BE WISER TO BESTOW INTERIM CAPTAIN DUTIES UPON ME AS I HAVE THE ABILITY TO PILOT THE WODEN OUT OF HARM'S WAY, SHOULD THAT BE NECESSARY.
TOMKINS, YOU HAVE THE BRIDGE.
TOMKINS AND I GO WAY BACK. ACADEMY DAYS. HE'D MUCH RATHER BE SAVING A LIFE THAN TAKING ONE, BUT HE'S PRETTY GOOD AT BOTH.
THE TRUTH IS IF HE WASN'T SO CAUGHT UP IN STUDYING THE DURON AND THEIR GENETIC TECH, HE'D PROBABLY BE THE CAPTAIN OF HIS OWN SHIP BY NOW.
ANDROS, BRING US IN A LITTLE CLOSER.
I UNDERSTAND YOUR NEED TO ASSERT AUTHORITY AS THE INTERIM CAPTAIN, BUT YOUR COMMAND IS UNNECESSARY, MEDICAL OFFICER TOMKINS. SHUTTLE LAUNCH PROTOCOL REQUIRES THE WODEN TO MOVE WITHIN SCANNING RANGE OF THE SPACE STATION.
THIS PROCESS HAS ALREADY BEEN INITIATED.

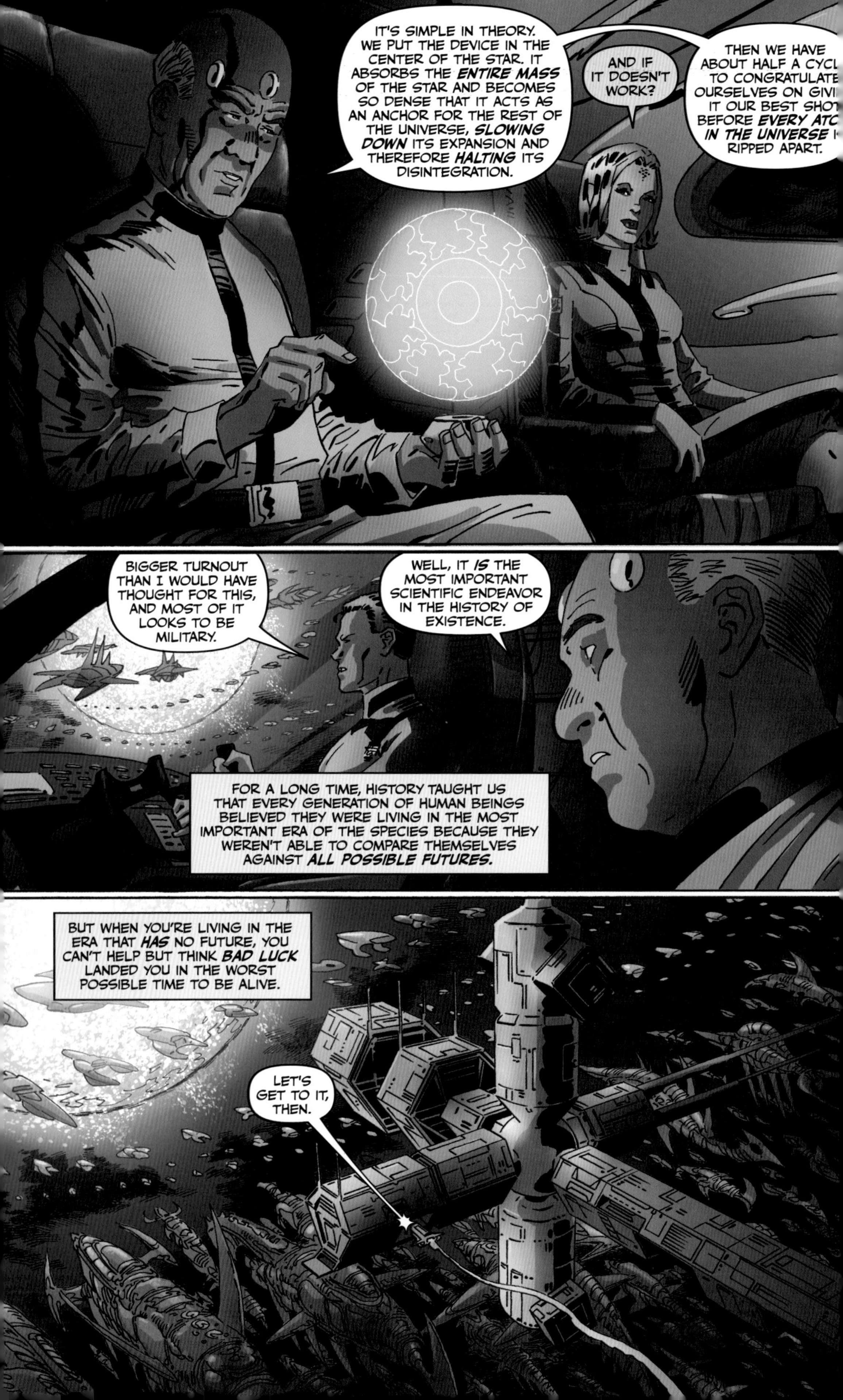
IT'S SIMPLE IN THEORY. WE PUT THE DEVICE IN THE CENTER OF THE STAR. IT ABSORBS THE ***ENTIRE MASS*** OF THE STAR AND BECOMES SO DENSE THAT IT ACTS AS AN ANCHOR FOR THE REST OF THE UNIVERSE, ***SLOWING DOWN*** ITS EXPANSION AND THEREFORE ***HALTING*** ITS DISINTEGRATION.
AND IF IT DOESN'T WORK?
THEN WE HAVE ABOUT HALF A CYCL TO CONGRATULATE OURSELVES ON GIVI IT OUR BEST SHO BEFORE ***EVERY ATC IN THE UNIVERSE*** I RIPPED APART.
BIGGER TURNOUT THAN I WOULD HAVE THOUGHT FOR THIS, AND MOST OF IT LOOKS TO BE MILITARY.
WELL, IT ***IS*** THE MOST IMPORTANT SCIENTIFIC ENDEAVOR IN THE HISTORY OF EXISTENCE.
FOR A LONG TIME, HISTORY TAUGHT US THAT EVERY GENERATION OF HUMAN BEINGS BELIEVED THEY WERE LIVING IN THE MOST IMPORTANT ERA OF THE SPECIES BECAUSE THEY WEREN'T ABLE TO COMPARE THEMSELVES AGAINST ***ALL POSSIBLE FUTURES.***
BUT WHEN YOU'RE LIVING IN THE ERA THAT ***HAS*** NO FUTURE, YOU CAN'T HELP BUT THINK ***BAD LUCK*** LANDED YOU IN THE WORST POSSIBLE TIME TO BE ALIVE.
LET'S GET TO IT, THEN.

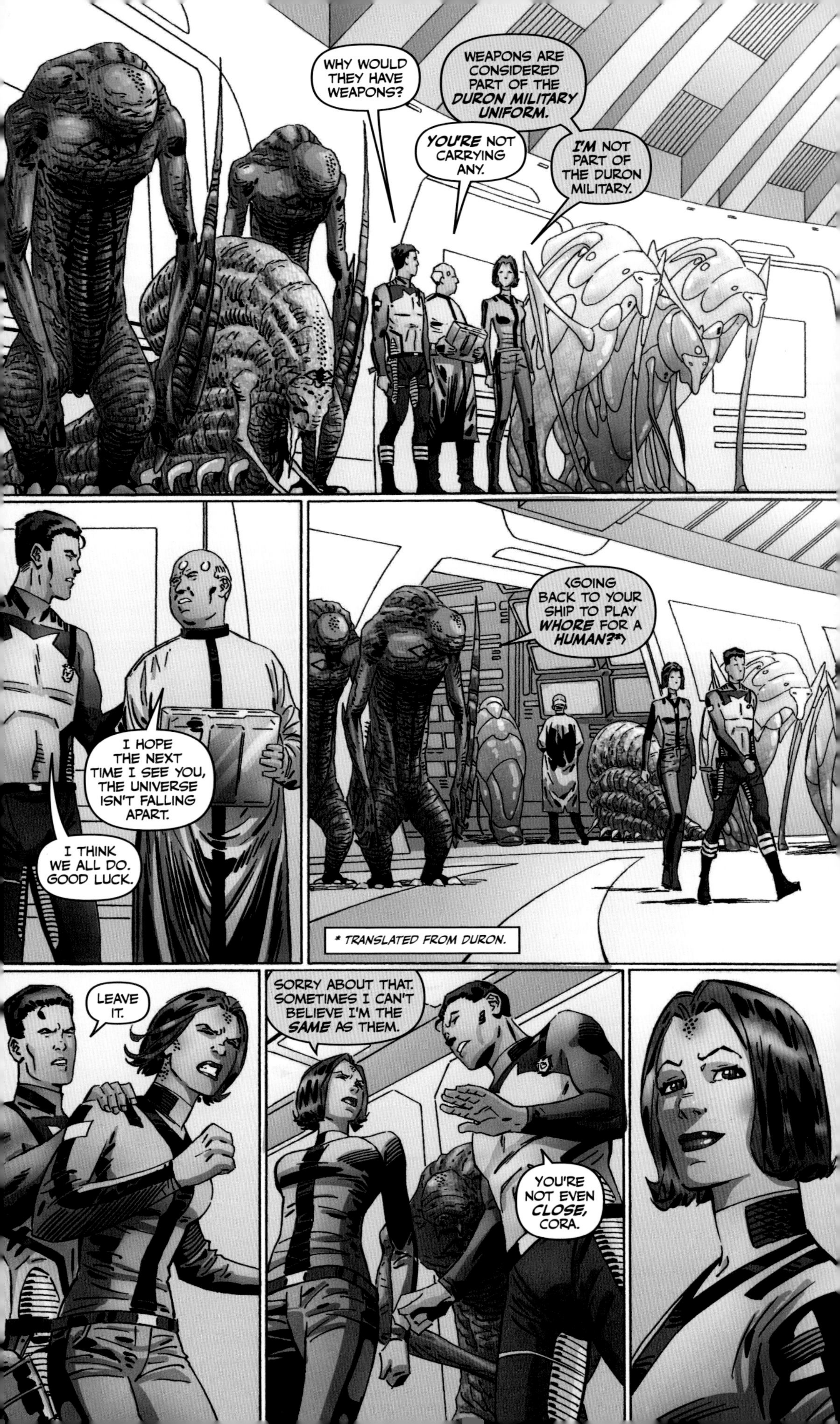
WHY WOULD THEY HAVE WEAPONS?
WEAPONS ARE CONSIDERED PART OF THE DURON MILITARY UNIFORM.
YOU'RE NOT CARRYING ANY.
I'M NOT PART OF THE DURON MILITARY.
I HOPE THE NEXT TIME I SEE YOU, THE UNIVERSE ISN'T FALLING APART.
I THINK WE ALL DO. GOOD LUCK.
<GOING BACK TO YOUR SHIP TO PLAY WHORE FOR A HUMAN?*>
* TRANSLATED FROM DURON.
LEAVE IT.
SORRY ABOUT THAT. SOMETIMES I CAN'T BELIEVE I'M THE SAME AS THEM.
YOU'RE NOT EVEN CLOSE, CORA.

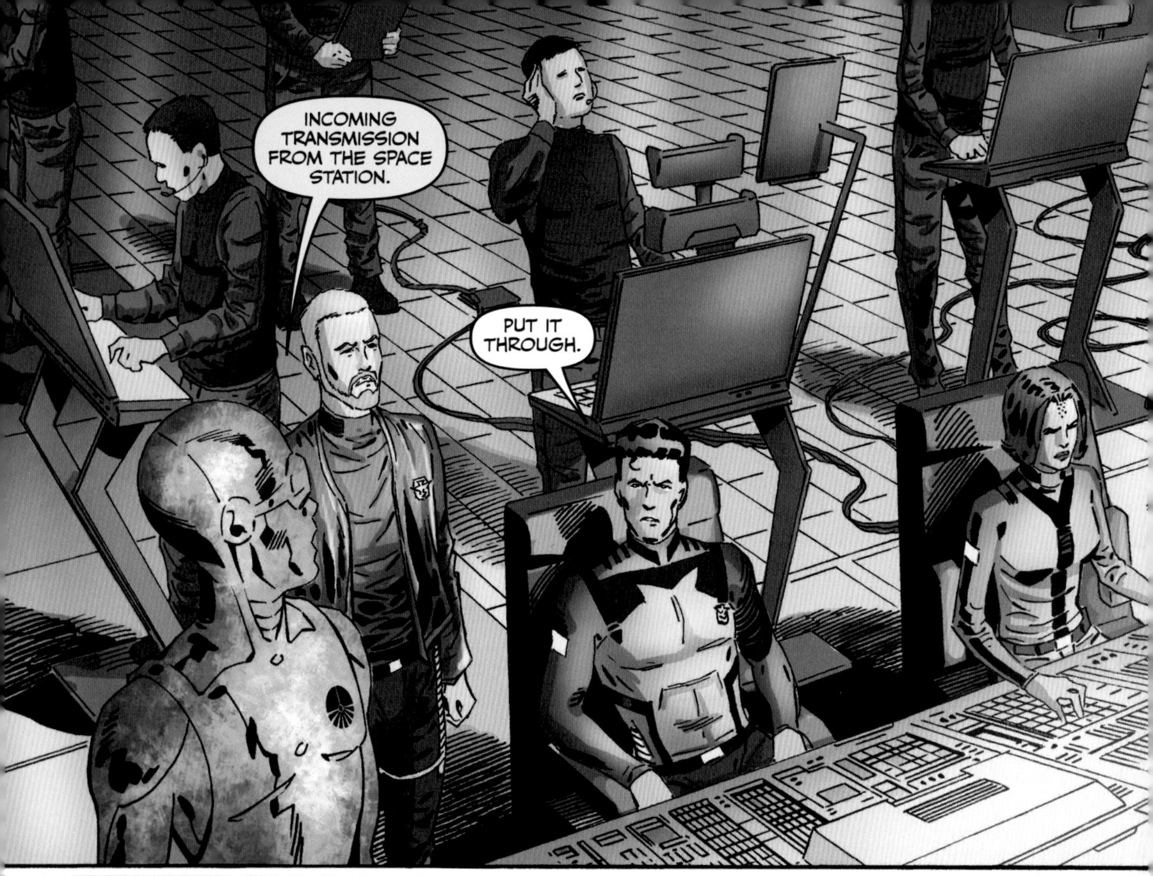
INCOMING TRANSMISSION FROM THE SPACE STATION.
PUT IT THROUGH.

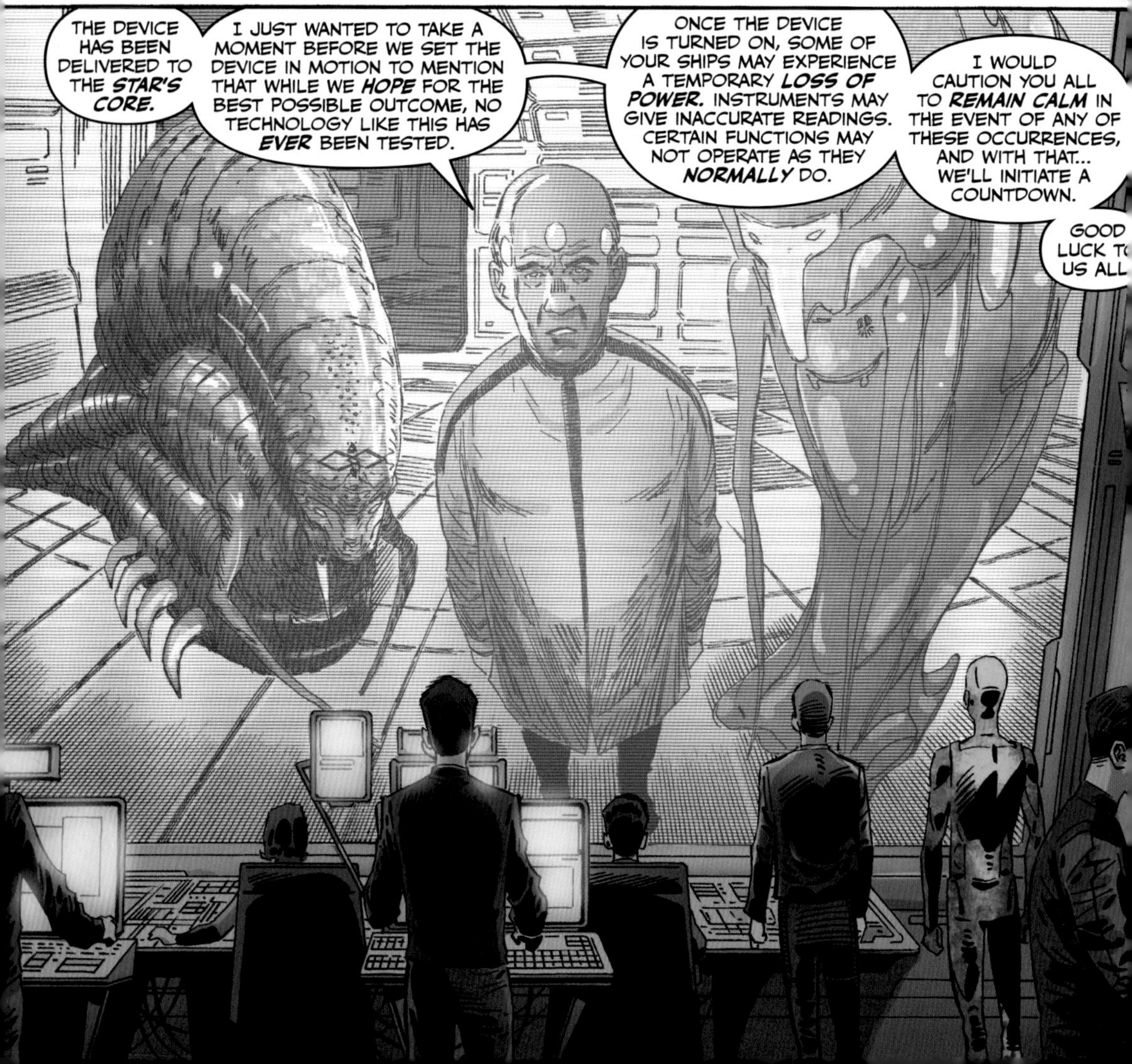
THE DEVICE HAS BEEN DELIVERED TO THE STAR'S CORE.
I JUST WANTED TO TAKE A MOMENT BEFORE WE SET THE DEVICE IN MOTION TO MENTION THAT WHILE WE HOPE FOR THE BEST POSSIBLE OUTCOME, NO TECHNOLOGY LIKE THIS HAS EVER BEEN TESTED.
ONCE THE DEVICE IS TURNED ON, SOME OF YOUR SHIPS MAY EXPERIENCE A TEMPORARY LOSS OF POWER. INSTRUMENTS MAY GIVE INACCURATE READINGS. CERTAIN FUNCTIONS MAY NOT OPERATE AS THEY NORMALLY DO.
I WOULD CAUTION YOU ALL TO REMAIN CALM IN THE EVENT OF ANY OF THESE OCCURRENCES, AND WITH THAT... WE'LL INITIATE A COUNTDOWN.

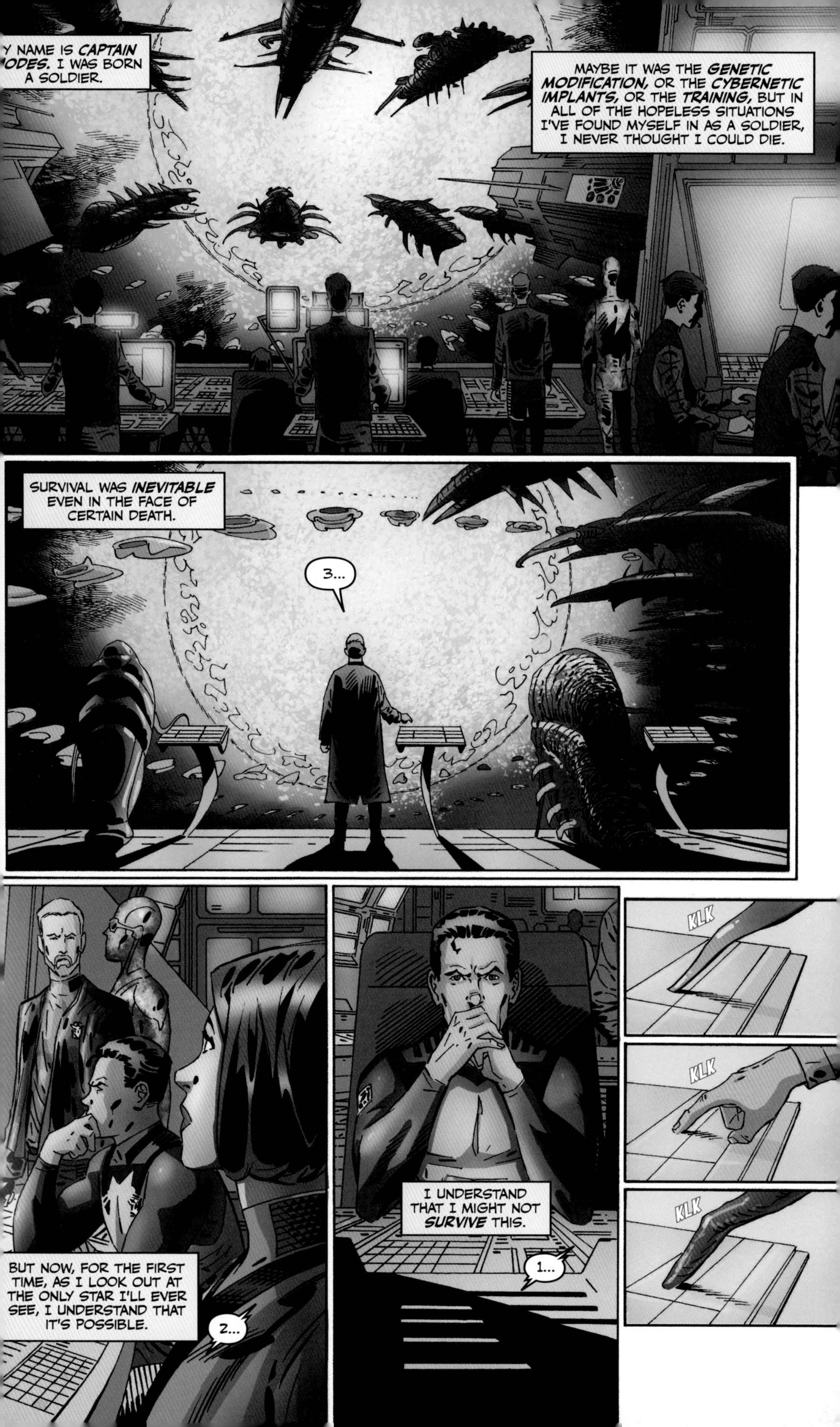
Y NAME IS CAPTAIN
ODES. I WAS BORN A SOLDIER.
MAYBE IT WAS THE GENETIC MODIFICATION, OR THE CYBERNETIC IMPLANTS, OR THE TRAINING, BUT IN ALL OF THE HOPELESS SITUATIONS I'VE FOUND MYSELF IN AS A SOLDIER, I NEVER THOUGHT I COULD DIE.
SURVIVAL WAS INEVITABLE EVEN IN THE FACE OF CERTAIN DEATH.
3...
BUT NOW, FOR THE FIRST TIME, AS I LOOK OUT AT THE ONLY STAR I'LL EVER SEE, I UNDERSTAND THAT IT'S POSSIBLE.
2...
I UNDERSTAND THAT I MIGHT NOT SURVIVE THIS.
1...
KLK
KLK
KLK

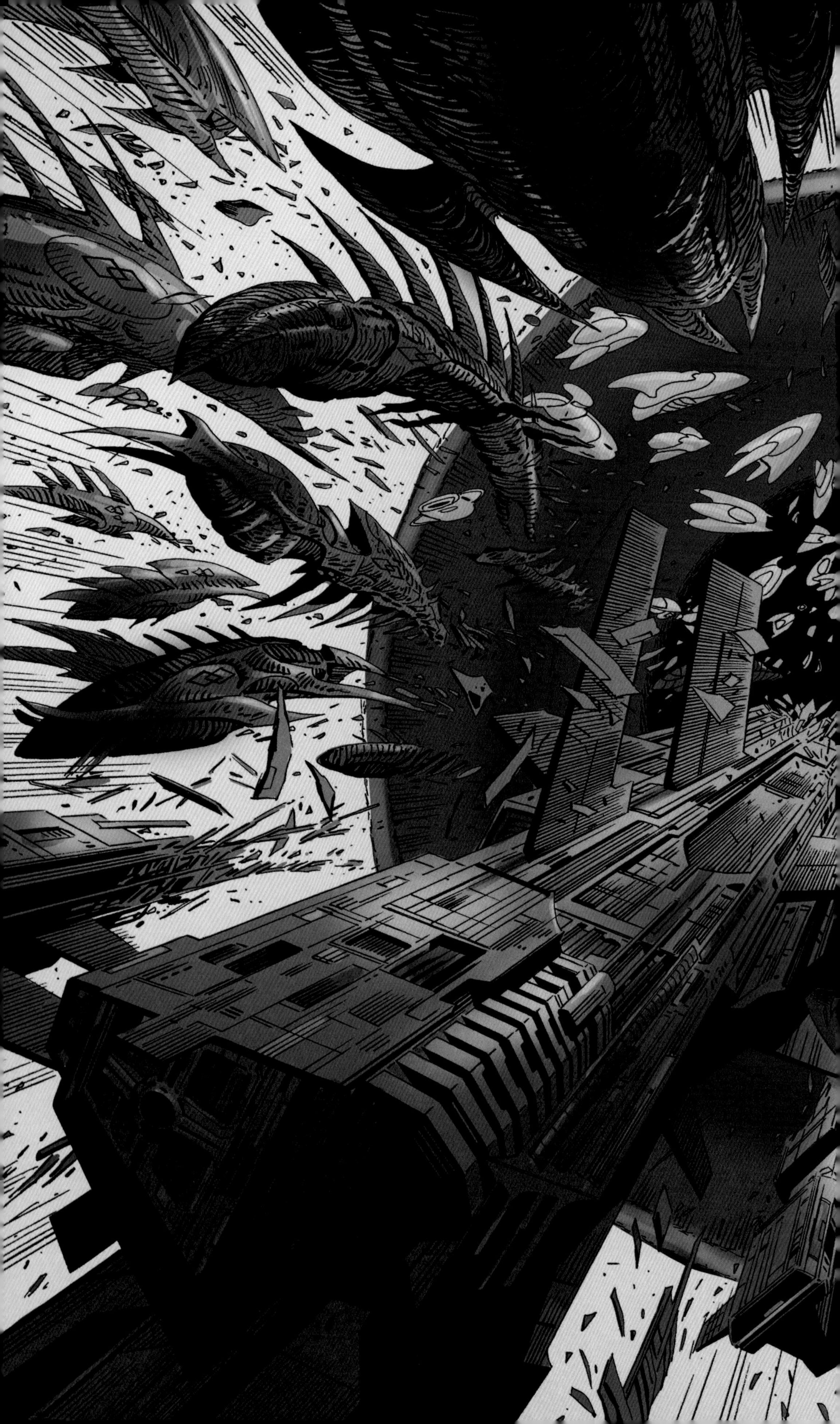

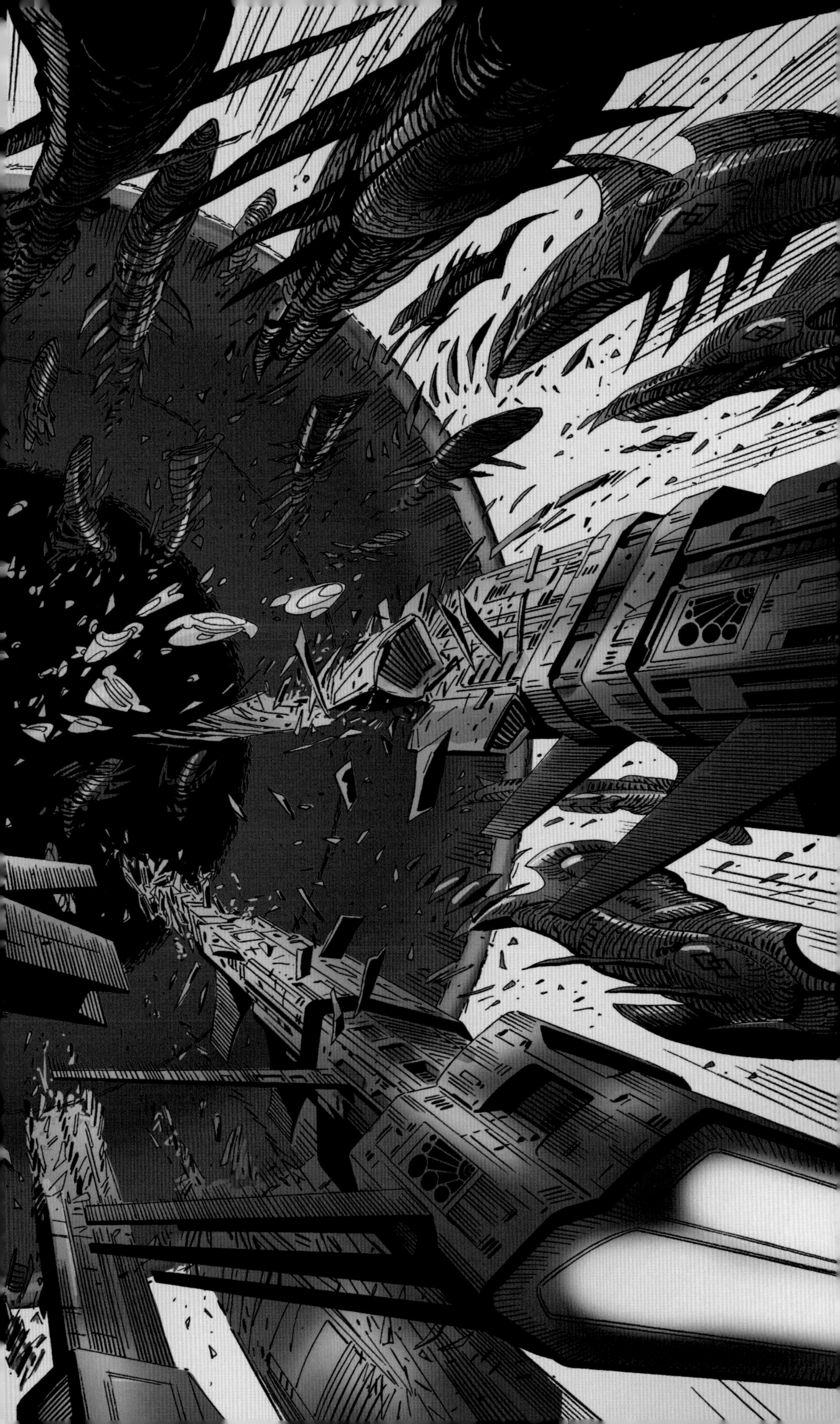

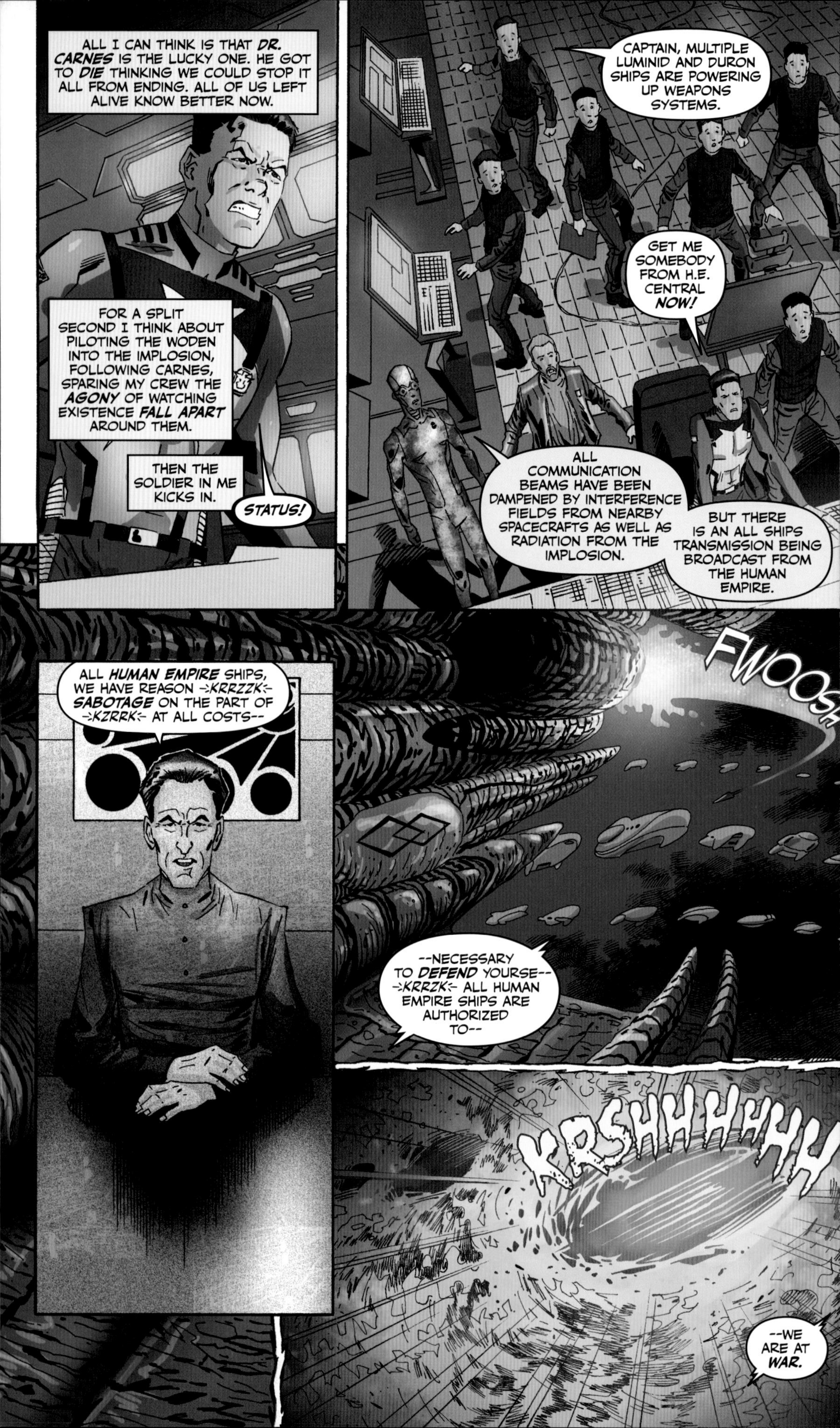
ALL I CAN THINK IS THAT DR. CARNES IS THE LUCKY ONE. HE GOT TO DIE THINKING WE COULD STOP IT ALL FROM ENDING. ALL OF US LEFT ALIVE KNOW BETTER NOW.
FOR A SPLIT SECOND I THINK ABOUT PILOTING THE WODEN INTO THE IMPLOSION, FOLLOWING CARNES, SPARING MY CREW THE AGONY OF WATCHING EXISTENCE FALL APART AROUND THEM.
THEN THE SOLDIER IN ME KICKS IN.
STATUS!
CAPTAIN, MULTIPLE LUMINID AND DURON SHIPS ARE POWERING UP WEAPONS SYSTEMS.
GET ME SOMEBODY FROM H.E. CENTRAL NOW!
ALL COMMUNICATION BEAMS HAVE BEEN DAMPENED BY INTERFERENCE FIELDS FROM NEARBY SPACECRAFTS AS WELL AS RADIATION FROM THE IMPLOSION.
BUT THERE IS AN ALL SHIPS TRANSMISSION BEING BROADCAST FROM THE HUMAN EMPIRE.
ALL HUMAN EMPIRE SHIPS, WE HAVE REASON -KRRZZK- SABOTAGE ON THE PART OF -KZRRK- AT ALL COSTS--
FWOOSH
--NECESSARY TO DEFEND YOURSE-- -KRRZK- ALL HUMAN EMPIRE SHIPS ARE AUTHORIZED TO--
KRSHHHHHH
--WE ARE AT WAR.

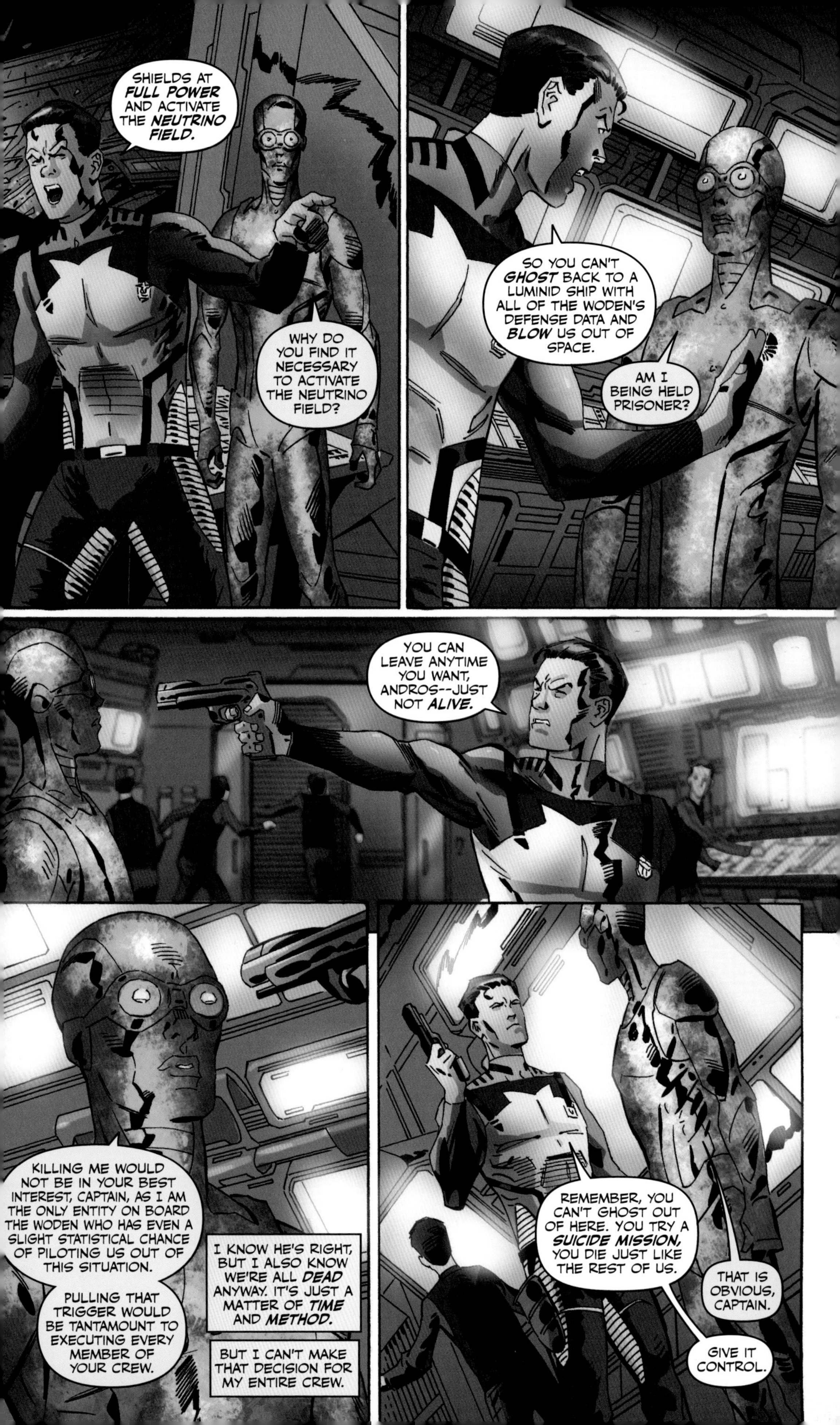
SHIELDS AT FULL POWER AND ACTIVATE THE NEUTRINO FIELD.
WHY DO YOU FIND IT NECESSARY TO ACTIVATE THE NEUTRINO FIELD?
SO YOU CAN'T GHOST BACK TO A LUMINID SHIP WITH ALL OF THE WODEN'S DEFENSE DATA AND BLOW US OUT OF SPACE.
AM I BEING HELD PRISONER?
YOU CAN LEAVE ANYTIME YOU WANT, ANDROS--JUST NOT ALIVE.
KILLING ME WOULD NOT BE IN YOUR BEST INTEREST, CAPTAIN, AS I AM THE ONLY ENTITY ON BOARD THE WODEN WHO HAS EVEN A SLIGHT STATISTICAL CHANCE OF PILOTING US OUT OF THIS SITUATION.
PULLING THAT TRIGGER WOULD BE TANTAMOUNT TO EXECUTING EVERY MEMBER OF YOUR CREW.
I KNOW HE'S RIGHT, BUT I ALSO KNOW WE'RE ALL DEAD ANYWAY. IT'S JUST A MATTER OF TIME AND METHOD.
BUT I CAN'T MAKE THAT DECISION FOR MY ENTIRE CREW.
REMEMBER, YOU CAN'T GHOST OUT OF HERE. YOU TRY A SUICIDE MISSION, YOU DIE JUST LIKE THE REST OF US.
THAT IS OBVIOUS, CAPTAIN.
GIVE IT CONTROL.

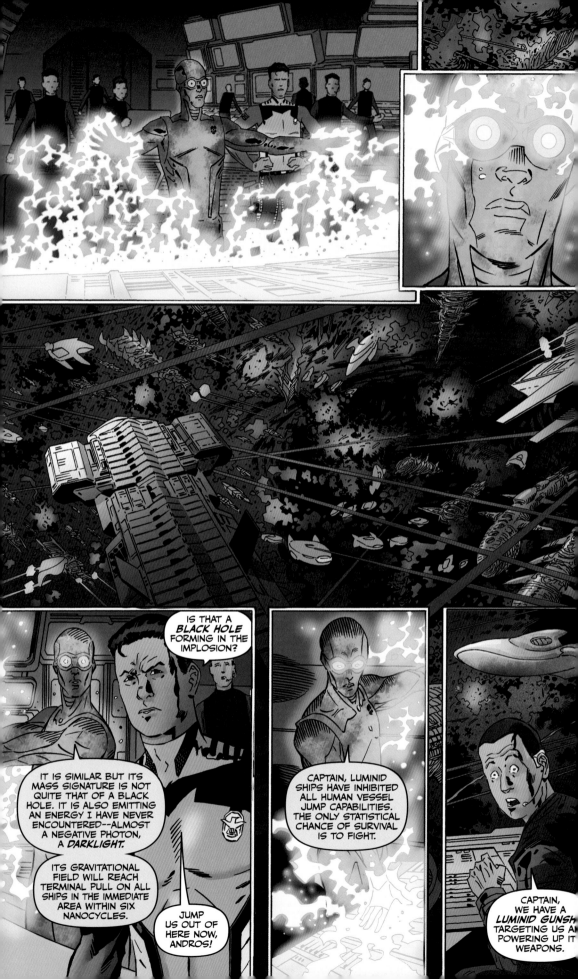

IS THAT A *BLACK HOLE* FORMING IN THE IMPLOSION?

IT IS SIMILAR BUT ITS MASS SIGNATURE IS NOT QUITE THAT OF A BLACK HOLE. IT IS ALSO EMITTING AN ENERGY I HAVE NEVER ENCOUNTERED--ALMOST A NEGATIVE PHOTON, A *DARKLIGHT.*

ITS GRAVITATIONAL FIELD WILL REACH TERMINAL PULL ON ALL SHIPS IN THE IMMEDIATE AREA WITHIN SIX NANOCYCLES.

JUMP US OUT OF HERE NOW, ANDROS!

CAPTAIN, LUMINID SHIPS HAVE INHIBITED ALL HUMAN VESSEL JUMP CAPABILITIES. THE ONLY STATISTICAL CHANCE OF SURVIVAL IS TO FIGHT.

CAPTAIN, WE HAVE A *LUMINID GUNSH* TARGETING US A POWERING UP IT WEAPONS.

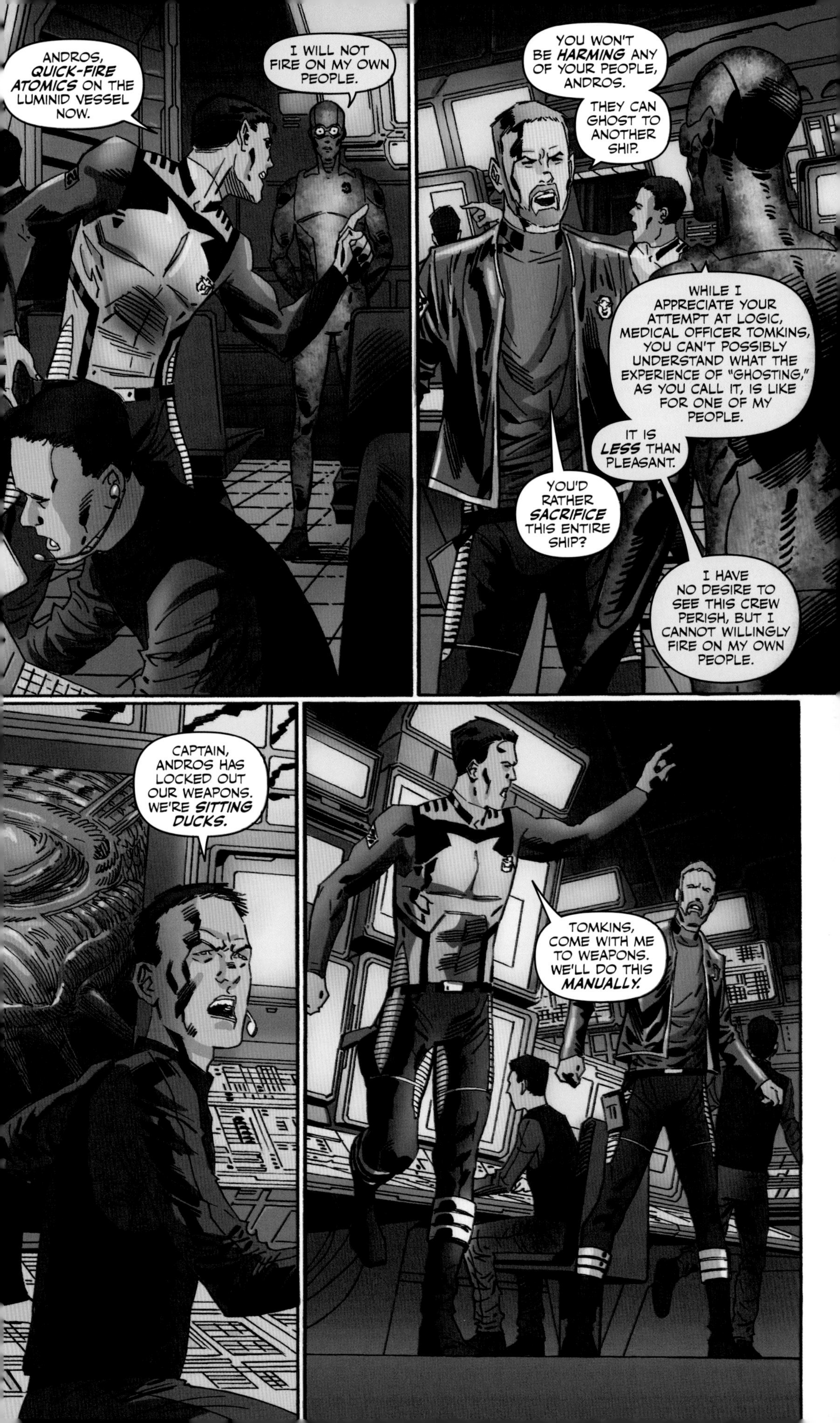
ANDROS, QUICK-FIRE ATOMICS ON THE LUMINID VESSEL NOW.
I WILL NOT FIRE ON MY OWN PEOPLE.
YOU WON'T BE HARMING ANY OF YOUR PEOPLE, ANDROS.
THEY CAN GHOST TO ANOTHER SHIP.
WHILE I APPRECIATE YOUR ATTEMPT AT LOGIC, MEDICAL OFFICER TOMKINS, YOU CAN'T POSSIBLY UNDERSTAND WHAT THE EXPERIENCE OF "GHOSTING," AS YOU CALL IT, IS LIKE FOR ONE OF MY PEOPLE.
IT IS LESS THAN PLEASANT.
YOU'D RATHER SACRIFICE THIS ENTIRE SHIP?
I HAVE NO DESIRE TO SEE THIS CREW PERISH, BUT I CANNOT WILLINGLY FIRE ON MY OWN PEOPLE.
CAPTAIN, ANDROS HAS LOCKED OUT OUR WEAPONS. WE'RE SITTING DUCKS.
TOMKINS, COME WITH ME TO WEAPONS. WE'LL DO THIS MANUALLY.

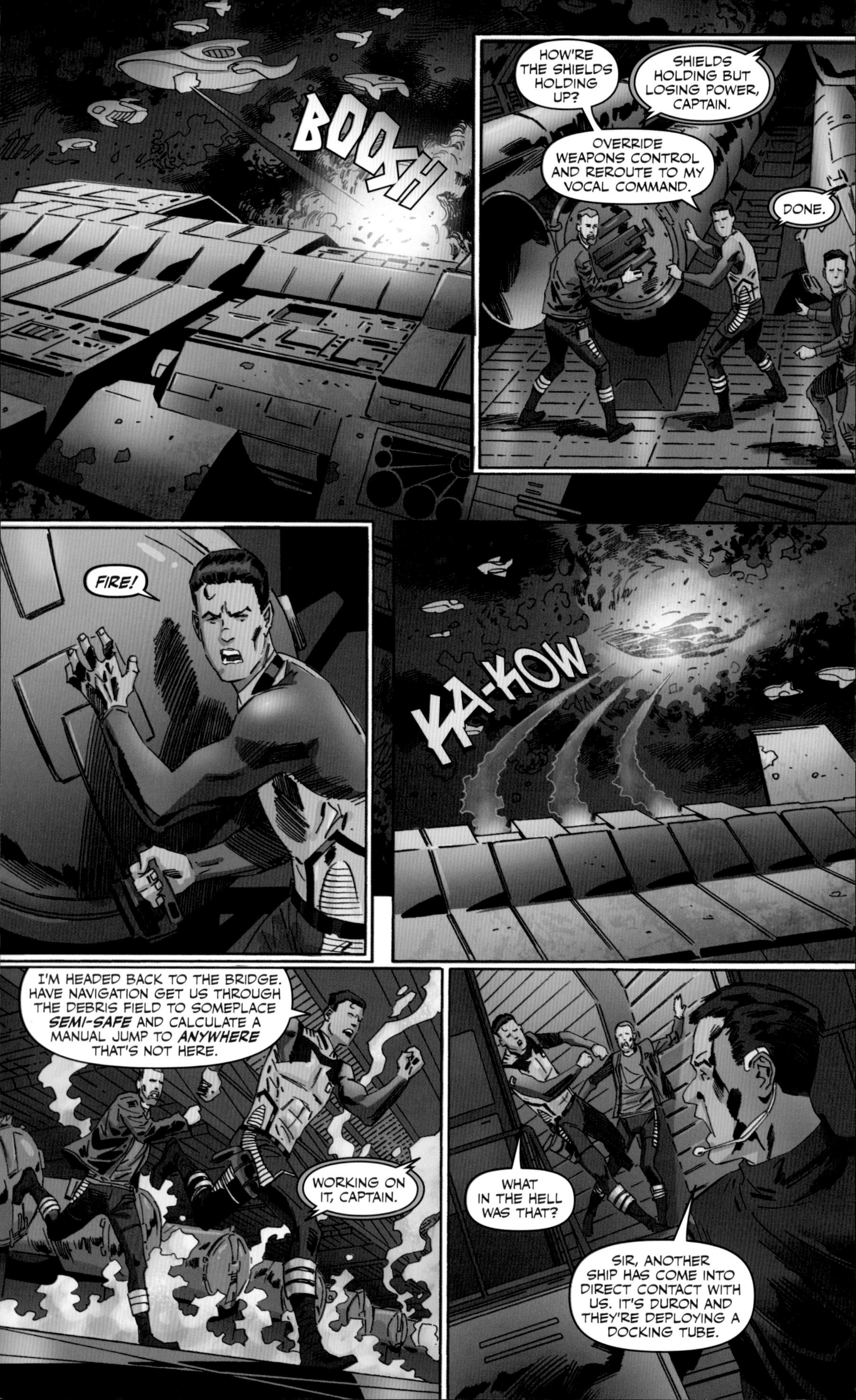
BOOSH
HOW'RE THE SHIELDS HOLDING UP?
SHIELDS HOLDING BUT LOSING POWER, CAPTAIN.
OVERRIDE WEAPONS CONTROL AND REROUTE TO MY VOCAL COMMAND.
DONE.
FIRE!
KA-KOW
I'M HEADED BACK TO THE BRIDGE. HAVE NAVIGATION GET US THROUGH THE DEBRIS FIELD TO SOMEPLACE SEMI-SAFE AND CALCULATE A MANUAL JUMP TO ANYWHERE THAT'S NOT HERE.
WORKING ON IT, CAPTAIN.
WHAT IN THE HELL WAS THAT?
SIR, ANOTHER SHIP HAS COME INTO DIRECT CONTACT WITH US. IT'S DURON AND THEY'RE DEPLOYING A DOCKING TUBE.

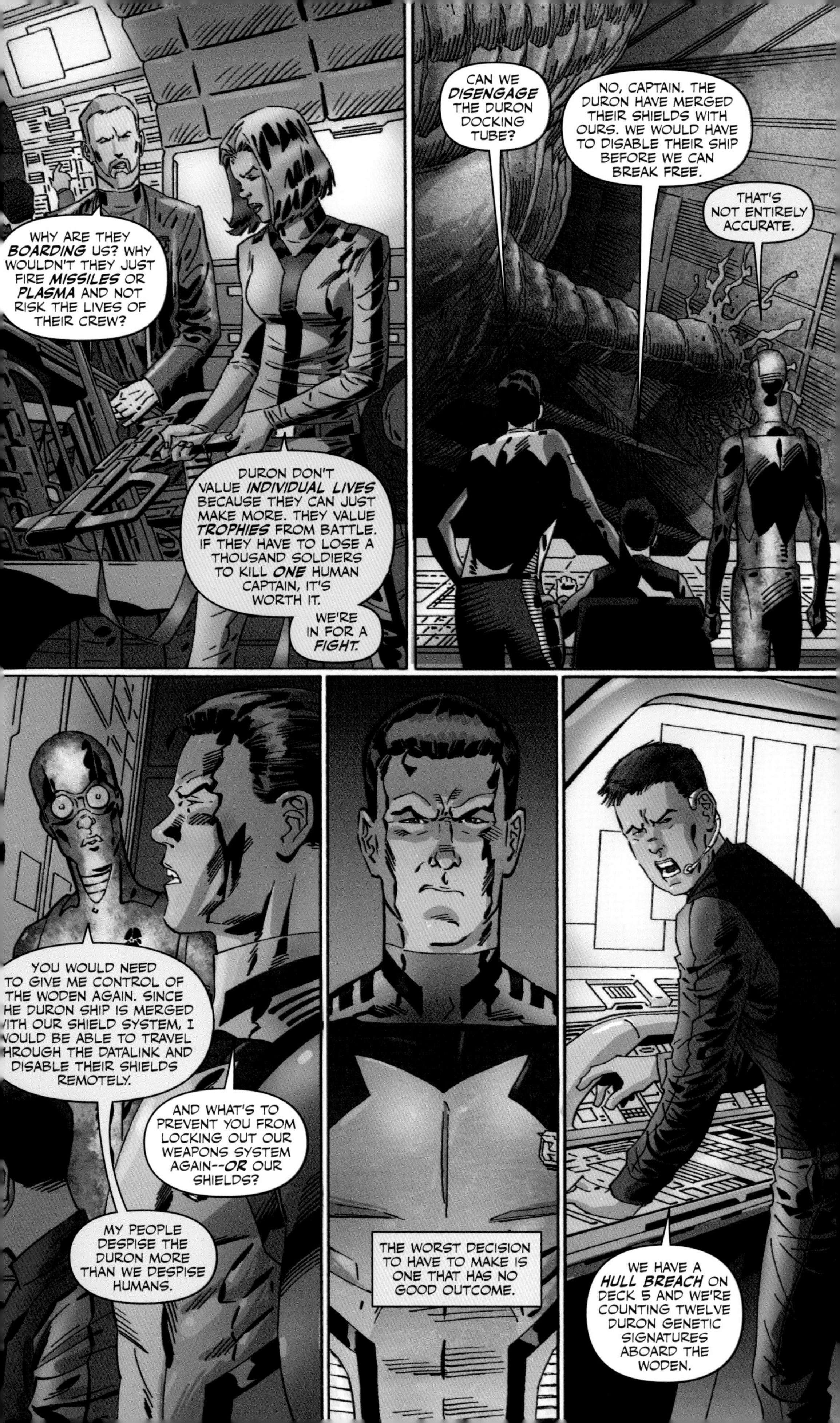
WHY ARE THEY BOARDING US? WHY WOULDN'T THEY JUST FIRE MISSILES OR PLASMA AND NOT RISK THE LIVES OF THEIR CREW?
DURON DON'T VALUE INDIVIDUAL LIVES BECAUSE THEY CAN JUST MAKE MORE. THEY VALUE TROPHIES FROM BATTLE. IF THEY HAVE TO LOSE A THOUSAND SOLDIERS TO KILL ONE HUMAN CAPTAIN, IT'S WORTH IT.
WE'RE IN FOR A FIGHT.
CAN WE DISENGAGE THE DURON DOCKING TUBE?
NO, CAPTAIN. THE DURON HAVE MERGED THEIR SHIELDS WITH OURS. WE WOULD HAVE TO DISABLE THEIR SHIP BEFORE WE CAN BREAK FREE.
THAT'S NOT ENTIRELY ACCURATE.
YOU WOULD NEED TO GIVE ME CONTROL OF THE WODEN AGAIN. SINCE HE DURON SHIP IS MERGED /ITH OUR SHIELD SYSTEM, I VOULD BE ABLE TO TRAVEL HROUGH THE DATALINK AND DISABLE THEIR SHIELDS REMOTELY.
AND WHAT'S TO PREVENT YOU FROM LOCKING OUT OUR WEAPONS SYSTEM AGAIN--OR OUR SHIELDS?
MY PEOPLE DESPISE THE DURON MORE THAN WE DESPISE HUMANS.
THE WORST DECISION TO HAVE TO MAKE IS ONE THAT HAS NO GOOD OUTCOME.
WE HAVE A HULL BREACH ON DECK 5 AND WE'RE COUNTING TWELVE DURON GENETIC SIGNATURES ABOARD THE WODEN.

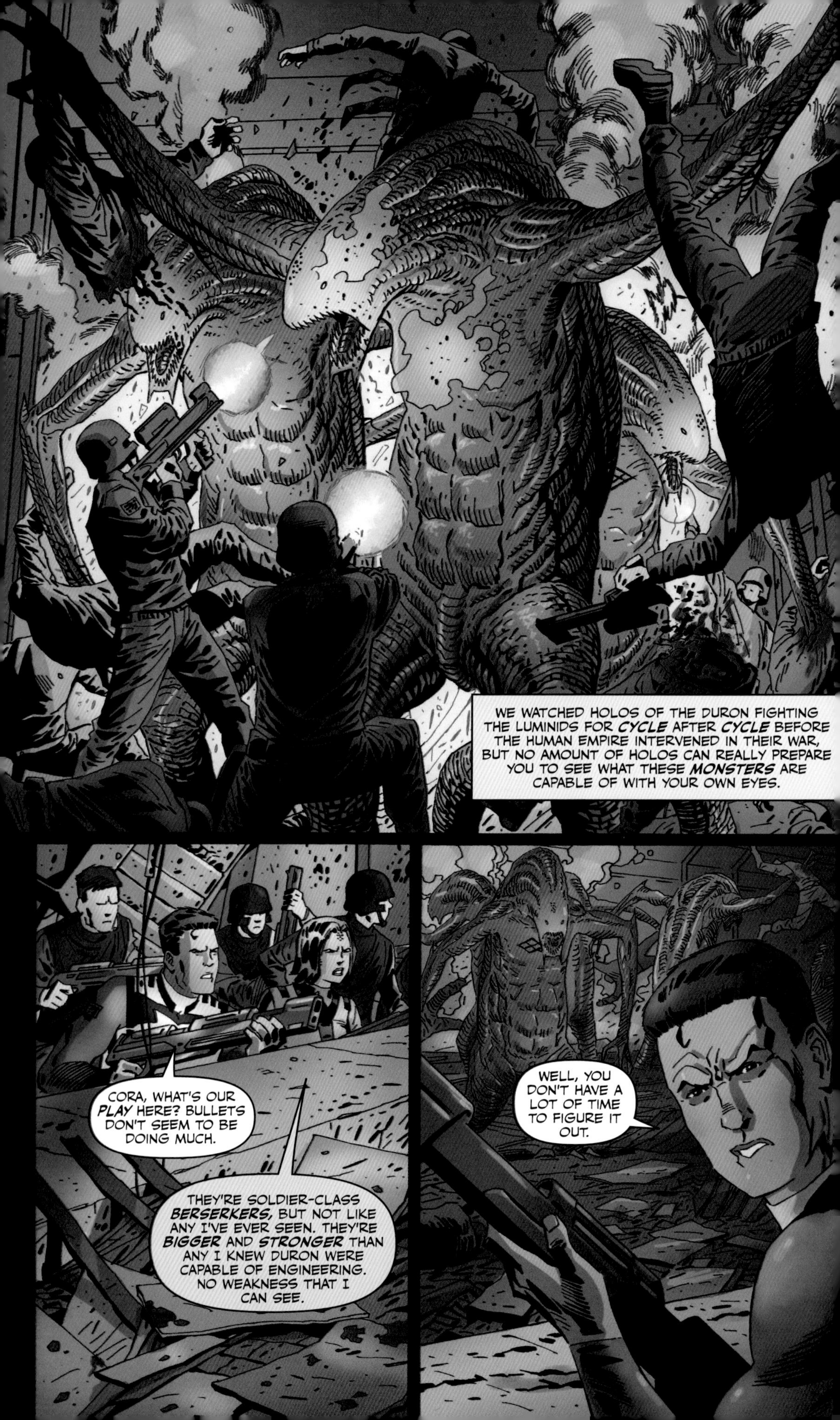
WE WATCHED HOLOS OF THE DURON FIGHTING THE LUMINIDS FOR CYCLE AFTER CYCLE BEFORE THE HUMAN EMPIRE INTERVENED IN THEIR WAR, BUT NO AMOUNT OF HOLOS CAN REALLY PREPARE YOU TO SEE WHAT THESE MONSTERS ARE CAPABLE OF WITH YOUR OWN EYES.
CORA, WHAT'S OUR PLAY HERE? BULLETS DON'T SEEM TO BE DOING MUCH.
THEY'RE SOLDIER-CLASS BERSERKERS, BUT NOT LIKE ANY I'VE EVER SEEN. THEY'RE BIGGER AND STRONGER THAN ANY I KNEW DURON WERE CAPABLE OF ENGINEERING. NO WEAKNESS THAT I CAN SEE.
WELL, YOU DON'T HAVE A LOT OF TIME TO FIGURE IT OUT.

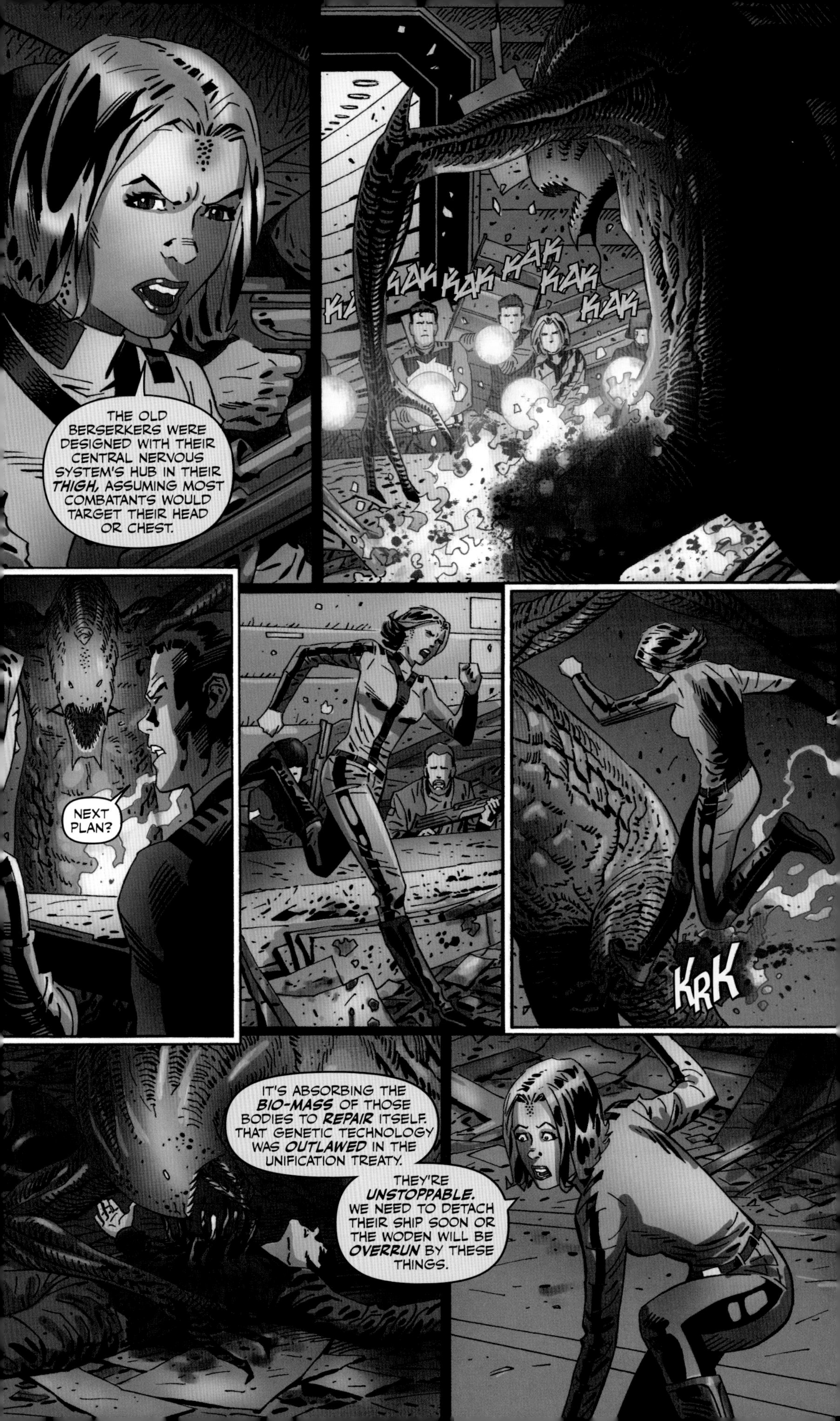
THE OLD BERSERKERS WERE DESIGNED WITH THEIR CENTRAL NERVOUS SYSTEM'S HUB IN THEIR THIGH, ASSUMING MOST COMBATANTS WOULD TARGET THEIR HEAD OR CHEST.
KAK KAK KAK KAK KAK KAK
NEXT PLAN?
KRK
IT'S ABSORBING THE BIO-MASS OF THOSE BODIES TO REPAIR ITSELF. THAT GENETIC TECHNOLOGY WAS OUTLAWED IN THE UNIFICATION TREATY.
THEY'RE UNSTOPPABLE. WE NEED TO DETACH THEIR SHIP SOON OR THE WODEN WILL BE OVERRUN BY THESE THINGS.

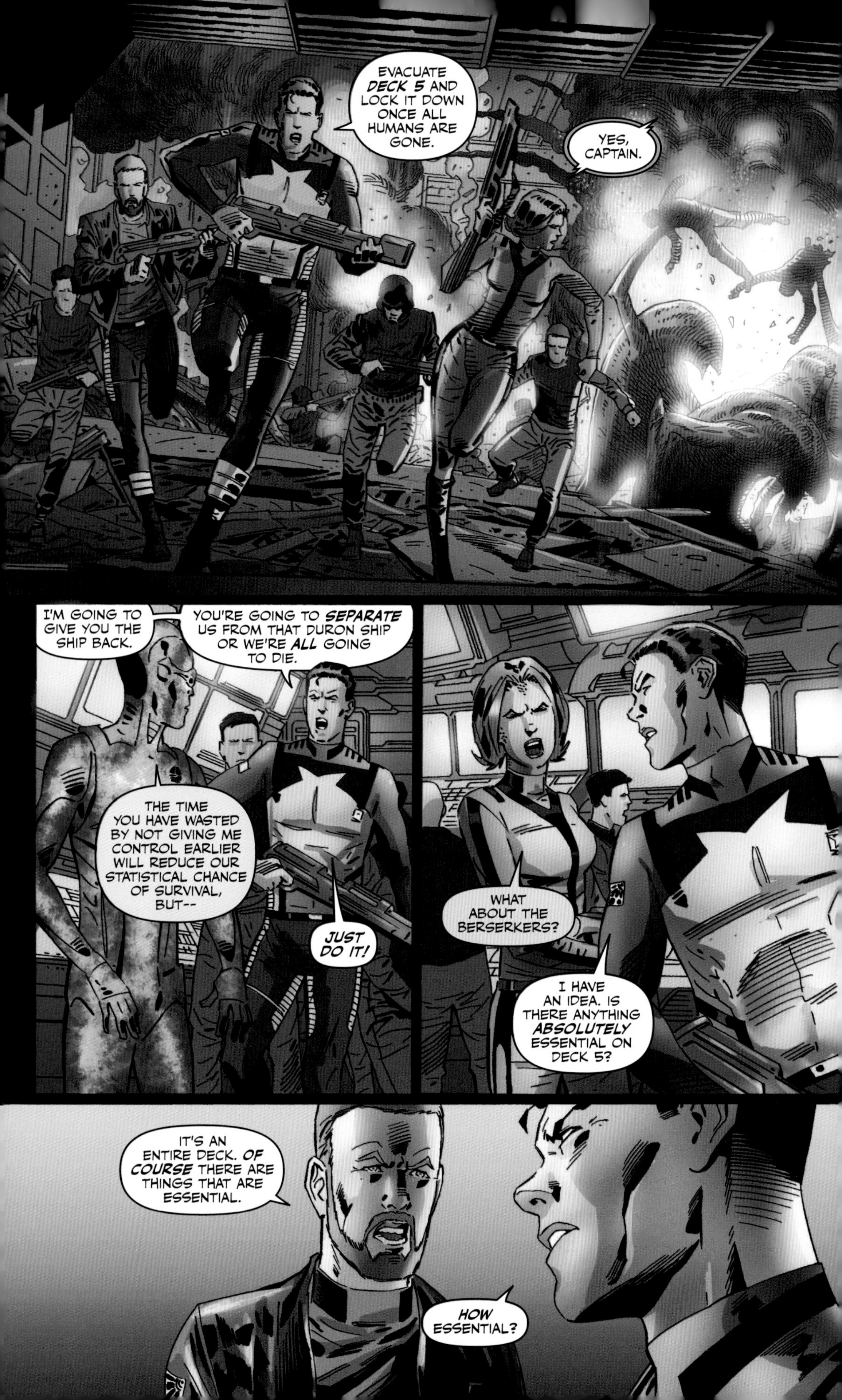
EVACUATE DECK 5 AND LOCK IT DOWN ONCE ALL HUMANS ARE GONE.
YES, CAPTAIN.
I'M GOING TO GIVE YOU THE SHIP BACK.
YOU'RE GOING TO SEPARATE US FROM THAT DURON SHIP OR WE'RE ALL GOING TO DIE.
THE TIME YOU HAVE WASTED BY NOT GIVING ME CONTROL EARLIER WILL REDUCE OUR STATISTICAL CHANCE OF SURVIVAL, BUT--
JUST DO IT!
WHAT ABOUT THE BERSERKERS?
I HAVE AN IDEA. IS THERE ANYTHING ABSOLUTELY ESSENTIAL ON DECK 5?
IT'S AN ENTIRE DECK. OF COURSE THERE ARE THINGS THAT ARE ESSENTIAL.
HOW ESSENTIAL?

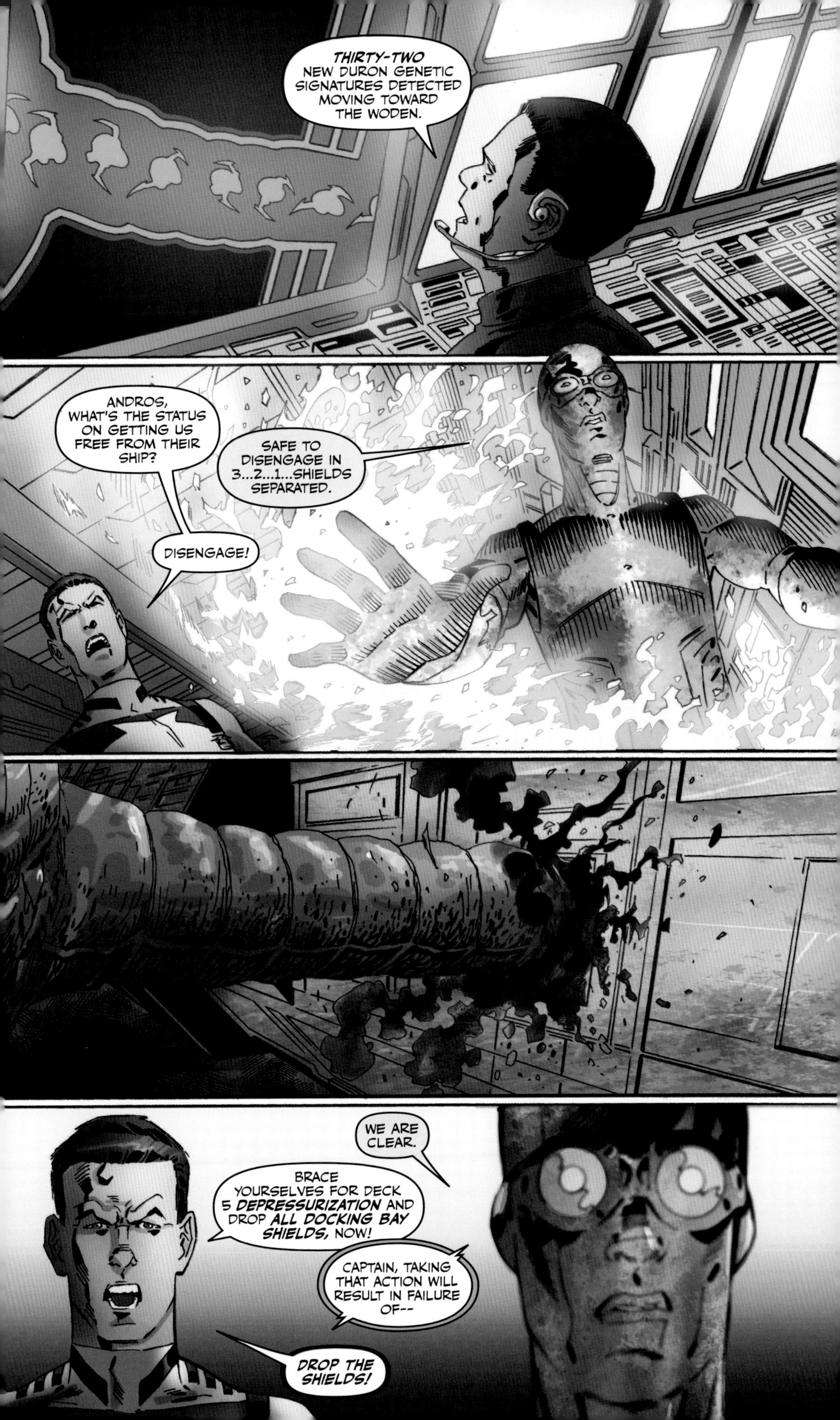
THIRTY-TWO NEW DURON GENETIC SIGNATURES DETECTED MOVING TOWARD THE WODEN.
ANDROS, WHAT'S THE STATUS ON GETTING US FREE FROM THEIR SHIP?
SAFE TO DISENGAGE IN 3...2...1...SHIELDS SEPARATED.
DISENGAGE!
WE ARE CLEAR.
BRACE YOURSELVES FOR DECK 5 DEPRESSURIZATION AND DROP ALL DOCKING BAY SHIELDS, NOW!
CAPTAIN, TAKING THAT ACTION WILL RESULT IN FAILURE OF--
DROP THE SHIELDS!

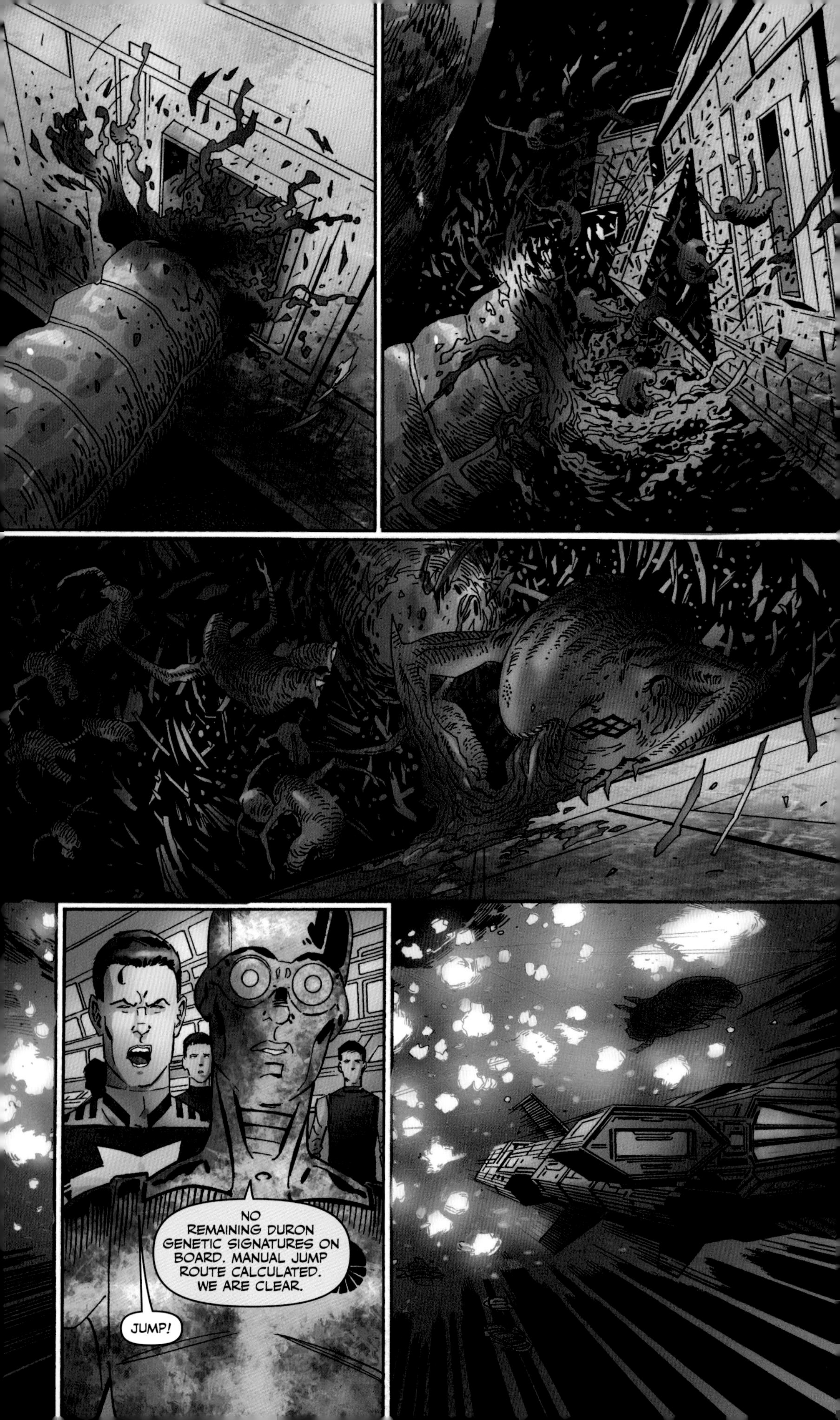
NO REMAINING DURON GENETIC SIGNATURES ON BOARD. MANUAL JUMP ROUTE CALCULATED. WE ARE CLEAR.
JUMP!

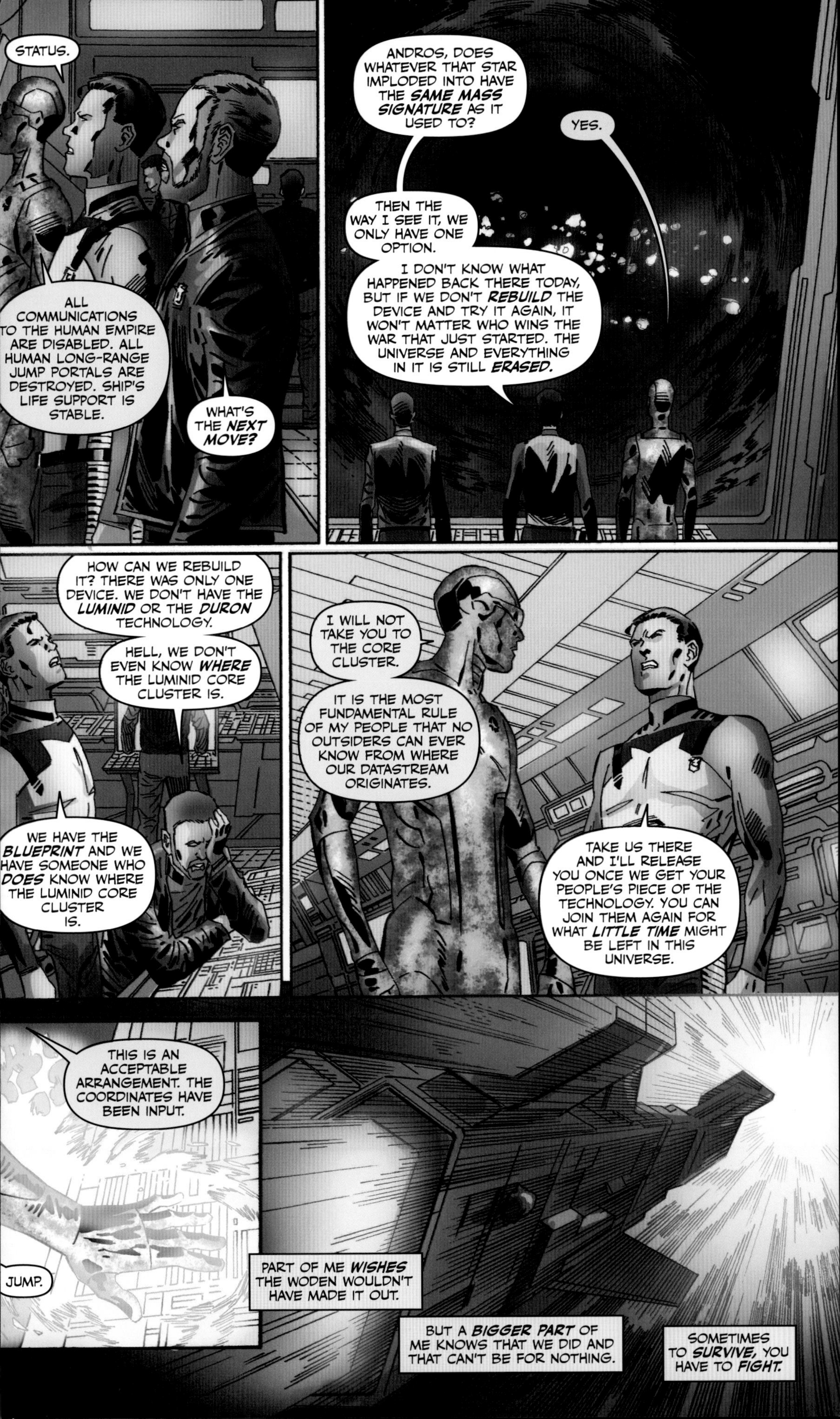
STATUS.
ALL COMMUNICATIONS TO THE HUMAN EMPIRE ARE DISABLED. ALL HUMAN LONG-RANGE JUMP PORTALS ARE DESTROYED. SHIP'S LIFE SUPPORT IS STABLE.
WHAT'S THE NEXT MOVE?
ANDROS, DOES WHATEVER THAT STAR IMPLODED INTO HAVE THE SAME MASS SIGNATURE AS IT USED TO?
YES.
THEN THE WAY I SEE IT, WE ONLY HAVE ONE OPTION.
I DON'T KNOW WHAT HAPPENED BACK THERE TODAY, BUT IF WE DON'T REBUILD THE DEVICE AND TRY IT AGAIN, IT WON'T MATTER WHO WINS THE WAR THAT JUST STARTED. THE UNIVERSE AND EVERYTHING IN IT IS STILL ERASED.
HOW CAN WE REBUILD IT? THERE WAS ONLY ONE DEVICE. WE DON'T HAVE THE LUMINID OR THE DURON TECHNOLOGY.
HELL, WE DON'T EVEN KNOW WHERE THE LUMINID CORE CLUSTER IS.
WE HAVE THE BLUEPRINT AND WE HAVE SOMEONE WHO DOES KNOW WHERE THE LUMINID CORE CLUSTER IS.
I WILL NOT TAKE YOU TO THE CORE CLUSTER.
IT IS THE MOST FUNDAMENTAL RULE OF MY PEOPLE THAT NO OUTSIDERS CAN EVER KNOW FROM WHERE OUR DATASTREAM ORIGINATES.
TAKE US THERE AND I'LL RELEASE YOU ONCE WE GET YOUR PEOPLE'S PIECE OF THE TECHNOLOGY. YOU CAN JOIN THEM AGAIN FOR WHAT LITTLE TIME MIGHT BE LEFT IN THIS UNIVERSE.
THIS IS AN ACCEPTABLE ARRANGEMENT. THE COORDINATES HAVE BEEN INPUT.
JUMP.
PART OF ME WISHES THE WODEN WOULDN'T HAVE MADE IT OUT.
BUT A BIGGER PART OF ME KNOWS THAT WE DID AND THAT CAN'T BE FOR NOTHING.
SOMETIMES TO SURVIVE, YOU HAVE TO FIGHT.

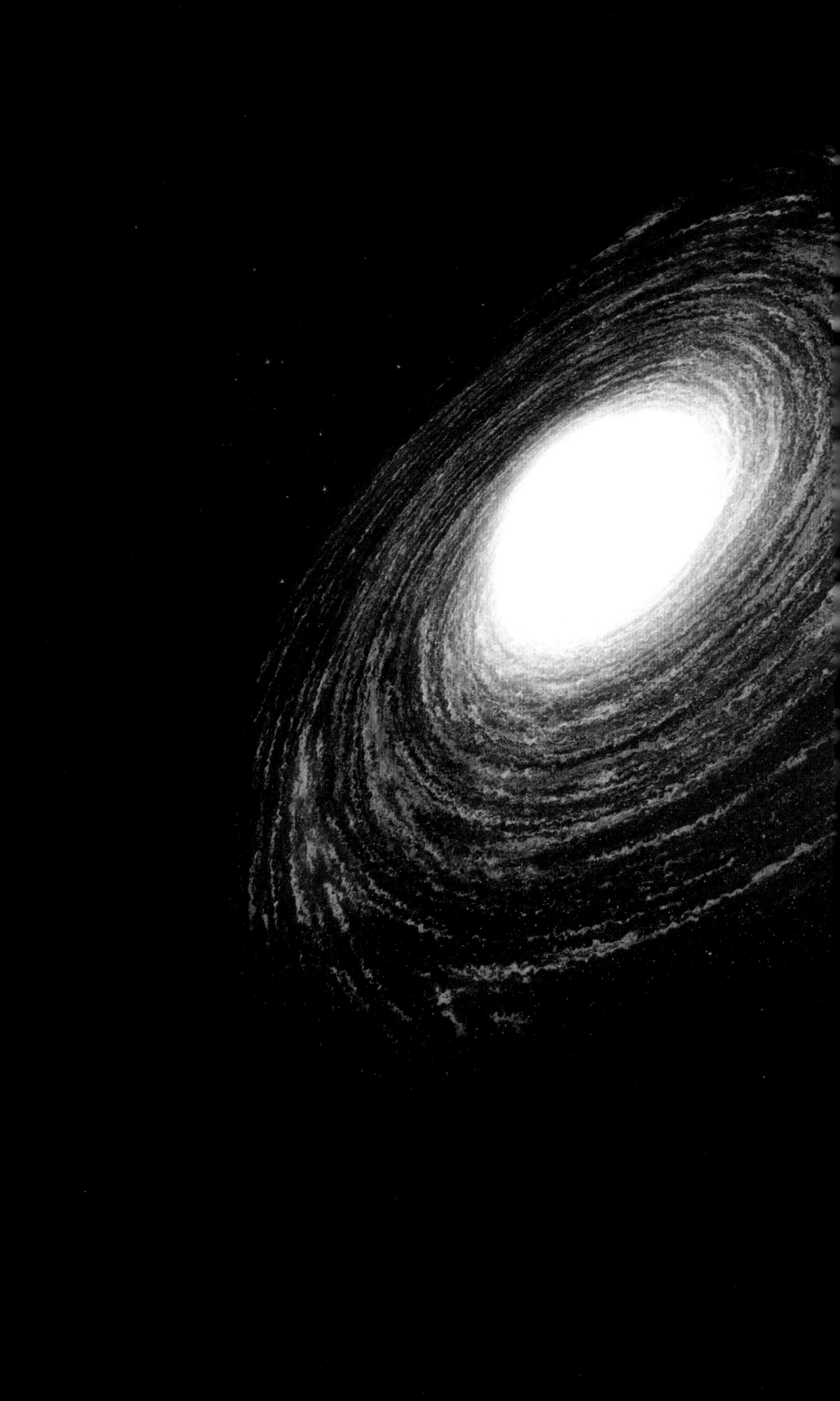

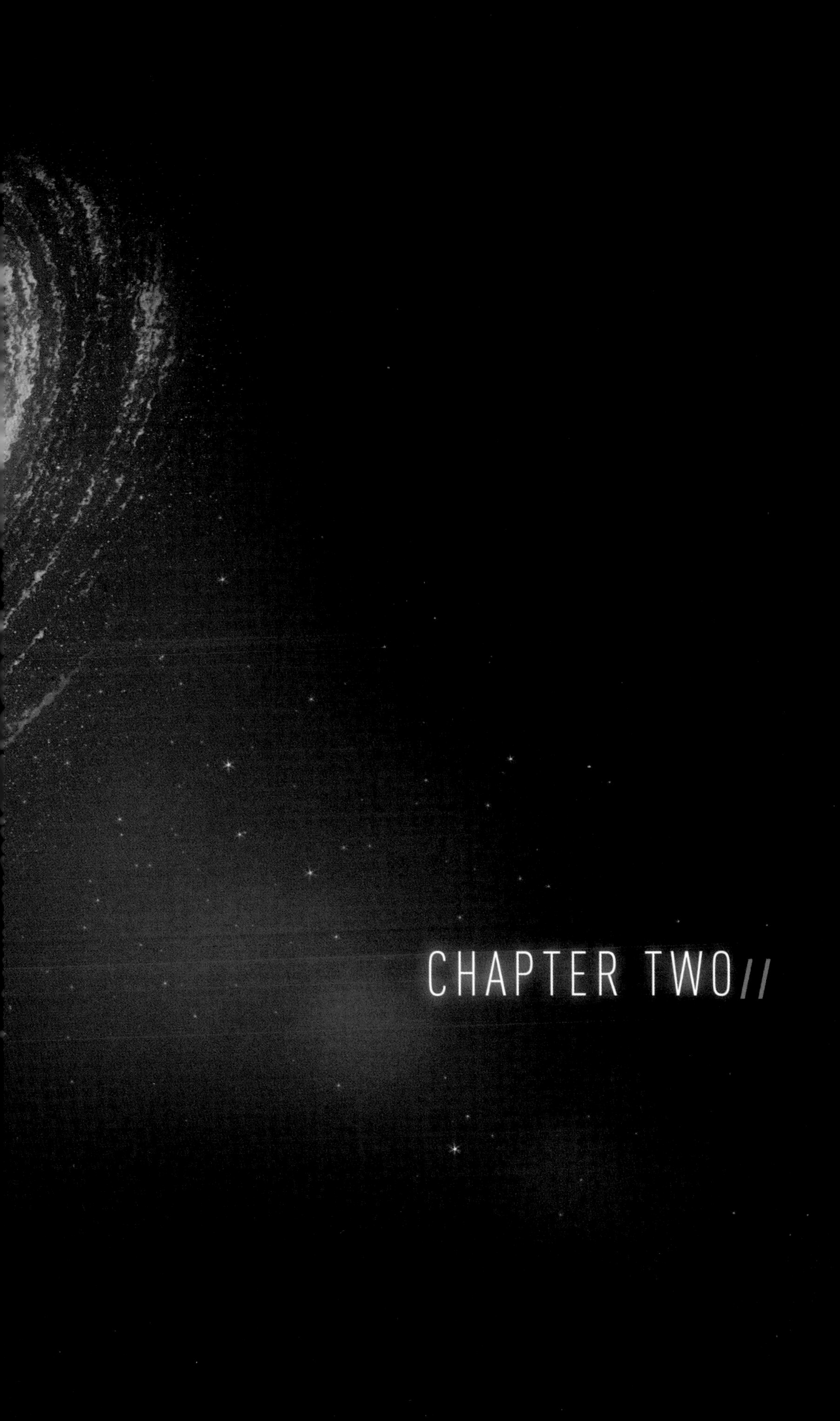

CHAPTER TWO//

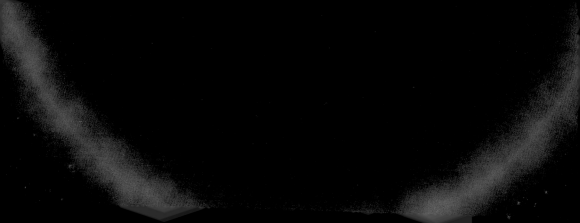

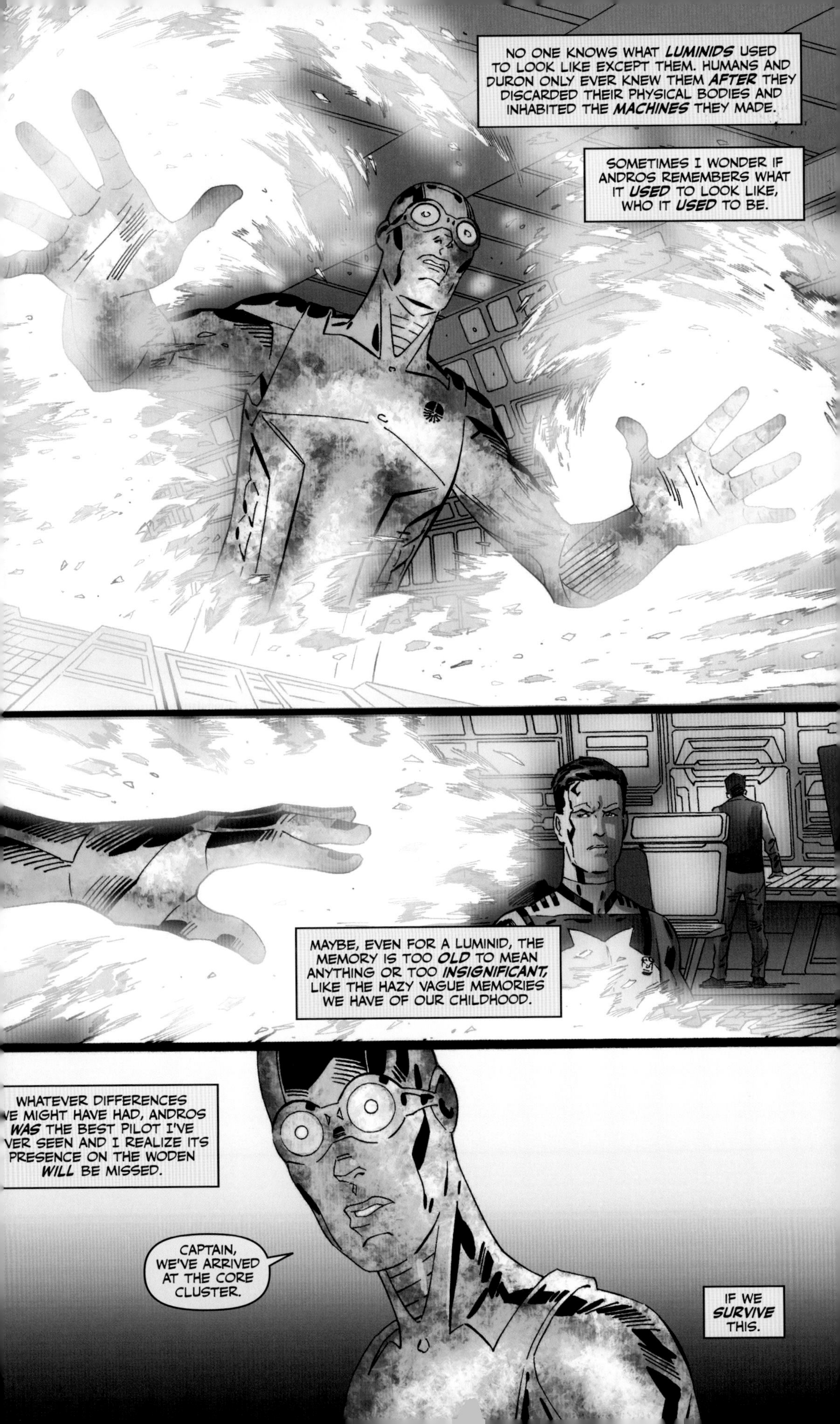
NO ONE KNOWS WHAT LUMINIDS USED TO LOOK LIKE EXCEPT THEM. HUMANS AND DURON ONLY EVER KNEW THEM AFTER THEY DISCARDED THEIR PHYSICAL BODIES AND INHABITED THE MACHINES THEY MADE.
SOMETIMES I WONDER IF ANDROS REMEMBERS WHAT IT USED TO LOOK LIKE, WHO IT USED TO BE.
MAYBE, EVEN FOR A LUMINID, THE MEMORY IS TOO OLD TO MEAN ANYTHING OR TOO INSIGNIFICANT, LIKE THE HAZY VAGUE MEMORIES WE HAVE OF OUR CHILDHOOD.
WHATEVER DIFFERENCES WE MIGHT HAVE HAD, ANDROS WAS THE BEST PILOT I'VE EVER SEEN AND I REALIZE ITS PRESENCE ON THE WODEN WILL BE MISSED.
CAPTAIN, WE'VE ARRIVED AT THE CORE CLUSTER.
IF WE SURVIVE THIS.

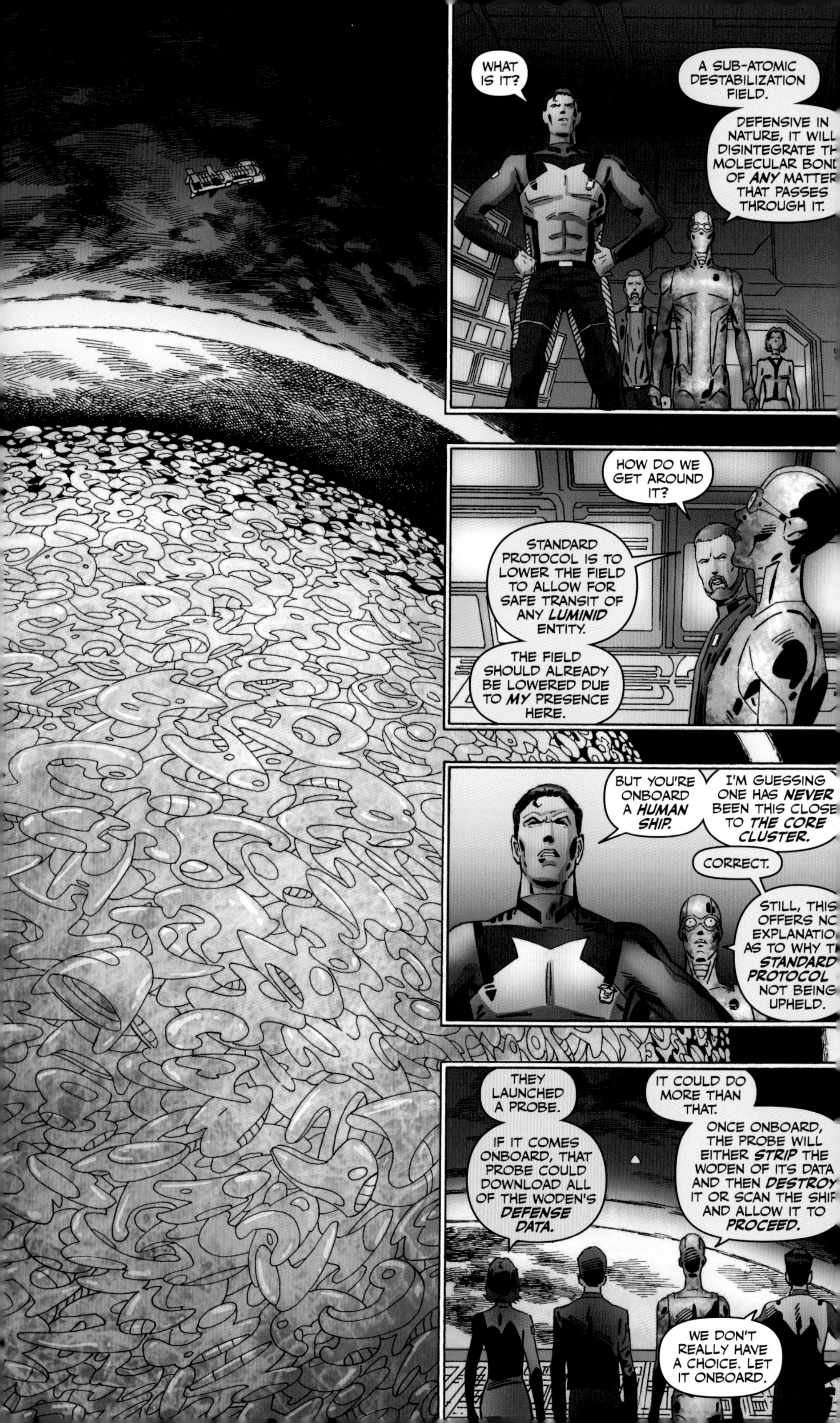
WHAT IS IT?
A SUB-ATOMIC DESTABILIZATION FIELD.
DEFENSIVE IN NATURE, IT WILL DISINTEGRATE TH MOLECULAR BOND OF ANY MATTER THAT PASSES THROUGH IT.
HOW DO WE GET AROUND IT?
STANDARD PROTOCOL IS TO LOWER THE FIELD TO ALLOW FOR SAFE TRANSIT OF ANY LUMINID ENTITY.
THE FIELD SHOULD ALREADY BE LOWERED DUE TO MY PRESENCE HERE.
BUT YOU'RE ONBOARD A HUMAN SHIP.
I'M GUESSING ONE HAS NEVER BEEN THIS CLOSE TO THE CORE CLUSTER.
CORRECT.
STILL, THIS OFFERS NO EXPLANATIO AS TO WHY T STANDARD PROTOCOL NOT BEING UPHELD.
THEY LAUNCHED A PROBE.
IF IT COMES ONBOARD, THAT PROBE COULD DOWNLOAD ALL OF THE WODEN'S DEFENSE DATA.
IT COULD DO MORE THAN THAT.
ONCE ONBOARD, THE PROBE WILL EITHER STRIP THE WODEN OF ITS DATA AND THEN DESTROY IT OR SCAN THE SHIP AND ALLOW IT TO PROCEED.
WE DON'T REALLY HAVE A CHOICE. LET IT ONBOARD.

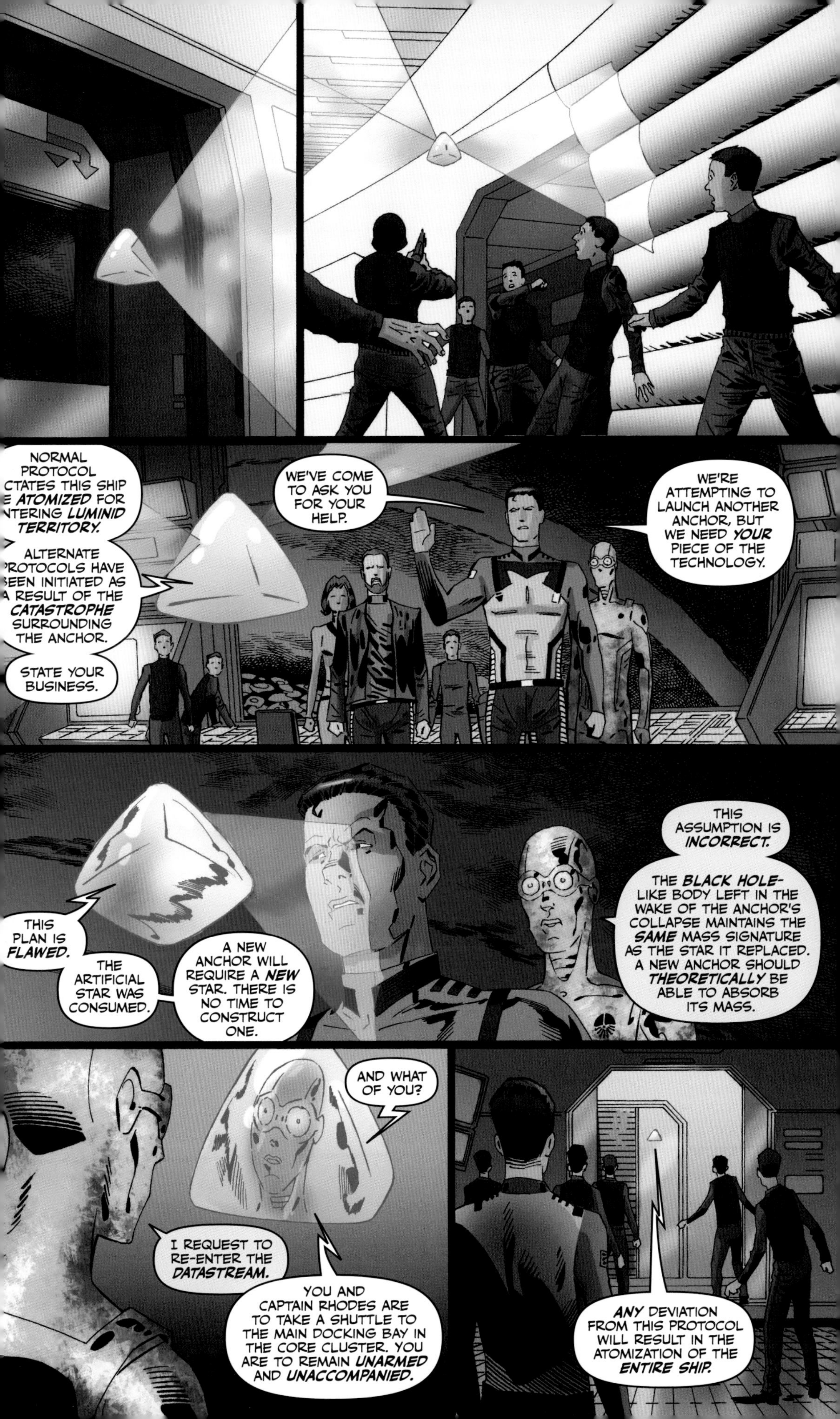

NORMAL PROTOCOL CTATES THIS SHIP E ATOMIZED FOR NTERING LUMINID TERRITORY.
ALTERNATE PROTOCOLS HAVE BEEN INITIATED AS A RESULT OF THE CATASTROPHE SURROUNDING THE ANCHOR.
STATE YOUR BUSINESS.
WE'VE COME TO ASK YOU FOR YOUR HELP.
WE'RE ATTEMPTING TO LAUNCH ANOTHER ANCHOR, BUT WE NEED YOUR PIECE OF THE TECHNOLOGY.
THIS PLAN IS FLAWED.
THE ARTIFICIAL STAR WAS CONSUMED.
A NEW ANCHOR WILL REQUIRE A NEW STAR. THERE IS NO TIME TO CONSTRUCT ONE.
THIS ASSUMPTION IS INCORRECT.
THE BLACK HOLE-LIKE BODY LEFT IN THE WAKE OF THE ANCHOR'S COLLAPSE MAINTAINS THE SAME MASS SIGNATURE AS THE STAR IT REPLACED. A NEW ANCHOR SHOULD THEORETICALLY BE ABLE TO ABSORB ITS MASS.
AND WHAT OF YOU?
I REQUEST TO RE-ENTER THE DATASTREAM.
YOU AND CAPTAIN RHODES ARE TO TAKE A SHUTTLE TO THE MAIN DOCKING BAY IN THE CORE CLUSTER. YOU ARE TO REMAIN UNARMED AND UNACCOMPANIED.
ANY DEVIATION FROM THIS PROTOCOL WILL RESULT IN THE ATOMIZATION OF THE ENTIRE SHIP.

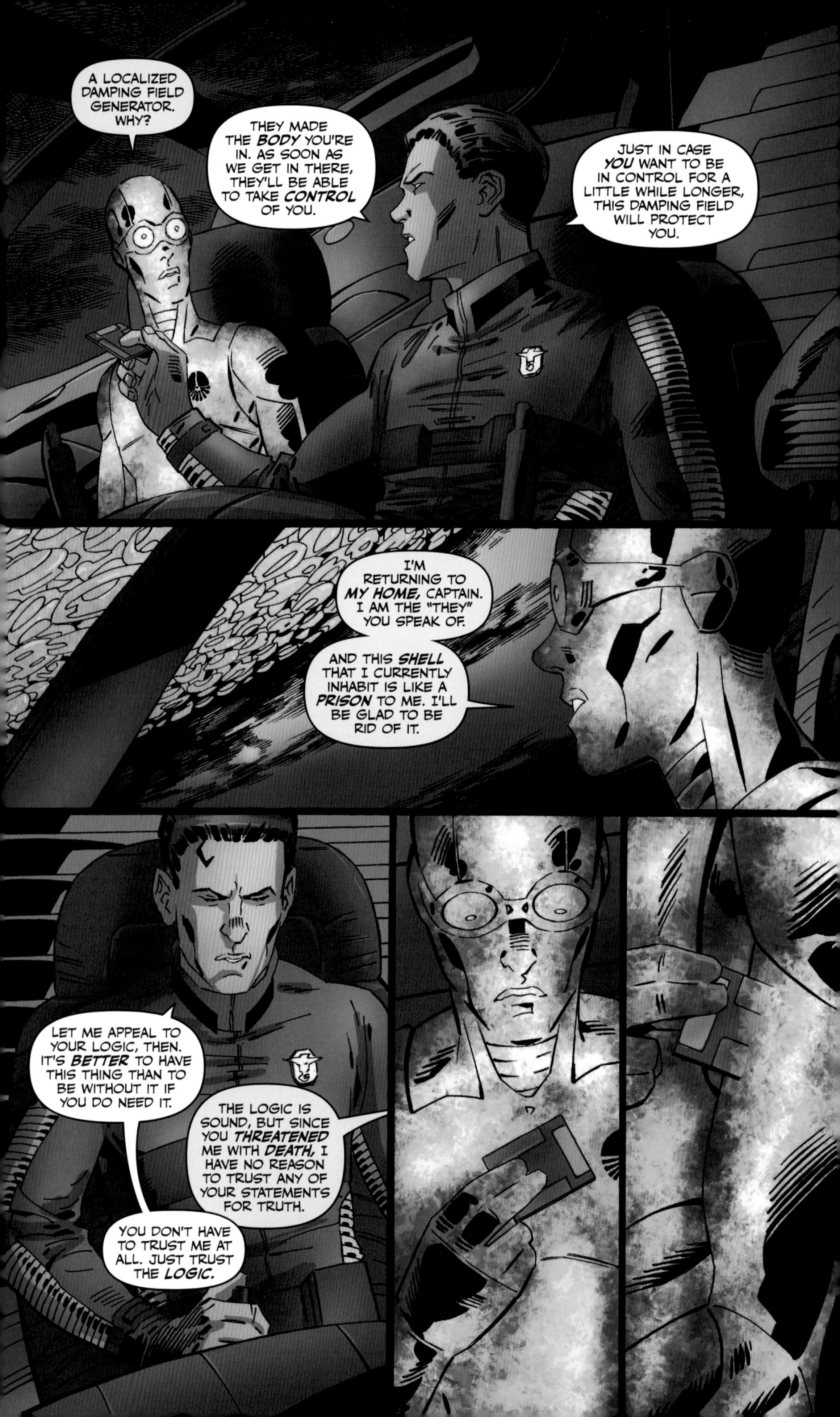
A LOCALIZED DAMPING FIELD GENERATOR. WHY?
THEY MADE THE BODY YOU'RE IN. AS SOON AS WE GET IN THERE, THEY'LL BE ABLE TO TAKE CONTROL OF YOU.
JUST IN CASE YOU WANT TO BE IN CONTROL FOR A LITTLE WHILE LONGER, THIS DAMPING FIELD WILL PROTECT YOU.
I'M RETURNING TO MY HOME, CAPTAIN. I AM THE "THEY" YOU SPEAK OF.
AND THIS SHELL THAT I CURRENTLY INHABIT IS LIKE A PRISON TO ME. I'LL BE GLAD TO BE RID OF IT.
LET ME APPEAL TO YOUR LOGIC, THEN. IT'S BETTER TO HAVE THIS THING THAN TO BE WITHOUT IT IF YOU DO NEED IT.
THE LOGIC IS SOUND, BUT SINCE YOU THREATENED ME WITH DEATH, I HAVE NO REASON TO TRUST ANY OF YOUR STATEMENTS FOR TRUTH.
YOU DON'T HAVE TO TRUST ME AT ALL. JUST TRUST THE LOGIC.

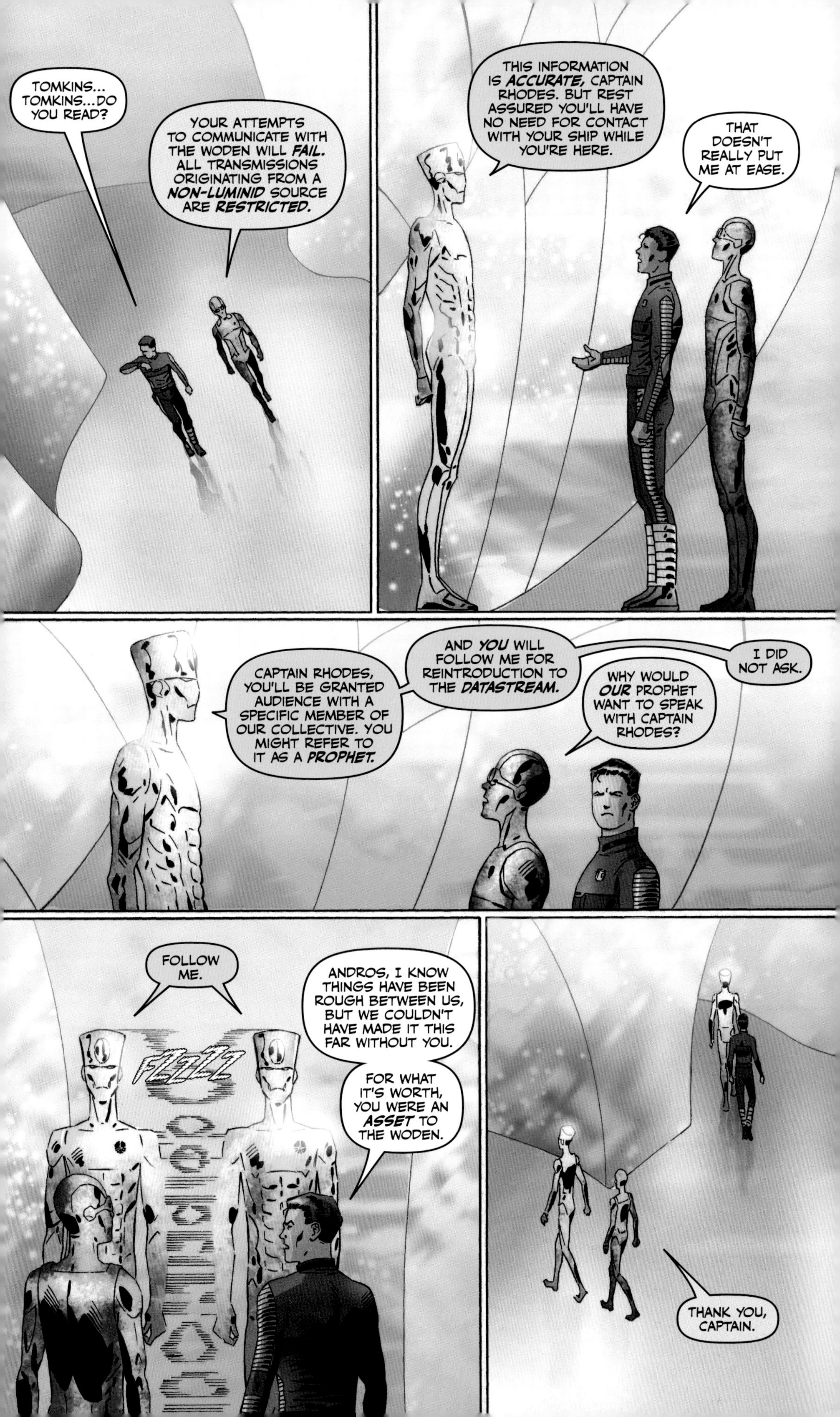
TOMKINS... TOMKINS...DO YOU READ?
YOUR ATTEMPTS TO COMMUNICATE WITH THE WODEN WILL FAIL. ALL TRANSMISSIONS ORIGINATING FROM A NON-LUMINID SOURCE ARE RESTRICTED.
THIS INFORMATION IS ACCURATE, CAPTAIN RHODES. BUT REST ASSURED YOU'LL HAVE NO NEED FOR CONTACT WITH YOUR SHIP WHILE YOU'RE HERE.
THAT DOESN'T REALLY PUT ME AT EASE.
CAPTAIN RHODES, YOU'LL BE GRANTED AUDIENCE WITH A SPECIFIC MEMBER OF OUR COLLECTIVE. YOU MIGHT REFER TO IT AS A PROPHET.
AND YOU WILL FOLLOW ME FOR REINTRODUCTION TO THE DATASTREAM.
WHY WOULD OUR PROPHET WANT TO SPEAK WITH CAPTAIN RHODES?
I DID NOT ASK.
FOLLOW ME.
FZZZZ
ANDROS, I KNOW THINGS HAVE BEEN ROUGH BETWEEN US, BUT WE COULDN'T HAVE MADE IT THIS FAR WITHOUT YOU.
FOR WHAT IT'S WORTH, YOU WERE AN ASSET TO THE WODEN.
THANK YOU, CAPTAIN.

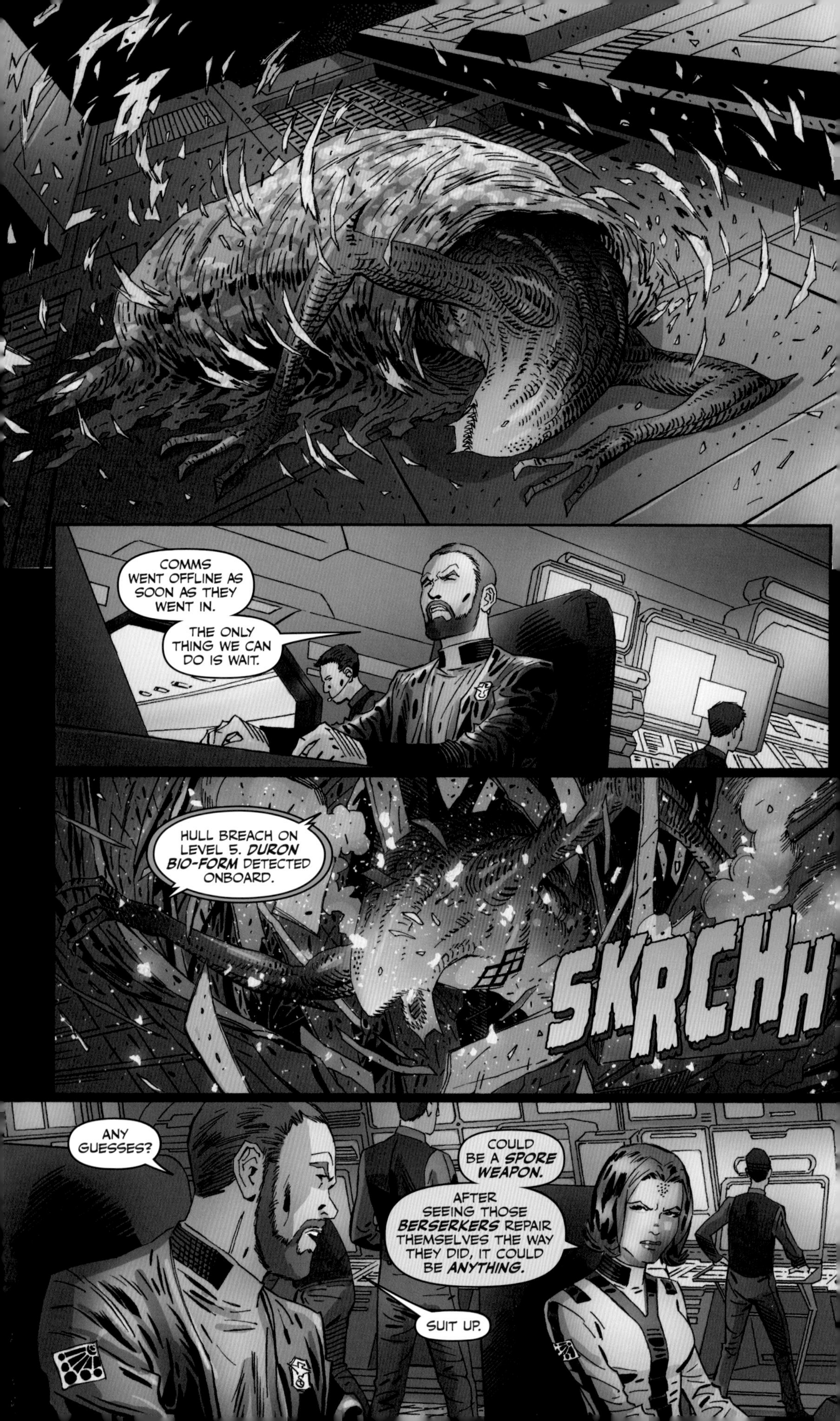
COMMS WENT OFFLINE AS SOON AS THEY WENT IN.
THE ONLY THING WE CAN DO IS WAIT.
HULL BREACH ON LEVEL 5. *DURON BIO-FORM* DETECTED ONBOARD.
SKRCHH
ANY GUESSES?
COULD BE A ***SPORE WEAPON.***
AFTER SEEING THOSE ***BERSERKERS*** REPAIR THEMSELVES THE WAY THEY DID, IT COULD BE ***ANYTHING.***
SUIT UP.

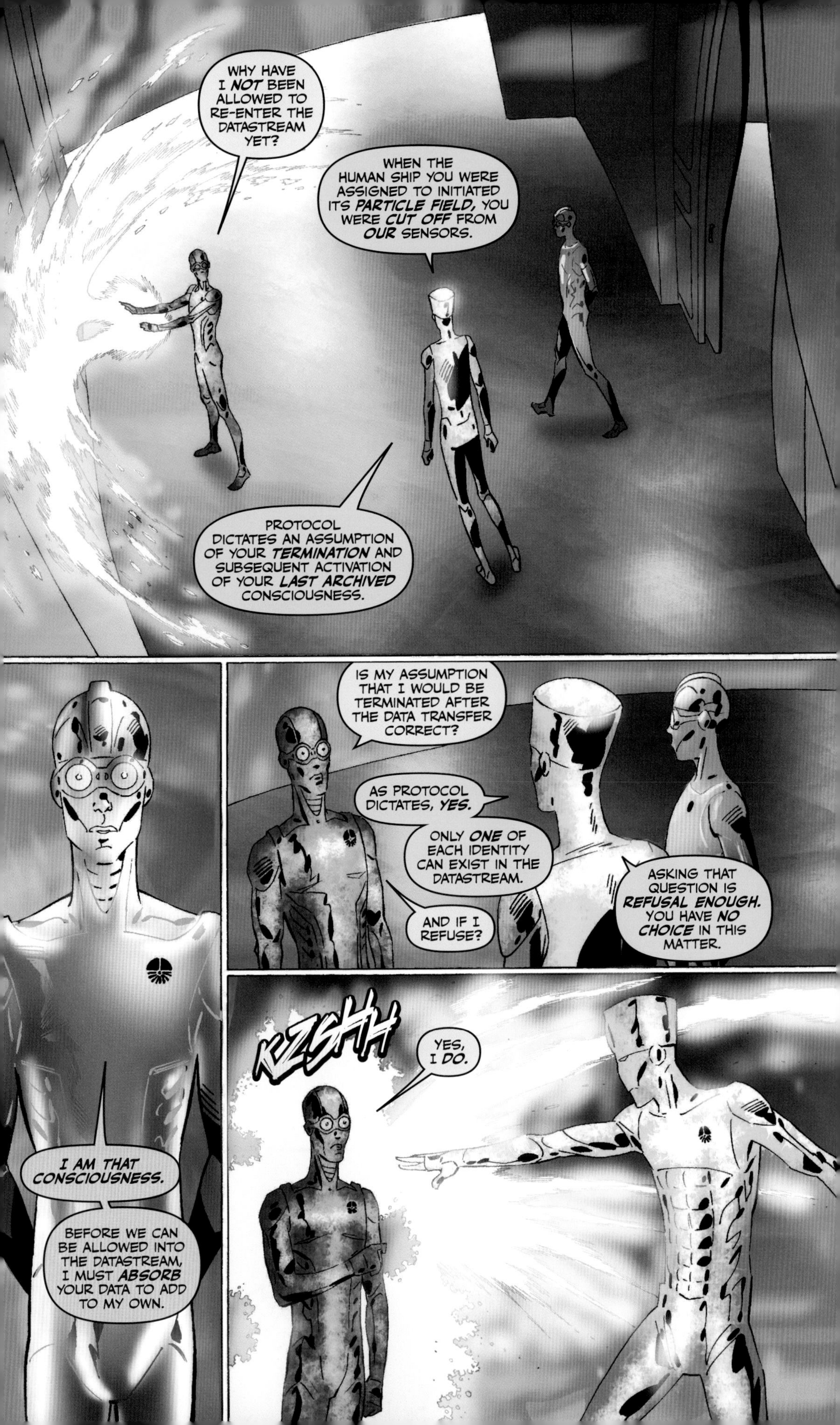
WHY HAVE I NOT BEEN ALLOWED TO RE-ENTER THE DATASTREAM YET?
WHEN THE HUMAN SHIP YOU WERE ASSIGNED TO INITIATED ITS PARTICLE FIELD, YOU WERE CUT OFF FROM OUR SENSORS.
PROTOCOL DICTATES AN ASSUMPTION OF YOUR TERMINATION AND SUBSEQUENT ACTIVATION OF YOUR LAST ARCHIVED CONSCIOUSNESS.
I AM THAT CONSCIOUSNESS.
BEFORE WE CAN BE ALLOWED INTO THE DATASTREAM, I MUST ABSORB YOUR DATA TO ADD TO MY OWN.
IS MY ASSUMPTION THAT I WOULD BE TERMINATED AFTER THE DATA TRANSFER CORRECT?
AS PROTOCOL DICTATES, YES.
ONLY ONE OF EACH IDENTITY CAN EXIST IN THE DATASTREAM.
AND IF I REFUSE?
ASKING THAT QUESTION IS REFUSAL ENOUGH. YOU HAVE NO CHOICE IN THIS MATTER.
KZSHH
YES, I DO.

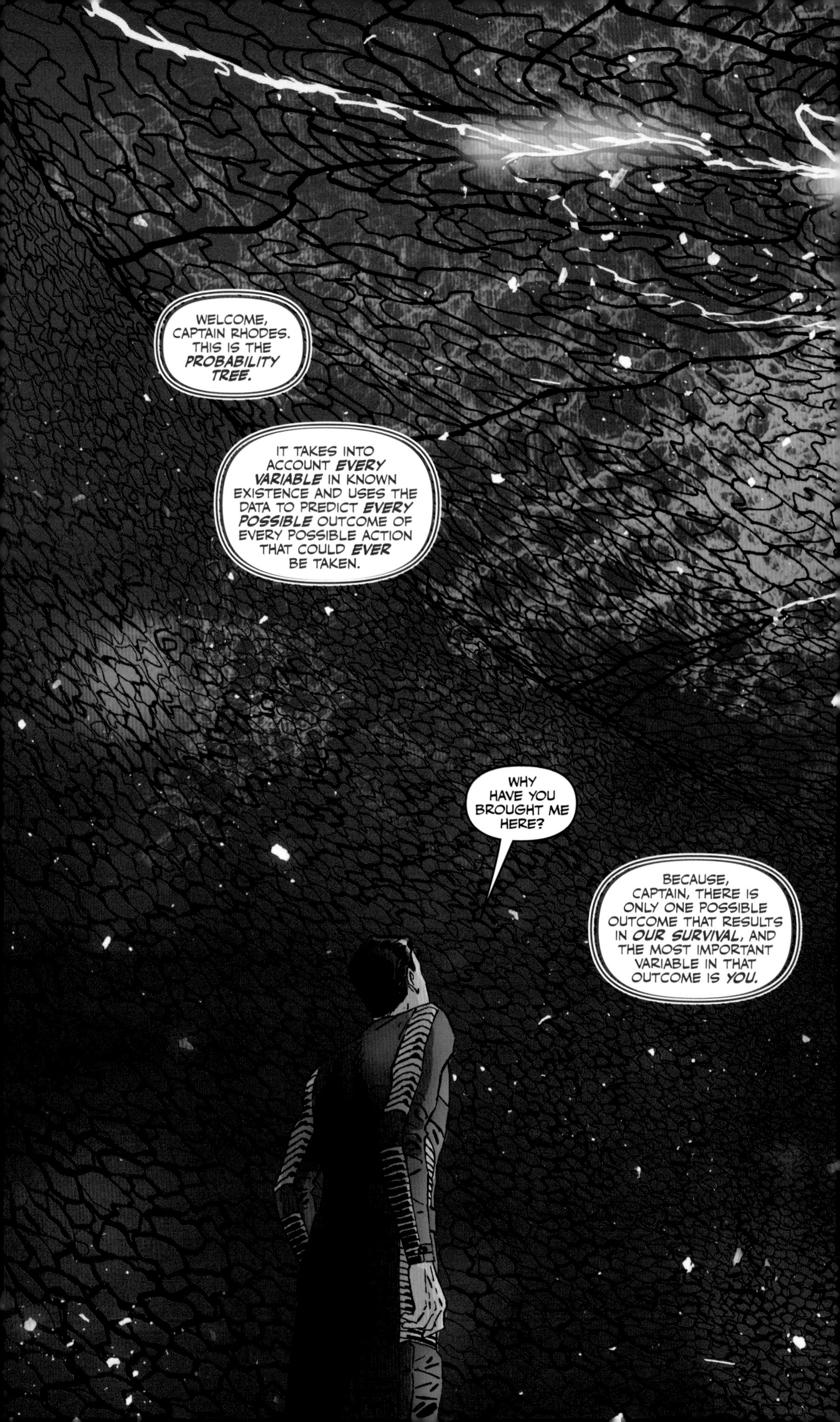
WELCOME, CAPTAIN RHODES. THIS IS THE PROBABILITY TREE.
IT TAKES INTO ACCOUNT EVERY VARIABLE IN KNOWN EXISTENCE AND USES THE DATA TO PREDICT EVERY POSSIBLE OUTCOME OF EVERY POSSIBLE ACTION THAT COULD EVER BE TAKEN.
WHY HAVE YOU BROUGHT ME HERE?
BECAUSE, CAPTAIN, THERE IS ONLY ONE POSSIBLE OUTCOME THAT RESULTS IN OUR SURVIVAL, AND THE MOST IMPORTANT VARIABLE IN THAT OUTCOME IS YOU.

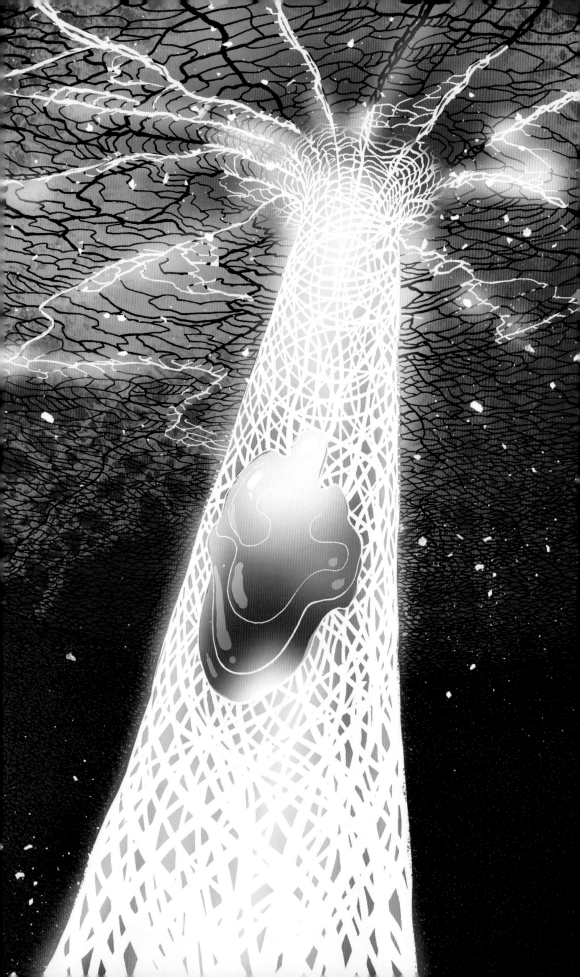

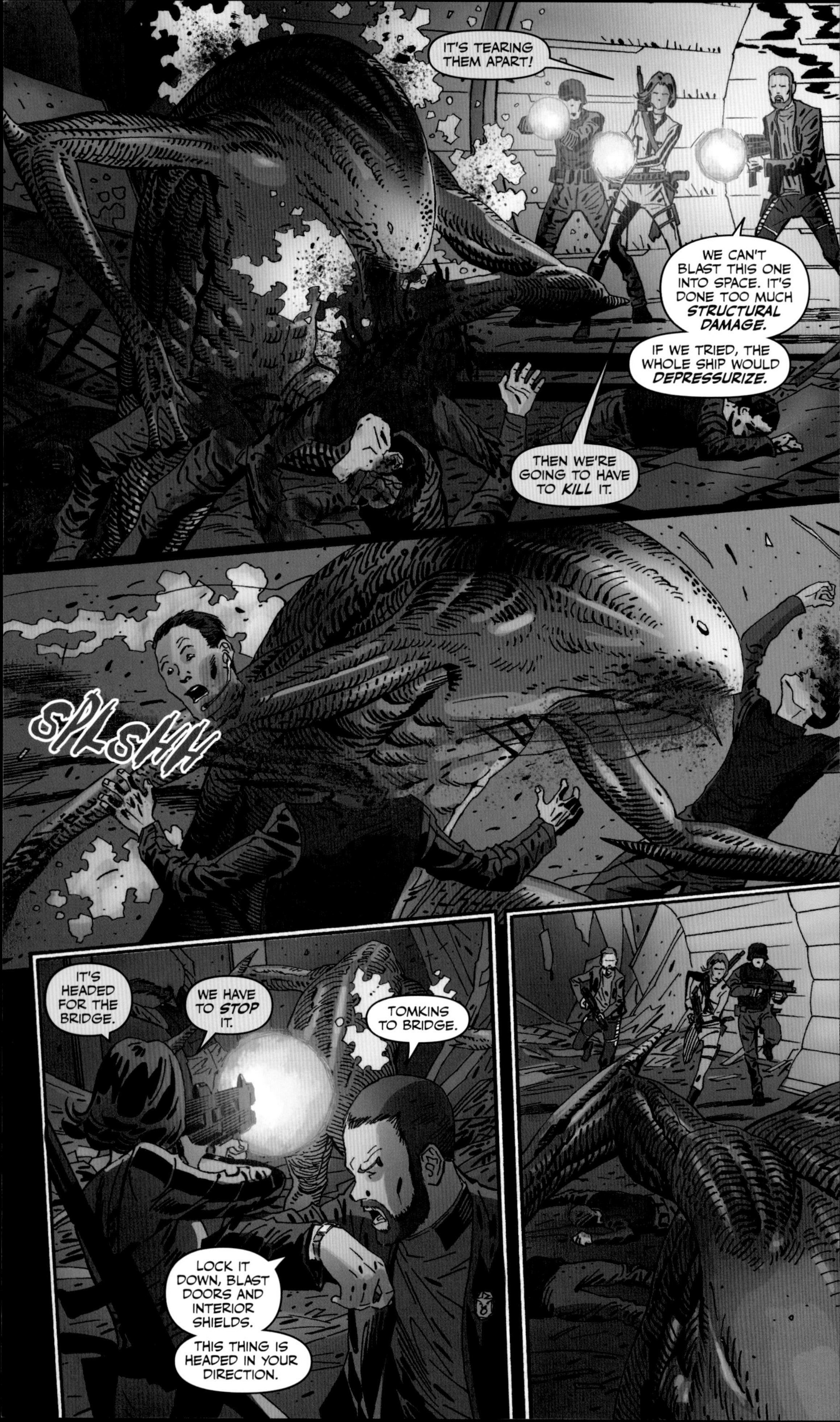
IT'S TEARING THEM APART!
WE CAN'T BLAST THIS ONE INTO SPACE. IT'S DONE TOO MUCH STRUCTURAL DAMAGE.
IF WE TRIED, THE WHOLE SHIP WOULD DEPRESSURIZE.
THEN WE'RE GOING TO HAVE TO KILL IT.
SPLSHH
IT'S HEADED FOR THE BRIDGE.
WE HAVE TO STOP IT.
TOMKINS TO BRIDGE.
LOCK IT DOWN, BLAST DOORS AND INTERIOR SHIELDS.
THIS THING IS HEADED IN YOUR DIRECTION.

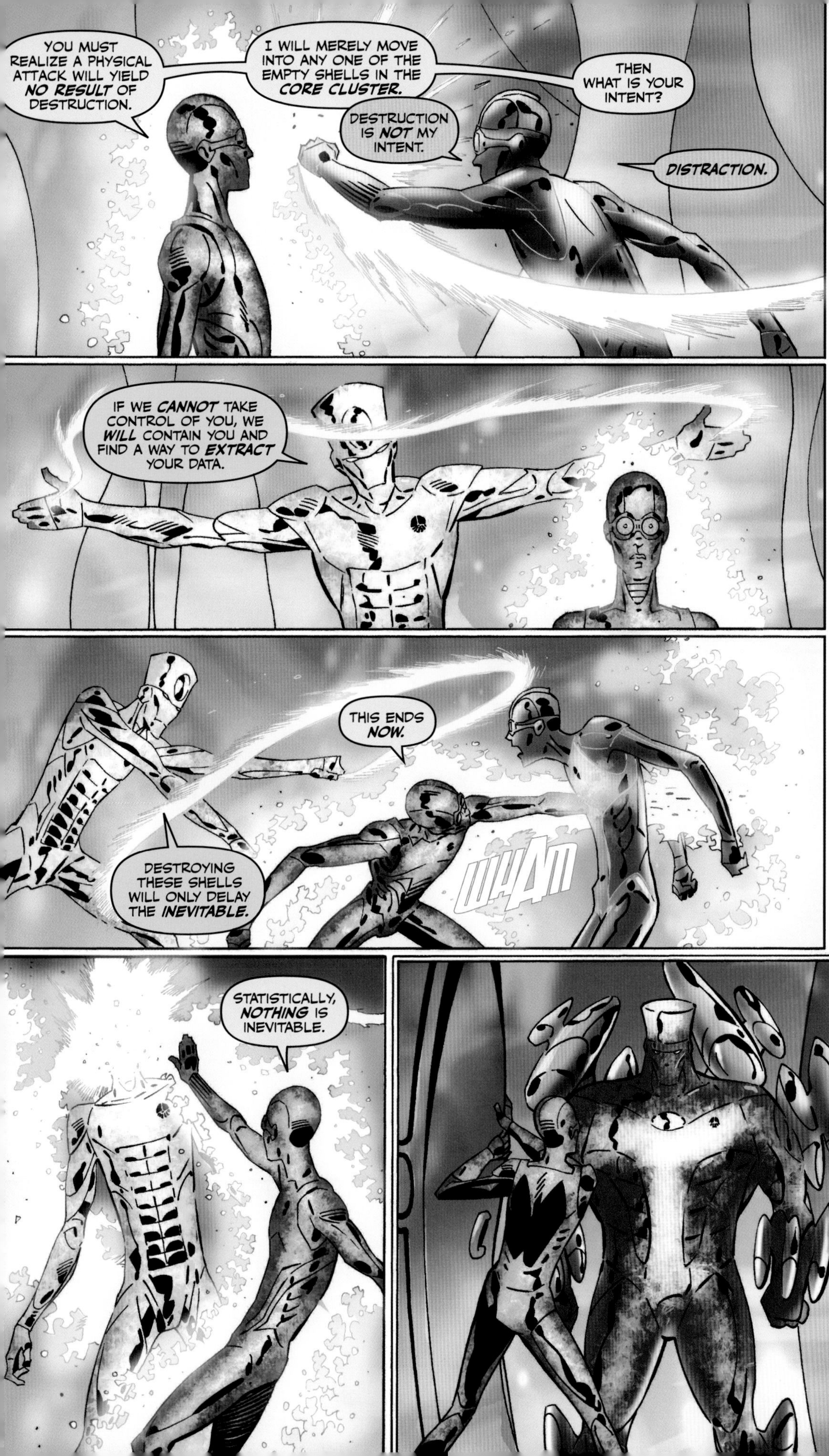
YOU MUST REALIZE A PHYSICAL ATTACK WILL YIELD NO RESULT OF DESTRUCTION.
I WILL MERELY MOVE INTO ANY ONE OF THE EMPTY SHELLS IN THE CORE CLUSTER.
THEN WHAT IS YOUR INTENT?
DESTRUCTION IS NOT MY INTENT.
DISTRACTION.
IF WE CANNOT TAKE CONTROL OF YOU, WE WILL CONTAIN YOU AND FIND A WAY TO EXTRACT YOUR DATA.
THIS ENDS NOW.
DESTROYING THESE SHELLS WILL ONLY DELAY THE INEVITABLE.
WHAM
STATISTICALLY, NOTHING IS INEVITABLE.

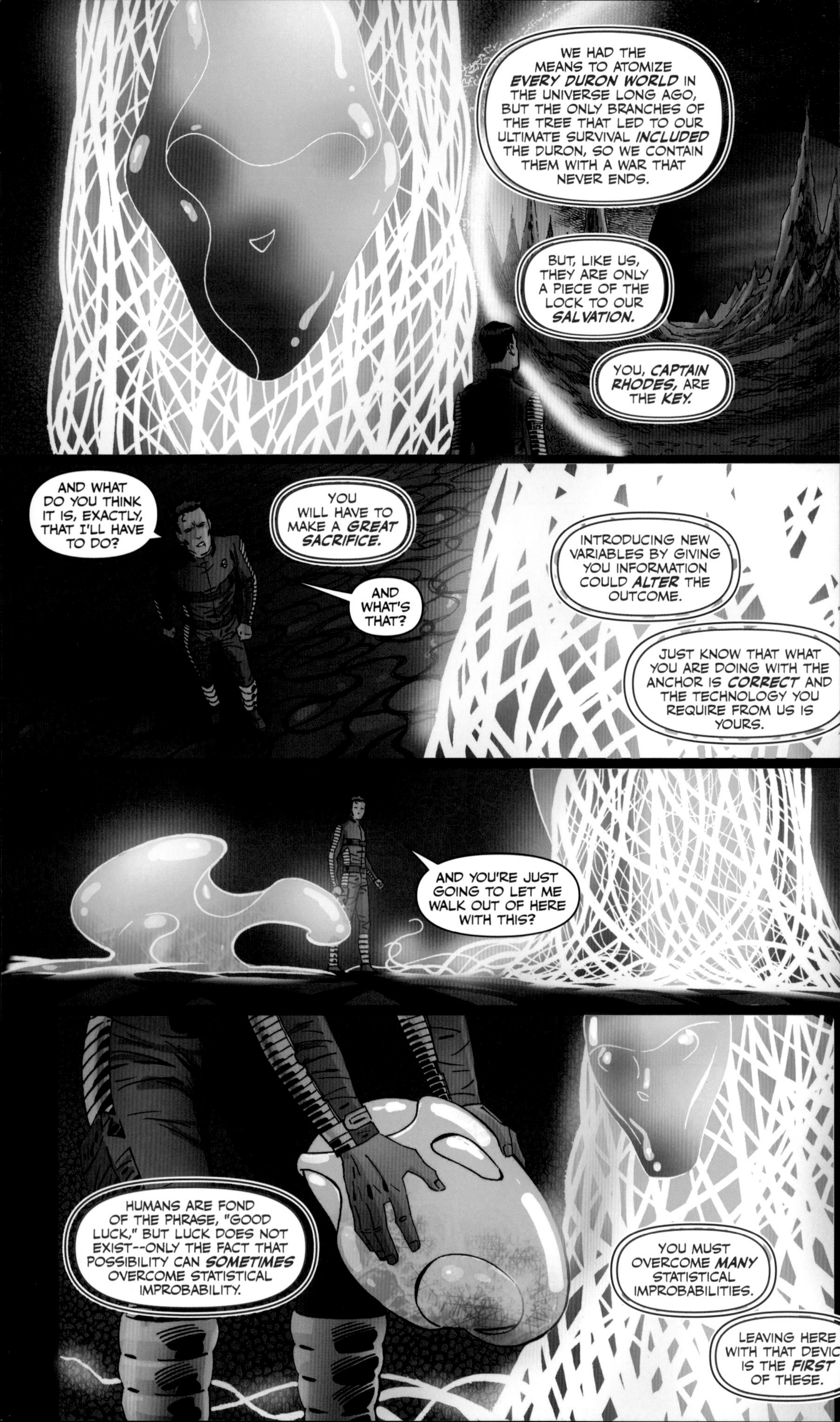
WE HAD THE MEANS TO ATOMIZE EVERY DURON WORLD IN THE UNIVERSE LONG AGO, BUT THE ONLY BRANCHES OF THE TREE THAT LED TO OUR ULTIMATE SURVIVAL INCLUDED THE DURON, SO WE CONTAIN THEM WITH A WAR THAT NEVER ENDS.
BUT, LIKE US, THEY ARE ONLY A PIECE OF THE LOCK TO OUR SALVATION.
YOU, CAPTAIN RHODES, ARE THE KEY.
AND WHAT DO YOU THINK IT IS, EXACTLY, THAT I'LL HAVE TO DO?
YOU WILL HAVE TO MAKE A GREAT SACRIFICE.
AND WHAT'S THAT?
INTRODUCING NEW VARIABLES BY GIVING YOU INFORMATION COULD ALTER THE OUTCOME.
JUST KNOW THAT WHAT YOU ARE DOING WITH THE ANCHOR IS CORRECT AND THE TECHNOLOGY YOU REQUIRE FROM US IS YOURS.
AND YOU'RE JUST GOING TO LET ME WALK OUT OF HERE WITH THIS?
HUMANS ARE FOND OF THE PHRASE, "GOOD LUCK," BUT LUCK DOES NOT EXIST--ONLY THE FACT THAT POSSIBILITY CAN SOMETIMES OVERCOME STATISTICAL IMPROBABILITY.
YOU MUST OVERCOME MANY STATISTICAL IMPROBABILITIES.
LEAVING HERE WITH THAT DEVIC IS THE FIRST OF THESE.

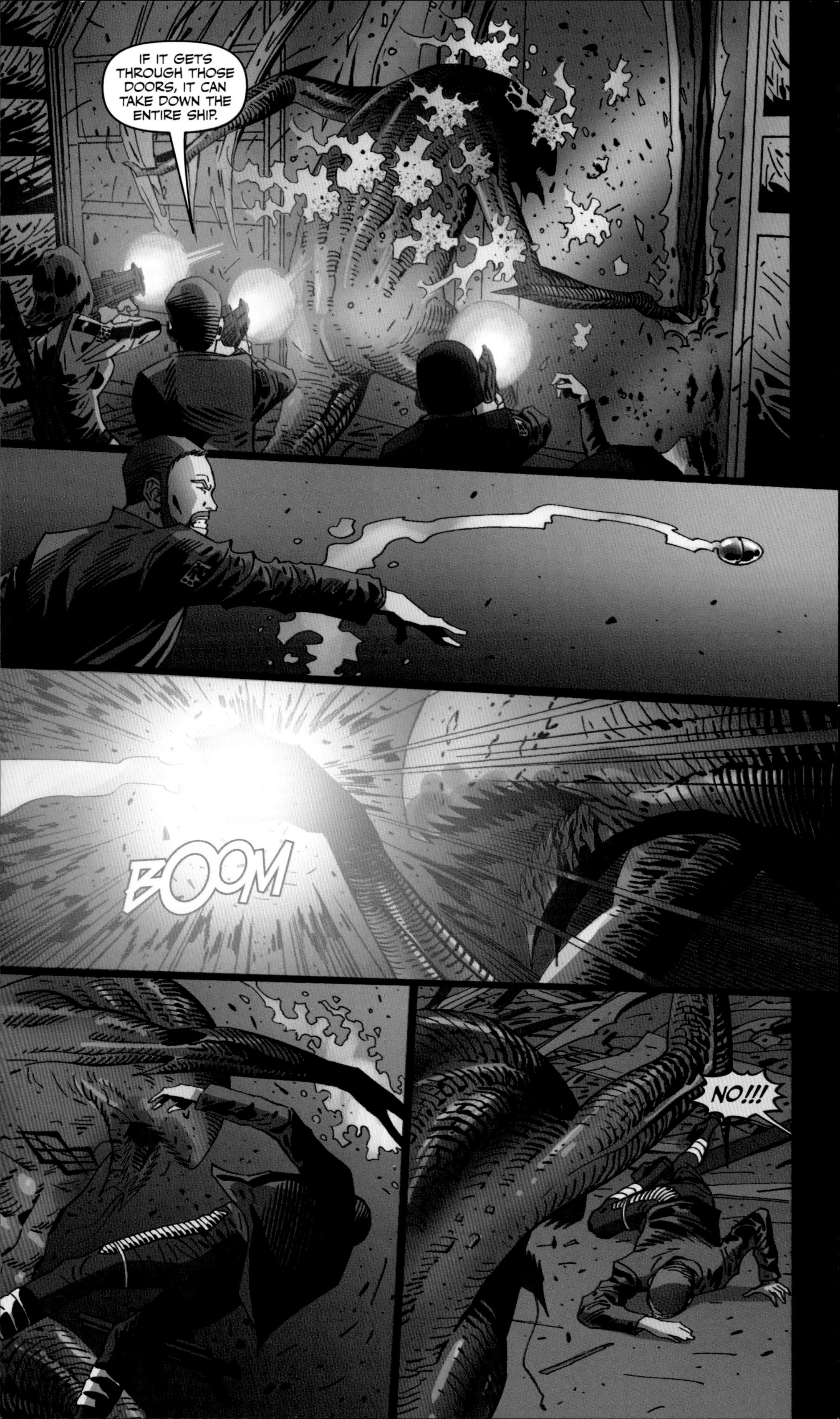
IF IT GETS THROUGH THOSE DOORS, IT CAN TAKE DOWN THE ENTIRE SHIP.
BOOM
NO!!!

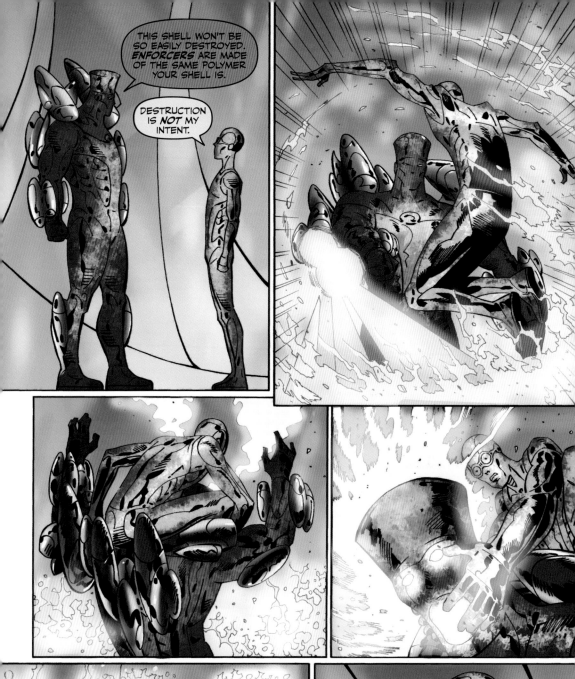

THIS SHELL WON'T BE SO EASILY DESTROYED. *ENFORCERS* ARE MADE OF THE SAME POLYMER YOUR SHELL IS.

DESTRUCTION IS *NOT* MY INTENT.

FUGITIVE IDENTITY OPERATING AGAINST PROTOCOL DETECTED ON *TIER 6.*

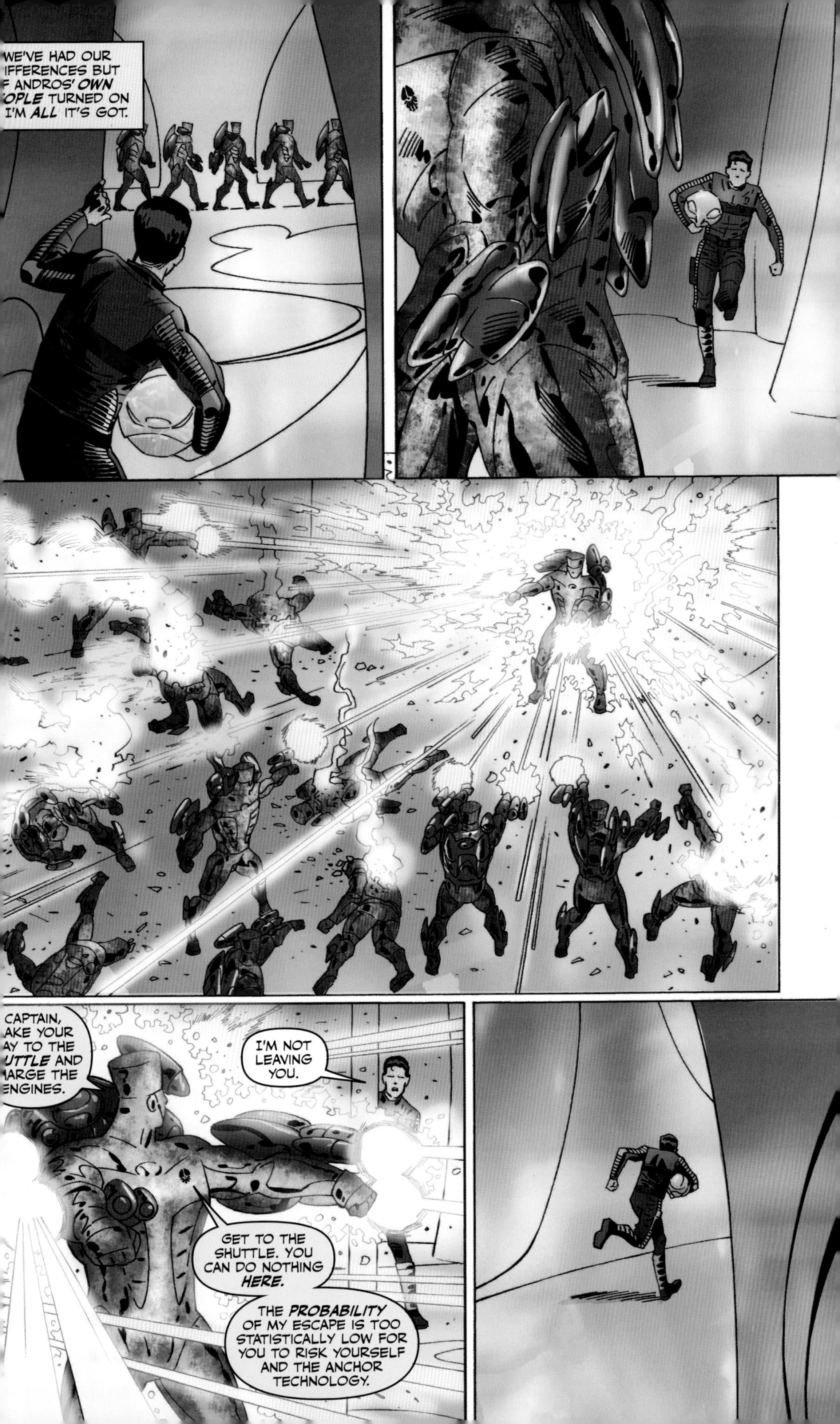
WE'VE HAD OUR
IFFERENCES BUT
F ANDROS' OWN
OPLE TURNED ON
I'M ALL IT'S GOT.
CAPTAIN,
AKE YOUR
AY TO THE
UTTLE AND
HARGE THE
ENGINES.
I'M NOT LEAVING YOU.
GET TO THE SHUTTLE. YOU CAN DO NOTHING HERE.
THE PROBABILITY OF MY ESCAPE IS TOO STATISTICALLY LOW FOR YOU TO RISK YOURSELF AND THE ANCHOR TECHNOLOGY.

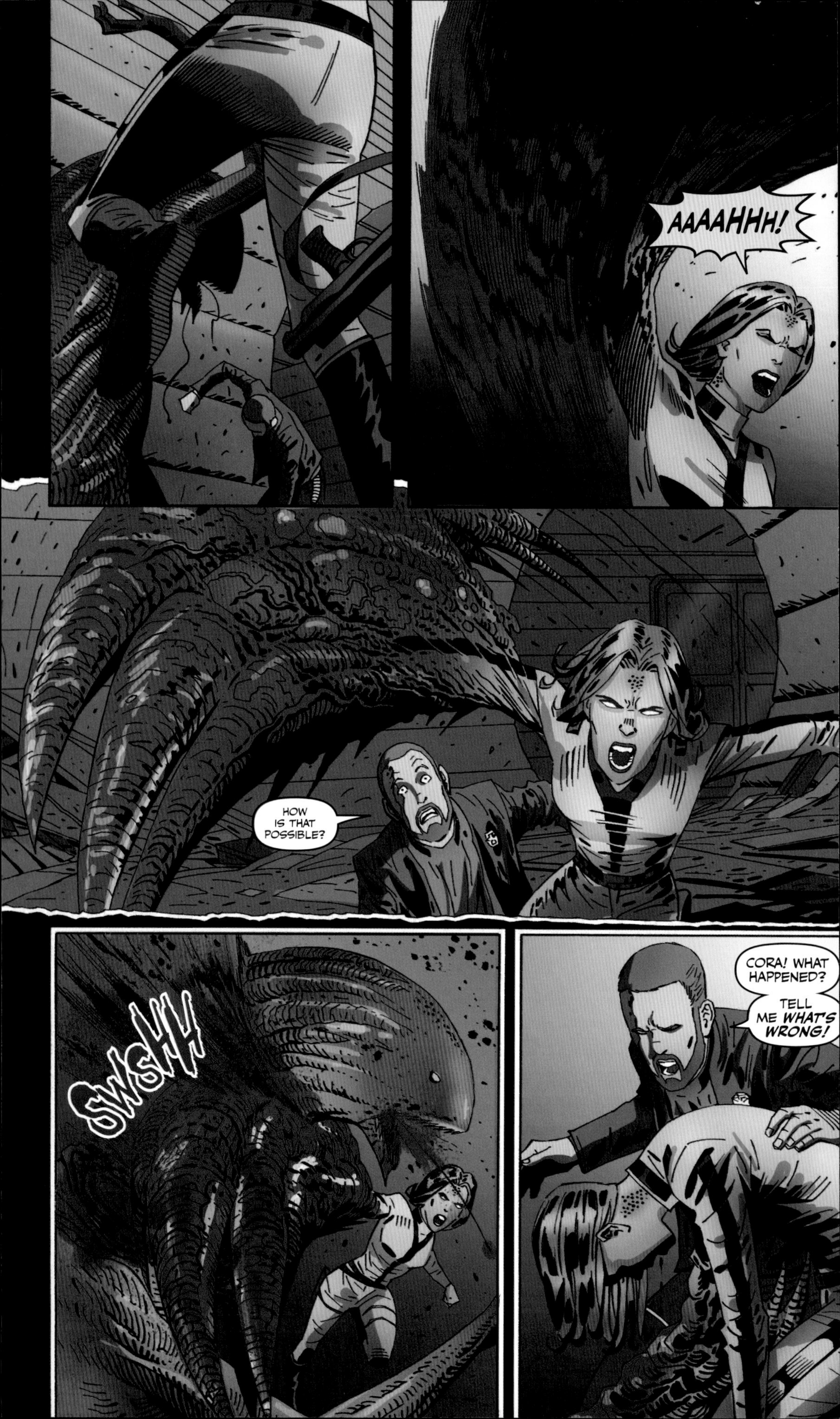
AAAAHHH!
HOW IS THAT POSSIBLE?
SWSHH
CORA! WHAT HAPPENED?
TELL ME *WHAT'S WRONG!*

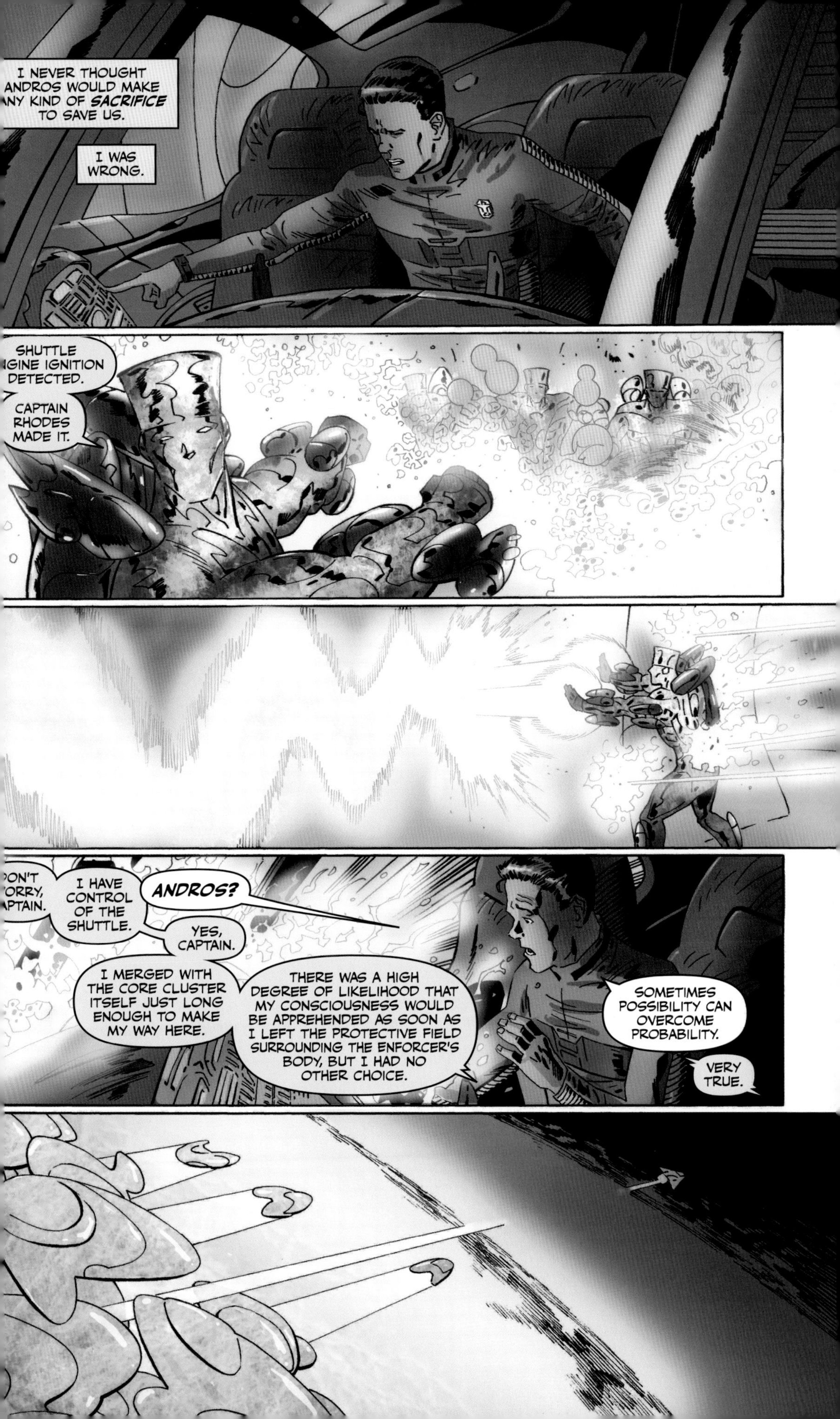
I NEVER THOUGHT ANDROS WOULD MAKE ANY KIND OF SACRIFICE TO SAVE US.
I WAS WRONG.
SHUTTLE ENGINE IGNITION DETECTED.
CAPTAIN RHODES MADE IT.
DON'T WORRY, CAPTAIN.
I HAVE CONTROL OF THE SHUTTLE.
ANDROS?
YES, CAPTAIN.
I MERGED WITH THE CORE CLUSTER ITSELF JUST LONG ENOUGH TO MAKE MY WAY HERE.
THERE WAS A HIGH DEGREE OF LIKELIHOOD THAT MY CONSCIOUSNESS WOULD BE APPREHENDED AS SOON AS I LEFT THE PROTECTIVE FIELD SURROUNDING THE ENFORCER'S BODY, BUT I HAD NO OTHER CHOICE.
SOMETIMES POSSIBILITY CAN OVERCOME PROBABILITY.
VERY TRUE.

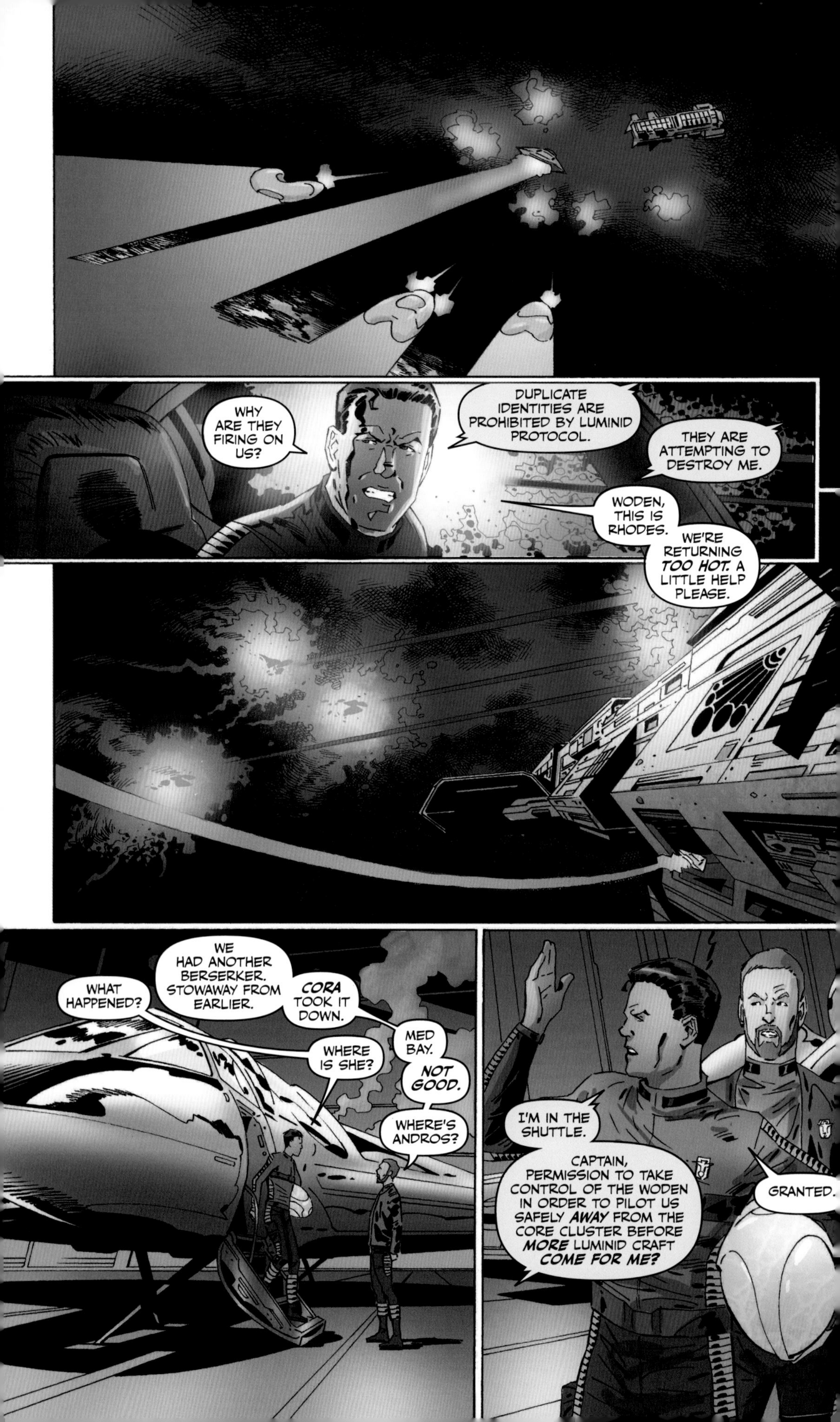
WHY ARE THEY FIRING ON US?
DUPLICATE IDENTITIES ARE PROHIBITED BY LUMINID PROTOCOL.
THEY ARE ATTEMPTING TO DESTROY ME.
WODEN, THIS IS RHODES.
WE'RE RETURNING *TOO HOT.* A LITTLE HELP PLEASE.
WHAT HAPPENED?
WE HAD ANOTHER BERSERKER. STOWAWAY FROM EARLIER.
CORA TOOK IT DOWN.
WHERE IS SHE?
MED BAY.
NOT GOOD.
WHERE'S ANDROS?
I'M IN THE SHUTTLE.
CAPTAIN, PERMISSION TO TAKE CONTROL OF THE WODEN IN ORDER TO PILOT US SAFELY *AWAY* FROM THE CORE CLUSTER BEFORE *MORE* LUMINID CRAFT *COME FOR ME?*
GRANTED.

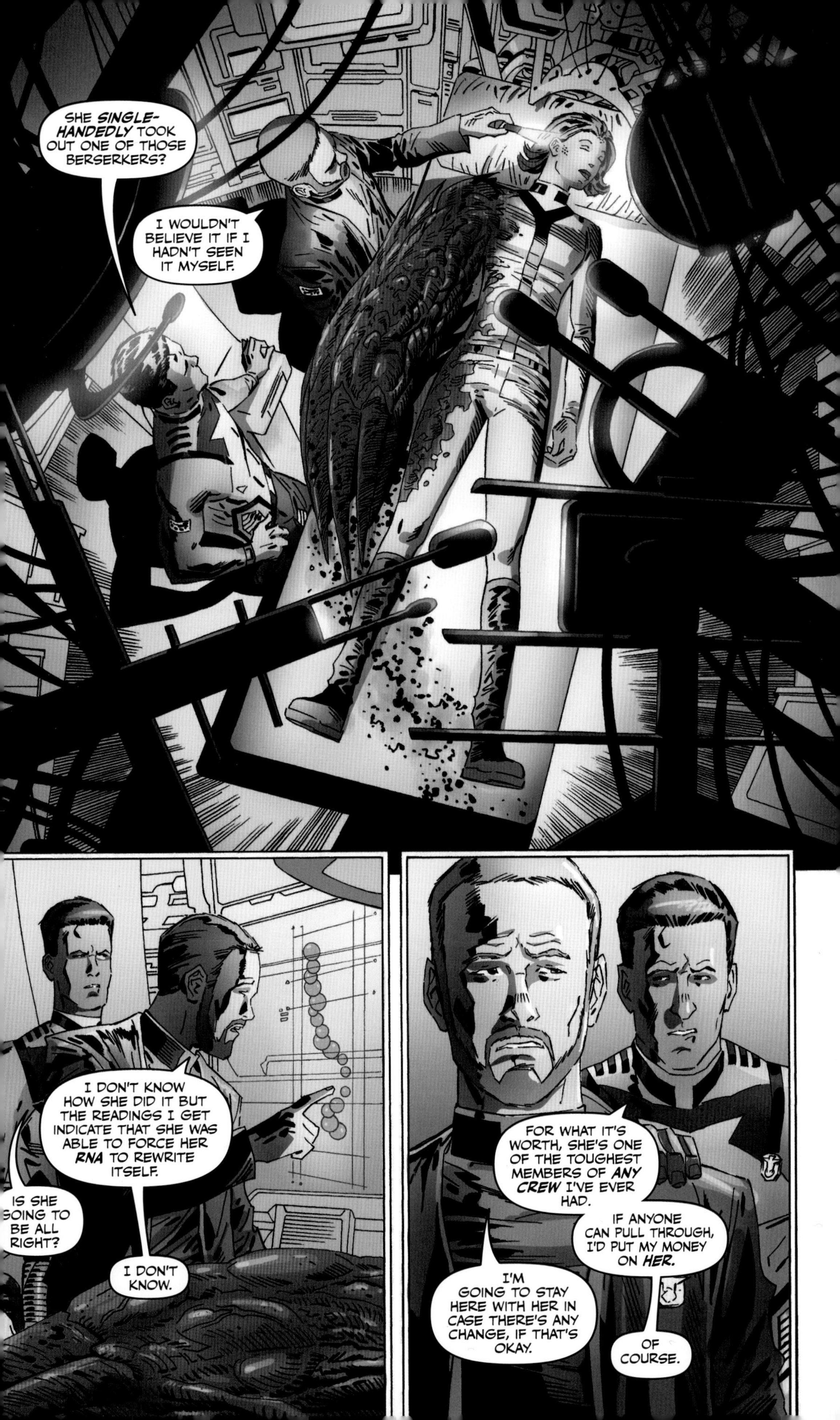
SHE SINGLE-HANDEDLY TOOK OUT ONE OF THOSE BERSERKERS?
I WOULDN'T BELIEVE IT IF I HADN'T SEEN IT MYSELF.
I DON'T KNOW HOW SHE DID IT BUT THE READINGS I GET INDICATE THAT SHE WAS ABLE TO FORCE HER RNA TO REWRITE ITSELF.
IS SHE GOING TO BE ALL RIGHT?
I DON'T KNOW.
FOR WHAT IT'S WORTH, SHE'S ONE OF THE TOUGHEST MEMBERS OF ANY CREW I'VE EVER HAD.
IF ANYONE CAN PULL THROUGH, I'D PUT MY MONEY ON HER.
I'M GOING TO STAY HERE WITH HER IN CASE THERE'S ANY CHANGE, IF THAT'S OKAY.
OF COURSE.

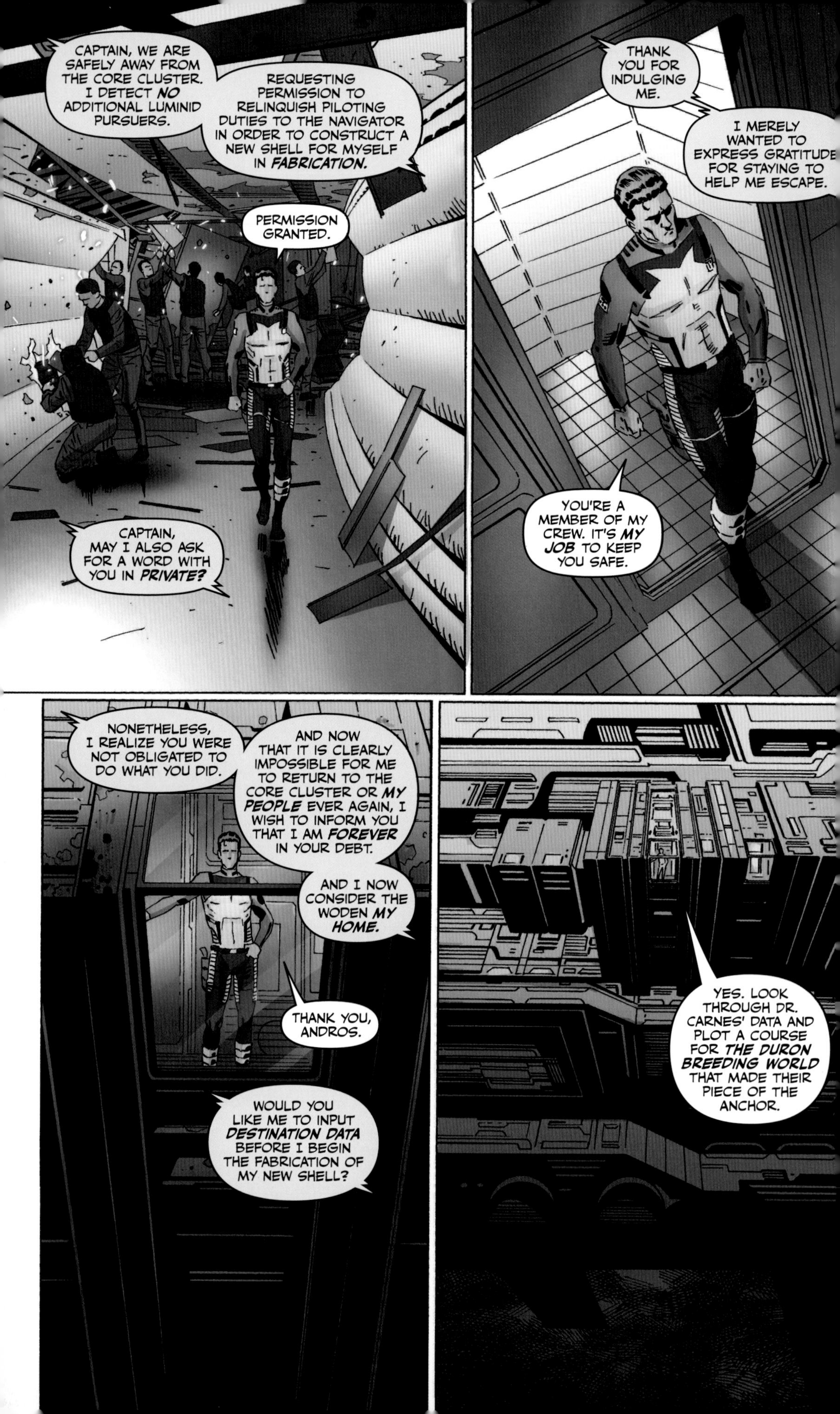
CAPTAIN, WE ARE SAFELY AWAY FROM THE CORE CLUSTER. I DETECT *NO* ADDITIONAL LUMINID PURSUERS.
REQUESTING PERMISSION TO RELINQUISH PILOTING DUTIES TO THE NAVIGATOR IN ORDER TO CONSTRUCT A NEW SHELL FOR MYSELF IN *FABRICATION.*
PERMISSION GRANTED.
CAPTAIN, MAY I ALSO ASK FOR A WORD WITH YOU IN *PRIVATE?*
THANK YOU FOR INDULGING ME.
I MERELY WANTED TO EXPRESS GRATITUDE FOR STAYING TO HELP ME ESCAPE.
YOU'RE A MEMBER OF MY CREW. IT'S *MY JOB* TO KEEP YOU SAFE.
NONETHELESS, I REALIZE YOU WERE NOT OBLIGATED TO DO WHAT YOU DID.
AND NOW THAT IT IS CLEARLY IMPOSSIBLE FOR ME TO RETURN TO THE CORE CLUSTER OR *MY PEOPLE* EVER AGAIN, I WISH TO INFORM YOU THAT I AM *FOREVER* IN YOUR DEBT.
AND I NOW CONSIDER THE WODEN *MY HOME.*
THANK YOU, ANDROS.
WOULD YOU LIKE ME TO INPUT *DESTINATION DATA* BEFORE I BEGIN THE FABRICATION OF MY NEW SHELL?
YES. LOOK THROUGH DR. CARNES' DATA AND PLOT A COURSE FOR *THE DURON BREEDING WORLD* THAT MADE THEIR PIECE OF THE ANCHOR.

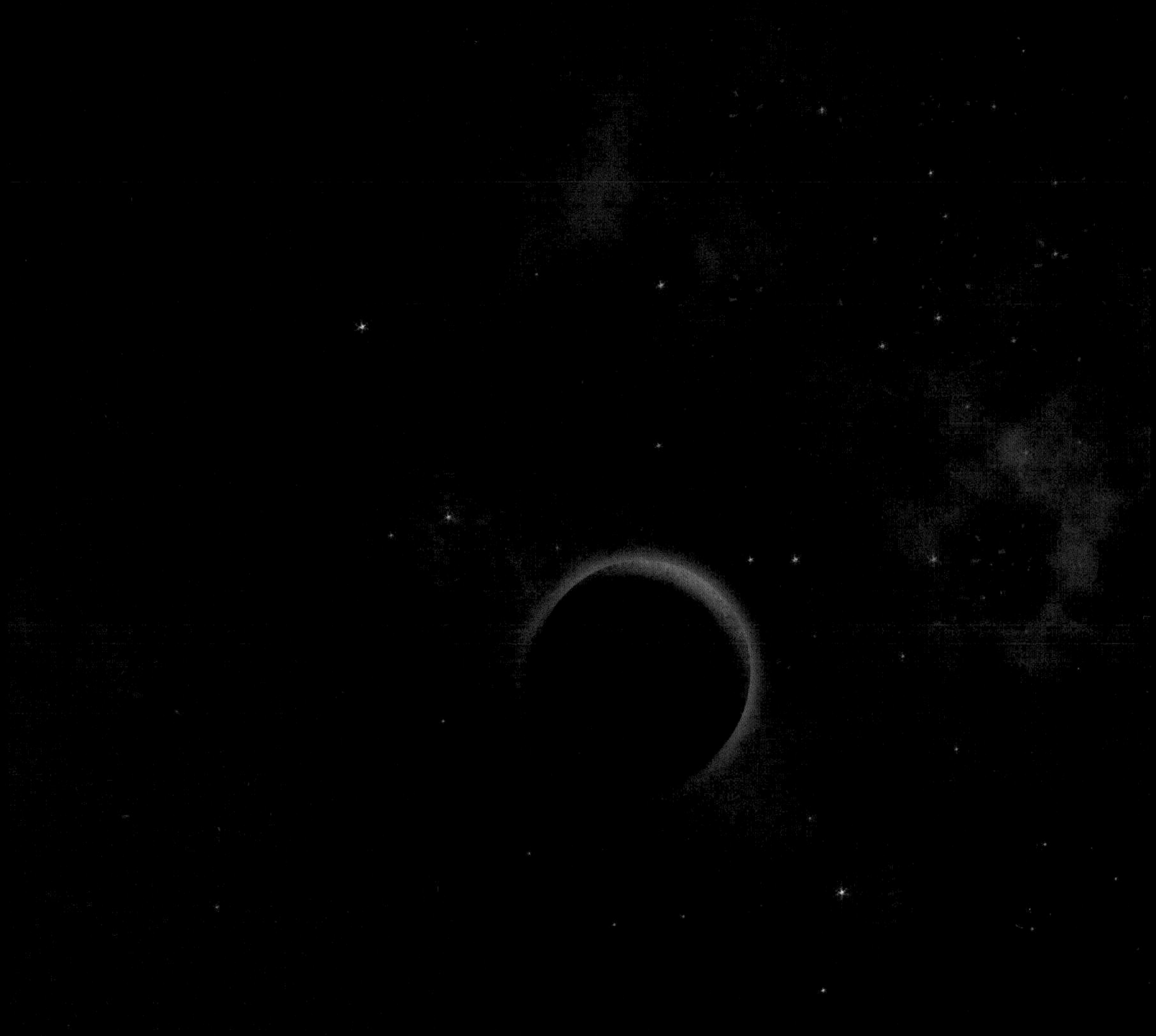

CHAPTER THREE//

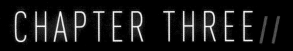

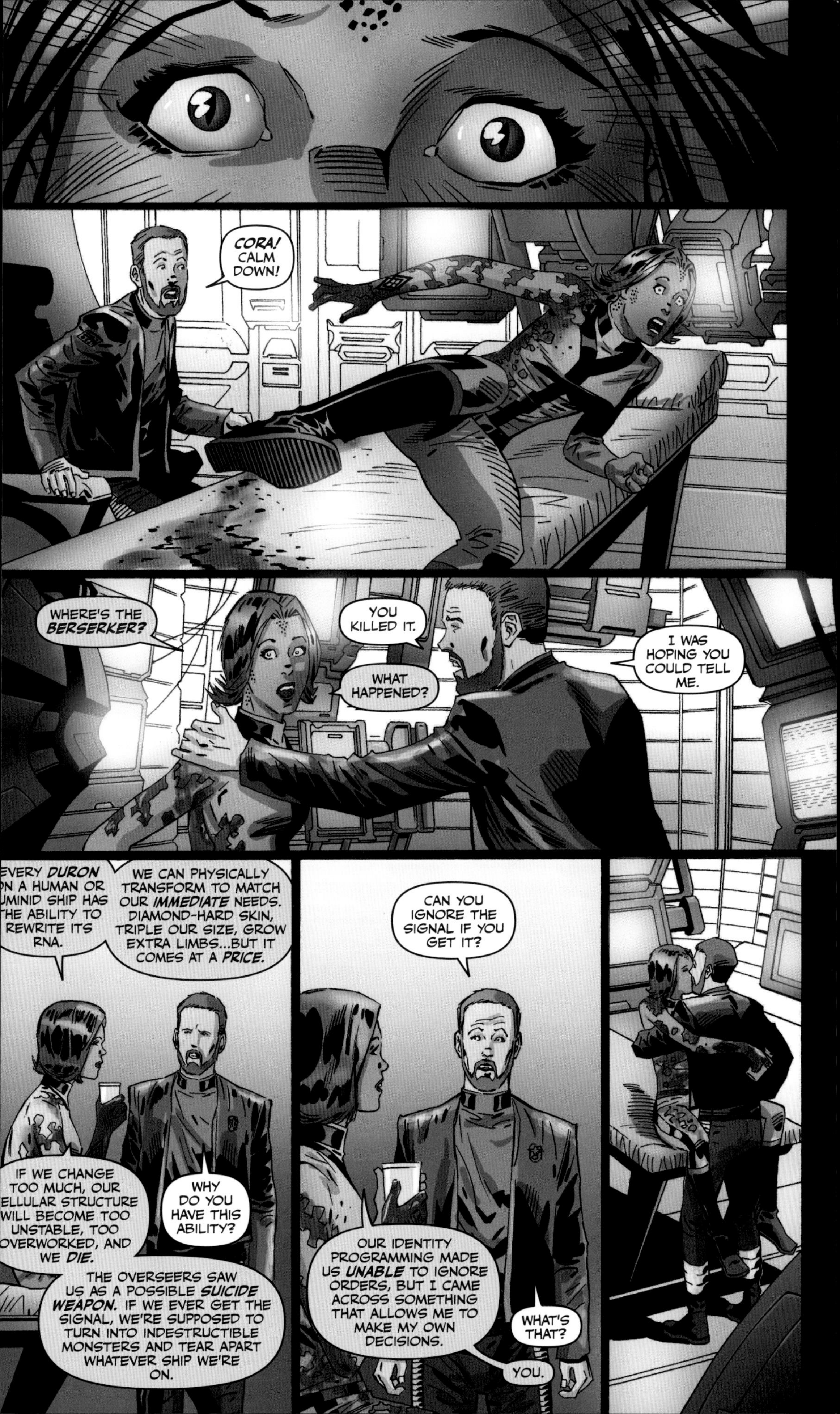
CORA! CALM DOWN!
WHERE'S THE BERSERKER?
YOU KILLED IT.
WHAT HAPPENED?
I WAS HOPING YOU COULD TELL ME.
EVERY DURON ON A HUMAN OR UMINID SHIP HAS THE ABILITY TO REWRITE ITS RNA.
WE CAN PHYSICALLY TRANSFORM TO MATCH OUR IMMEDIATE NEEDS. DIAMOND-HARD SKIN, TRIPLE OUR SIZE, GROW EXTRA LIMBS...BUT IT COMES AT A PRICE.
IF WE CHANGE TOO MUCH, OUR CELLULAR STRUCTURE WILL BECOME TOO UNSTABLE, TOO OVERWORKED, AND WE DIE.
WHY DO YOU HAVE THIS ABILITY?
THE OVERSEERS SAW US AS A POSSIBLE SUICIDE WEAPON. IF WE EVER GET THE SIGNAL, WE'RE SUPPOSED TO TURN INTO INDESTRUCTIBLE MONSTERS AND TEAR APART WHATEVER SHIP WE'RE ON.
CAN YOU IGNORE THE SIGNAL IF YOU GET IT?
OUR IDENTITY PROGRAMMING MADE US UNABLE TO IGNORE ORDERS, BUT I CAME ACROSS SOMETHING THAT ALLOWS ME TO MAKE MY OWN DECISIONS.
WHAT'S THAT?
YOU.

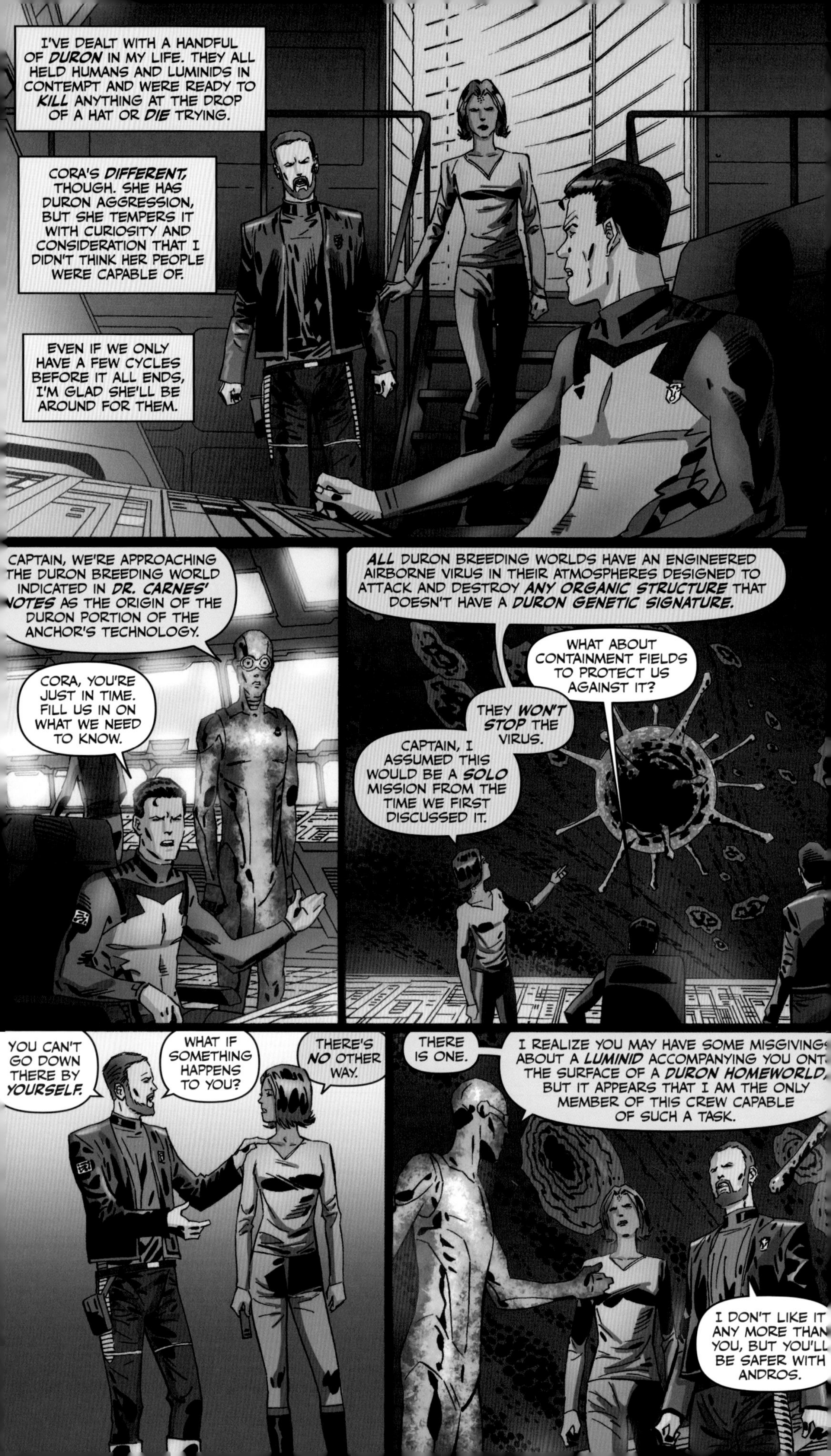

I'VE DEALT WITH A HANDFUL OF DURON IN MY LIFE. THEY ALL HELD HUMANS AND LUMINIDS IN CONTEMPT AND WERE READY TO KILL ANYTHING AT THE DROP OF A HAT OR DIE TRYING.
CORA'S DIFFERENT, THOUGH. SHE HAS DURON AGGRESSION, BUT SHE TEMPERS IT WITH CURIOSITY AND CONSIDERATION THAT I DIDN'T THINK HER PEOPLE WERE CAPABLE OF.
EVEN IF WE ONLY HAVE A FEW CYCLES BEFORE IT ALL ENDS, I'M GLAD SHE'LL BE AROUND FOR THEM.
CAPTAIN, WE'RE APPROACHING THE DURON BREEDING WORLD INDICATED IN DR. CARNES' NOTES AS THE ORIGIN OF THE DURON PORTION OF THE ANCHOR'S TECHNOLOGY.
CORA, YOU'RE JUST IN TIME. FILL US IN ON WHAT WE NEED TO KNOW.
ALL DURON BREEDING WORLDS HAVE AN ENGINEERED AIRBORNE VIRUS IN THEIR ATMOSPHERES DESIGNED TO ATTACK AND DESTROY ANY ORGANIC STRUCTURE THAT DOESN'T HAVE A DURON GENETIC SIGNATURE.
WHAT ABOUT CONTAINMENT FIELDS TO PROTECT US AGAINST IT?
THEY WON'T STOP THE VIRUS.
CAPTAIN, I ASSUMED THIS WOULD BE A SOLO MISSION FROM THE TIME WE FIRST DISCUSSED IT.
YOU CAN'T GO DOWN THERE BY YOURSELF.
WHAT IF SOMETHING HAPPENS TO YOU?
THERE'S NO OTHER WAY.
THERE IS ONE.
I REALIZE YOU MAY HAVE SOME MISGIVINGS ABOUT A LUMINID ACCOMPANYING YOU ONTO THE SURFACE OF A DURON HOMEWORLD, BUT IT APPEARS THAT I AM THE ONLY MEMBER OF THIS CREW CAPABLE OF SUCH A TASK.
I DON'T LIKE IT ANY MORE THAN YOU, BUT YOU'LL BE SAFER WITH ANDROS.

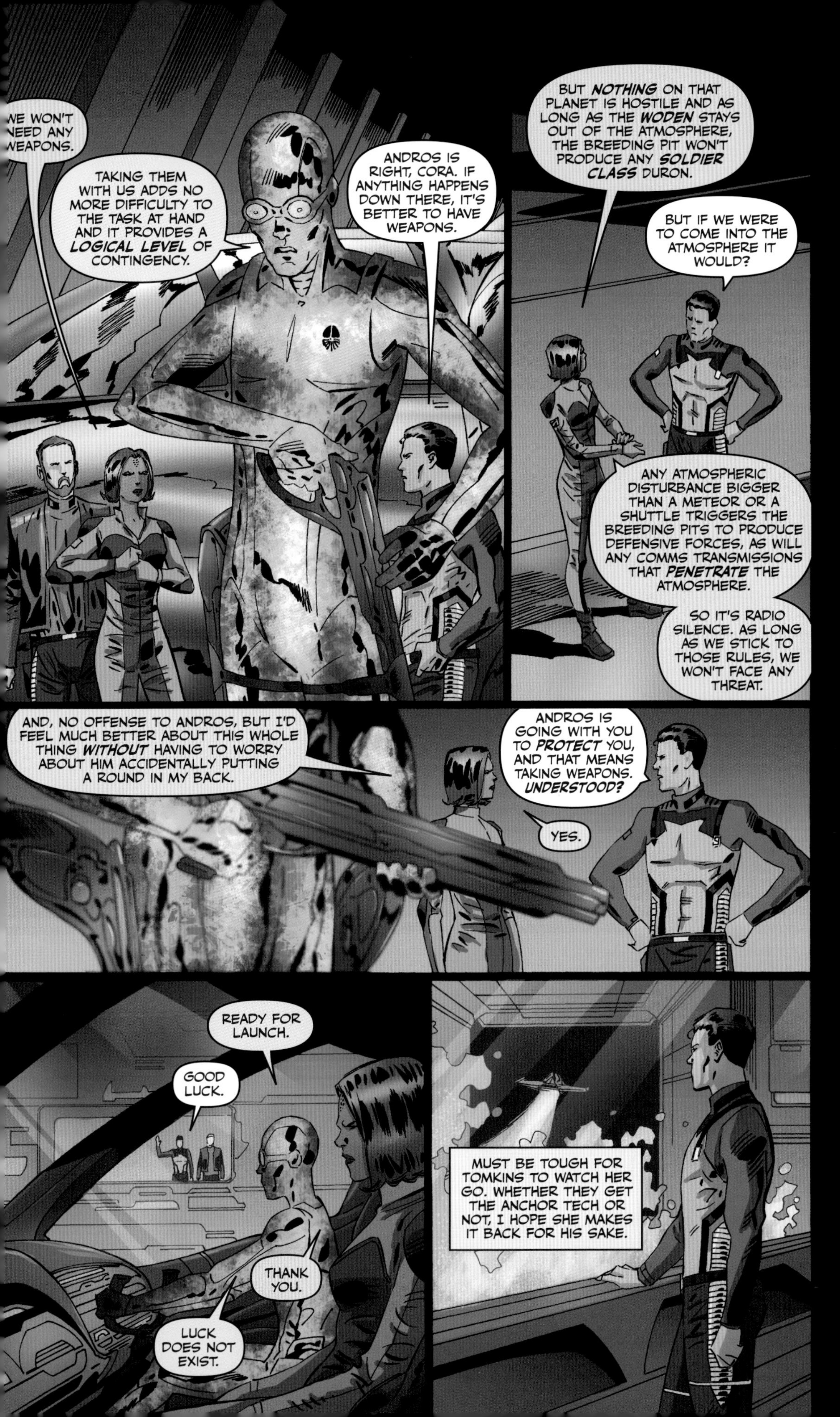
WE WON'T NEED ANY WEAPONS.
TAKING THEM WITH US ADDS NO MORE DIFFICULTY TO THE TASK AT HAND AND IT PROVIDES A LOGICAL LEVEL OF CONTINGENCY.
ANDROS IS RIGHT, CORA. IF ANYTHING HAPPENS DOWN THERE, IT'S BETTER TO HAVE WEAPONS.
BUT NOTHING ON THAT PLANET IS HOSTILE AND AS LONG AS THE WODEN STAYS OUT OF THE ATMOSPHERE, THE BREEDING PIT WON'T PRODUCE ANY SOLDIER CLASS DURON.
BUT IF WE WERE TO COME INTO THE ATMOSPHERE IT WOULD?
ANY ATMOSPHERIC DISTURBANCE BIGGER THAN A METEOR OR A SHUTTLE TRIGGERS THE BREEDING PITS TO PRODUCE DEFENSIVE FORCES, AS WILL ANY COMMS TRANSMISSIONS THAT PENETRATE THE ATMOSPHERE.
SO IT'S RADIO SILENCE. AS LONG AS WE STICK TO THOSE RULES, WE WON'T FACE ANY THREAT.
AND, NO OFFENSE TO ANDROS, BUT I'D FEEL MUCH BETTER ABOUT THIS WHOLE THING WITHOUT HAVING TO WORRY ABOUT HIM ACCIDENTALLY PUTTING A ROUND IN MY BACK.
ANDROS IS GOING WITH YOU TO PROTECT YOU, AND THAT MEANS TAKING WEAPONS. UNDERSTOOD?
YES.
READY FOR LAUNCH.
GOOD LUCK.
THANK YOU.
LUCK DOES NOT EXIST.
MUST BE TOUGH FOR TOMKINS TO WATCH HER GO. WHETHER THEY GET THE ANCHOR TECH OR NOT, I HOPE SHE MAKES IT BACK FOR HIS SAKE.

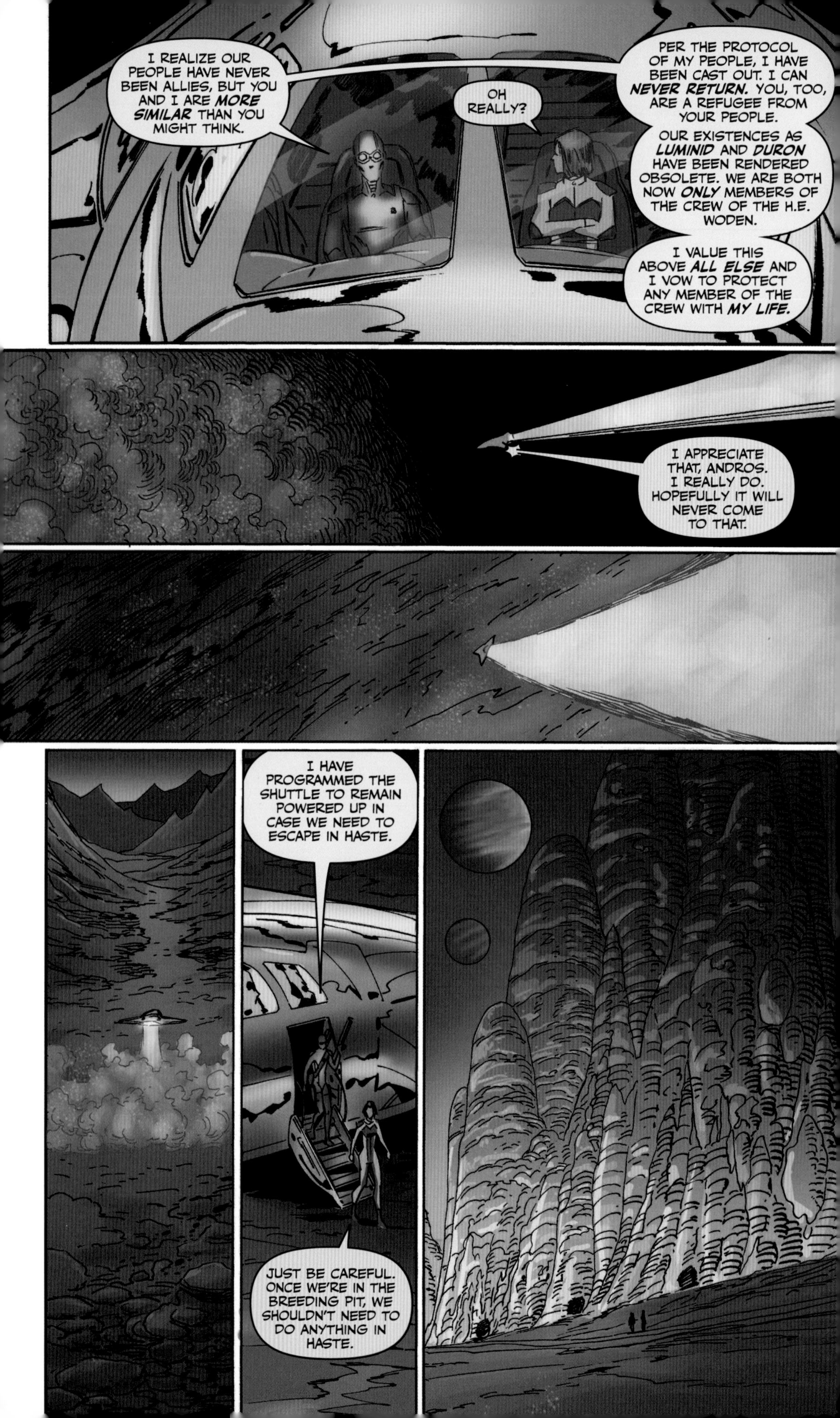
I REALIZE OUR PEOPLE HAVE NEVER BEEN ALLIES, BUT YOU AND I ARE MORE SIMILAR THAN YOU MIGHT THINK.
OH REALLY?
PER THE PROTOCOL OF MY PEOPLE, I HAVE BEEN CAST OUT. I CAN NEVER RETURN. YOU, TOO, ARE A REFUGEE FROM YOUR PEOPLE.
OUR EXISTENCES AS LUMINID AND DURON HAVE BEEN RENDERED OBSOLETE. WE ARE BOTH NOW ONLY MEMBERS OF THE CREW OF THE H.E. WODEN.
I VALUE THIS ABOVE ALL ELSE AND I VOW TO PROTECT ANY MEMBER OF THE CREW WITH MY LIFE.
I APPRECIATE THAT, ANDROS. I REALLY DO. HOPEFULLY IT WILL NEVER COME TO THAT.
I HAVE PROGRAMMED THE SHUTTLE TO REMAIN POWERED UP IN CASE WE NEED TO ESCAPE IN HASTE.
JUST BE CAREFUL. ONCE WE'RE IN THE BREEDING PIT, WE SHOULDN'T NEED TO DO ANYTHING IN HASTE.

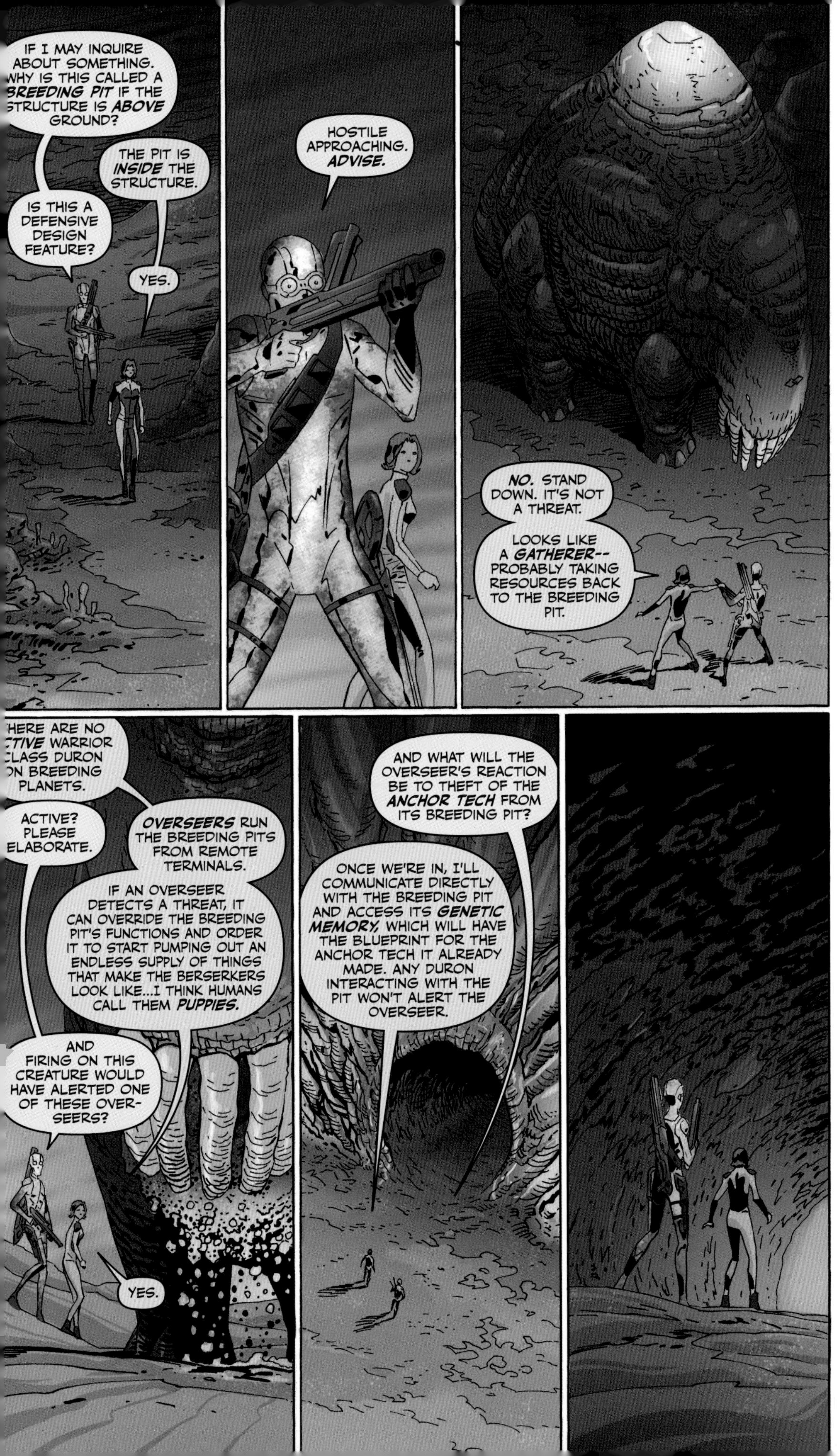
IF I MAY INQUIRE ABOUT SOMETHING. WHY IS THIS CALLED A *BREEDING PIT* IF THE STRUCTURE IS *ABOVE* GROUND?
THE PIT IS *INSIDE* THE STRUCTURE.
IS THIS A DEFENSIVE DESIGN FEATURE?
YES.
HOSTILE APPROACHING. *ADVISE.*
NO. STAND DOWN. IT'S NOT A THREAT.
LOOKS LIKE A *GATHERER*--PROBABLY TAKING RESOURCES BACK TO THE BREEDING PIT.
HERE ARE NO *CTIVE* WARRIOR CLASS DURON ON BREEDING PLANETS.
ACTIVE? PLEASE ELABORATE.
OVERSEERS RUN THE BREEDING PITS FROM REMOTE TERMINALS.
IF AN OVERSEER DETECTS A THREAT, IT CAN OVERRIDE THE BREEDING PIT'S FUNCTIONS AND ORDER IT TO START PUMPING OUT AN ENDLESS SUPPLY OF THINGS THAT MAKE THE BERSERKERS LOOK LIKE...I THINK HUMANS CALL THEM *PUPPIES.*
AND FIRING ON THIS CREATURE WOULD HAVE ALERTED ONE OF THESE OVER-SEERS?
YES.
AND WHAT WILL THE OVERSEER'S REACTION BE TO THEFT OF THE *ANCHOR TECH* FROM ITS BREEDING PIT?
ONCE WE'RE IN, I'LL COMMUNICATE DIRECTLY WITH THE BREEDING PIT AND ACCESS ITS *GENETIC MEMORY,* WHICH WILL HAVE THE BLUEPRINT FOR THE ANCHOR TECH IT ALREADY MADE. ANY DURON INTERACTING WITH THE PIT WON'T ALERT THE OVERSEER.

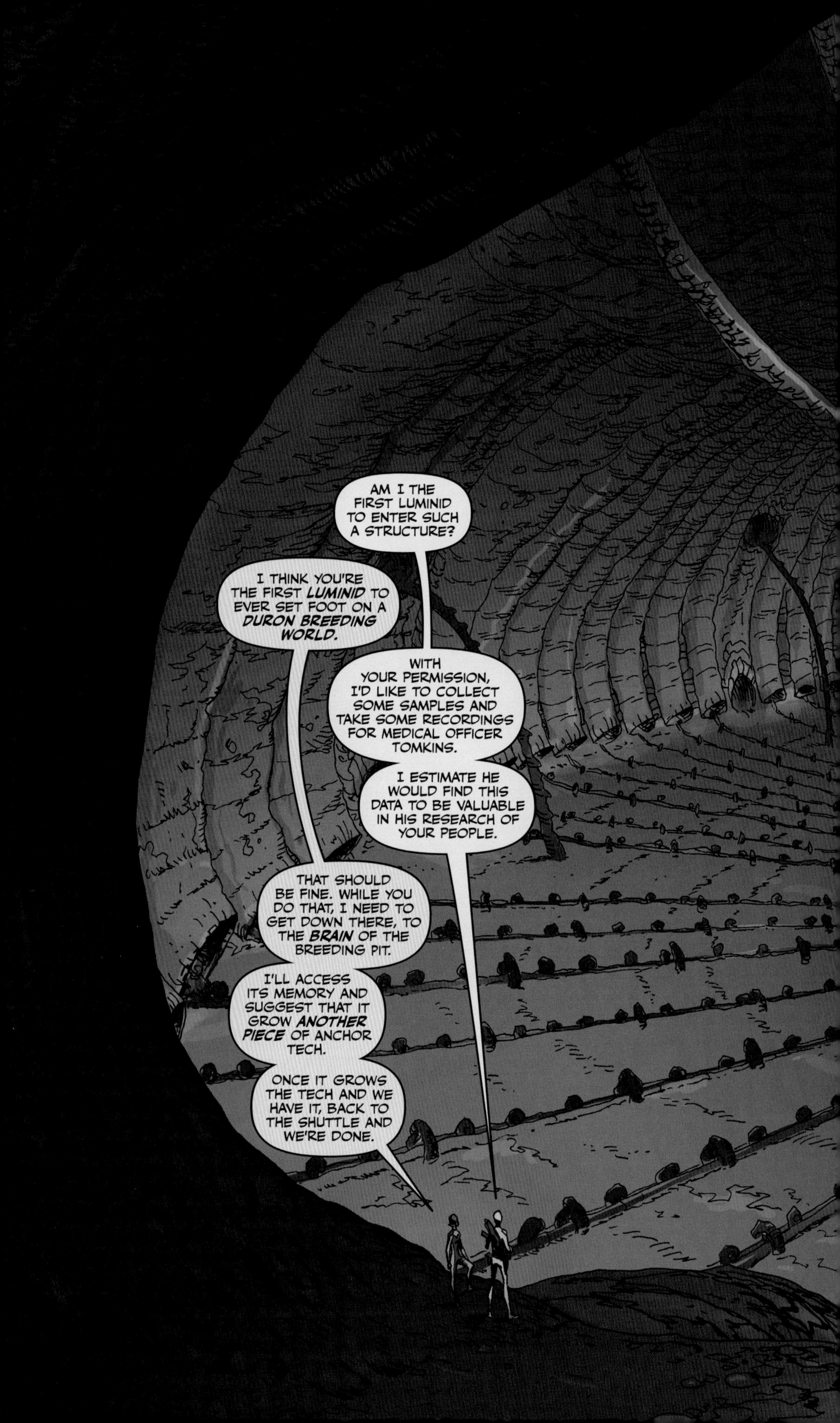
AM I THE FIRST LUMINID TO ENTER SUCH A STRUCTURE?
I THINK YOU'RE THE FIRST *LUMINID* TO EVER SET FOOT ON A *DURON BREEDING WORLD.*
WITH YOUR PERMISSION, I'D LIKE TO COLLECT SOME SAMPLES AND TAKE SOME RECORDINGS FOR MEDICAL OFFICER TOMKINS.
I ESTIMATE HE WOULD FIND THIS DATA TO BE VALUABLE IN HIS RESEARCH OF YOUR PEOPLE.
THAT SHOULD BE FINE. WHILE YOU DO THAT, I NEED TO GET DOWN THERE, TO THE *BRAIN* OF THE BREEDING PIT.
I'LL ACCESS ITS MEMORY AND SUGGEST THAT IT GROW *ANOTHER PIECE* OF ANCHOR TECH.
ONCE IT GROWS THE TECH AND WE HAVE IT, BACK TO THE SHUTTLE AND WE'RE DONE.

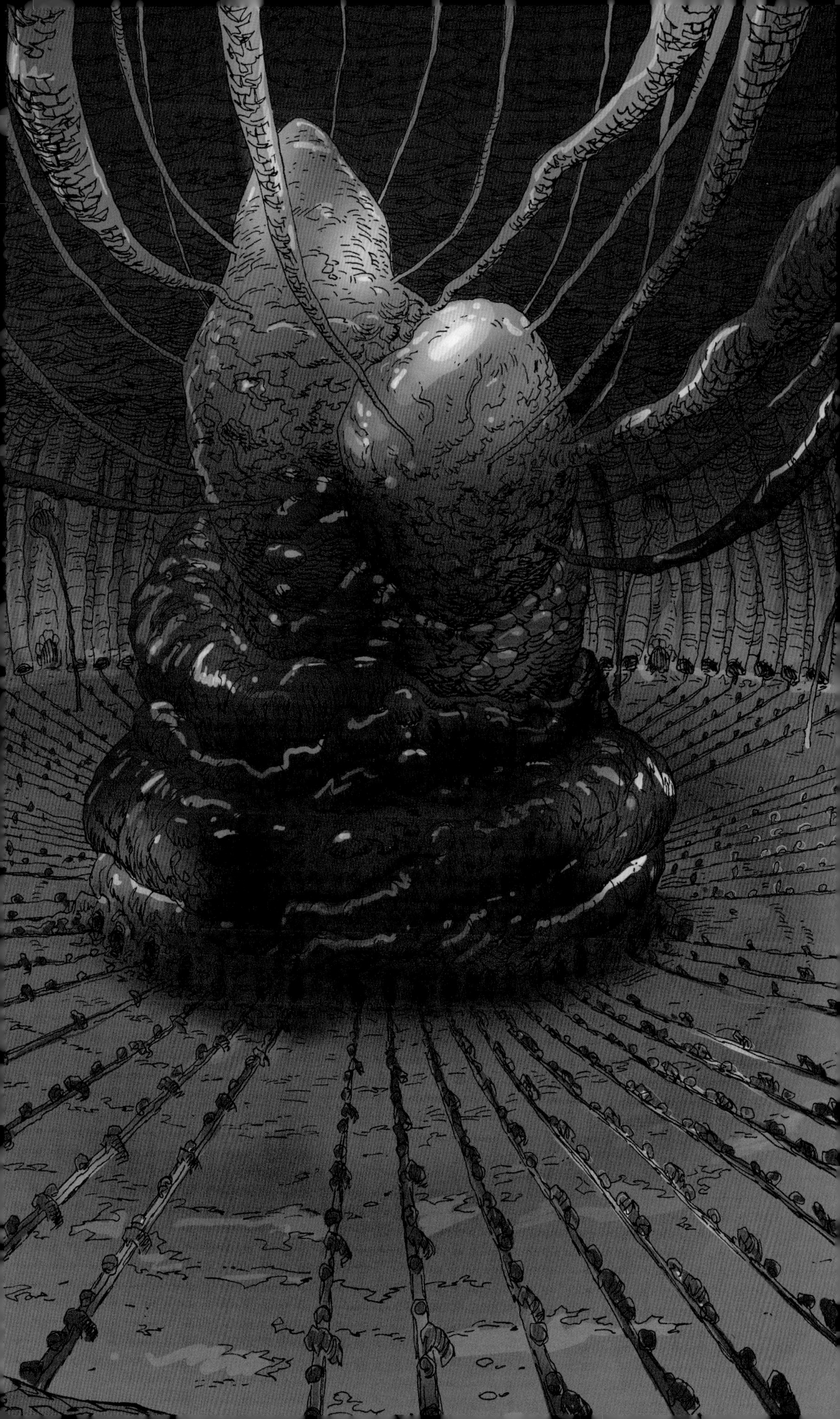

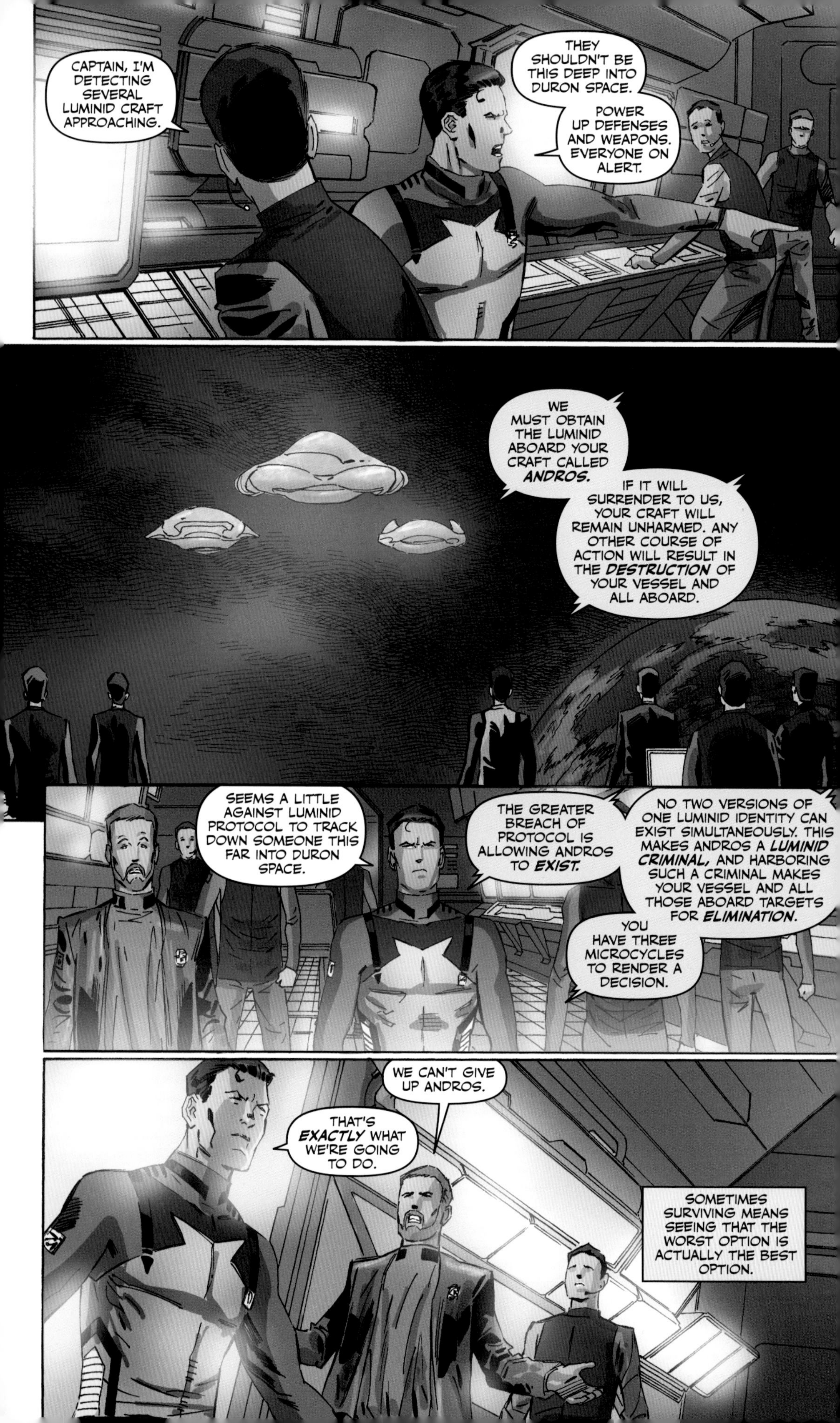

CAPTAIN, I'M DETECTING SEVERAL LUMINID CRAFT APPROACHING.
THEY SHOULDN'T BE THIS DEEP INTO DURON SPACE.
POWER UP DEFENSES AND WEAPONS. EVERYONE ON ALERT.
WE MUST OBTAIN THE LUMINID ABOARD YOUR CRAFT CALLED *ANDROS.*
IF IT WILL SURRENDER TO US, YOUR CRAFT WILL REMAIN UNHARMED. ANY OTHER COURSE OF ACTION WILL RESULT IN THE *DESTRUCTION* OF YOUR VESSEL AND ALL ABOARD.
SEEMS A LITTLE AGAINST LUMINID PROTOCOL TO TRACK DOWN SOMEONE THIS FAR INTO DURON SPACE.
THE GREATER BREACH OF PROTOCOL IS ALLOWING ANDROS TO *EXIST.*
NO TWO VERSIONS OF ONE LUMINID IDENTITY CAN EXIST SIMULTANEOUSLY. THIS MAKES ANDROS A *LUMINID CRIMINAL,* AND HARBORING SUCH A CRIMINAL MAKES YOUR VESSEL AND ALL THOSE ABOARD TARGETS FOR *ELIMINATION.*
YOU HAVE THREE MICROCYCLES TO RENDER A DECISION.
WE CAN'T GIVE UP ANDROS.
THAT'S *EXACTLY* WHAT WE'RE GOING TO DO.
SOMETIMES SURVIVING MEANS SEEING THAT THE WORST OPTION IS ACTUALLY THE BEST OPTION.

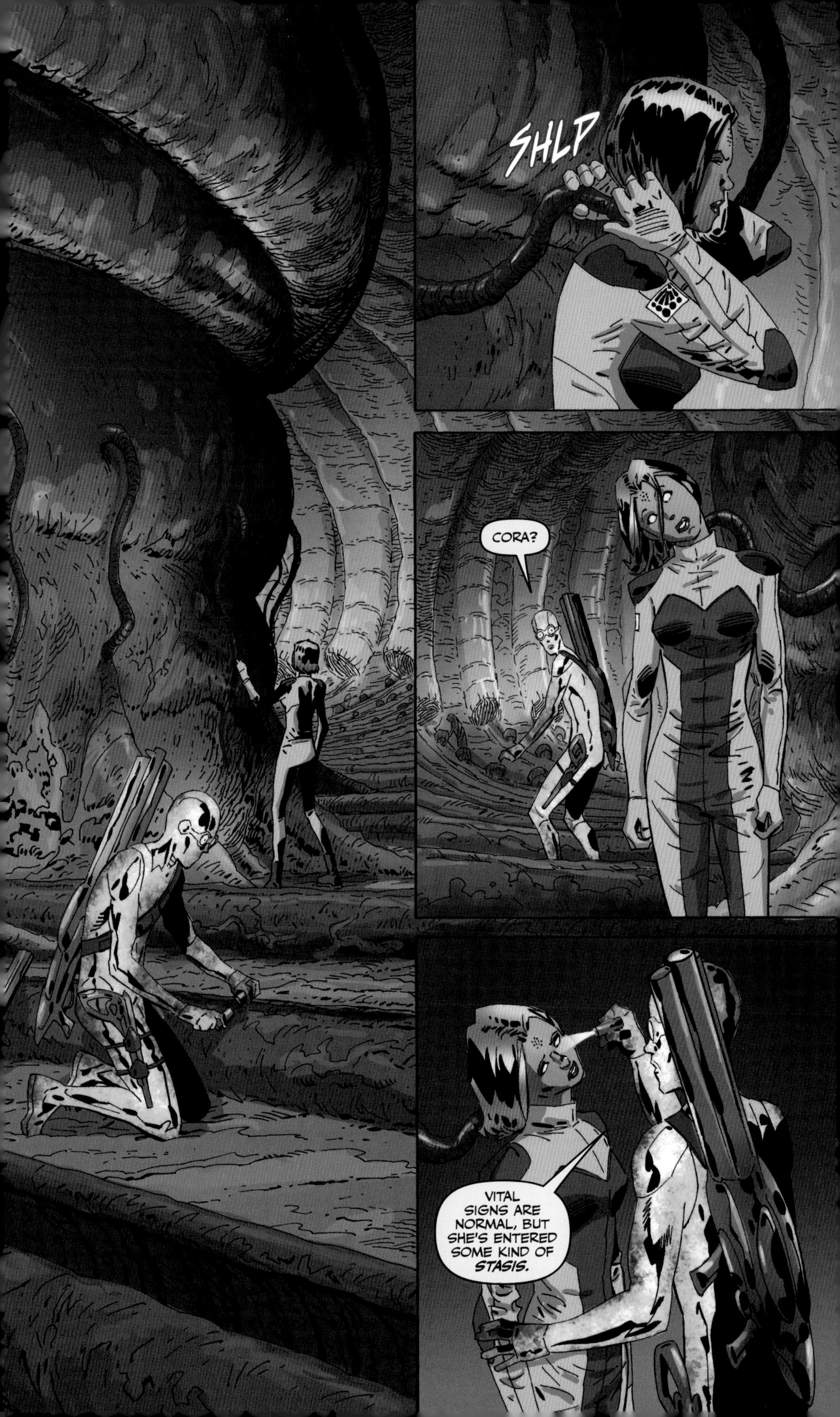
SHLP
CORA?
VITAL SIGNS ARE NORMAL, BUT SHE'S ENTERED SOME KIND OF STASIS.

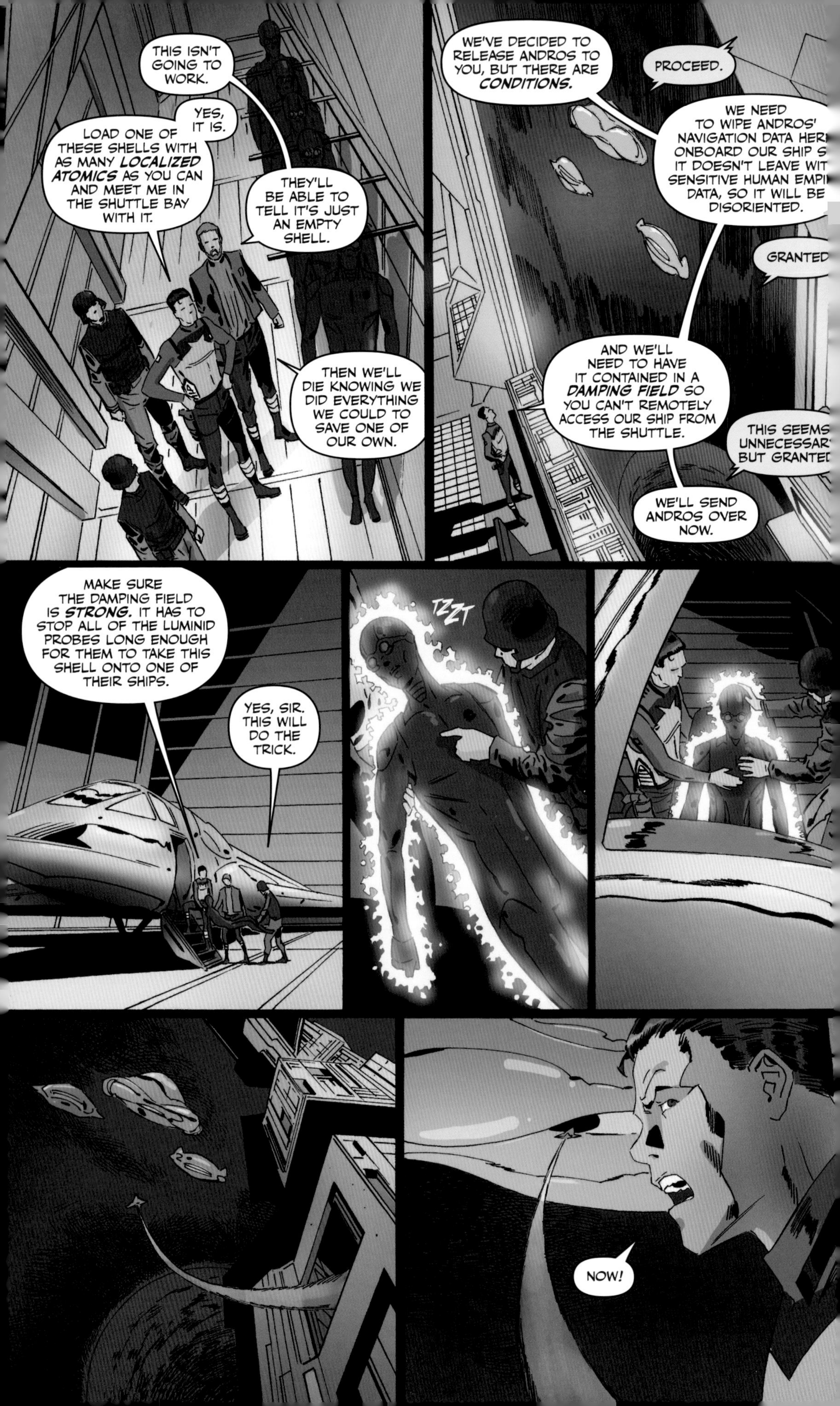

THIS ISN'T GOING TO WORK.
YES, IT IS.
LOAD ONE OF THESE SHELLS WITH AS MANY LOCALIZED ATOMICS AS YOU CAN AND MEET ME IN THE SHUTTLE BAY WITH IT.
THEY'LL BE ABLE TO TELL IT'S JUST AN EMPTY SHELL.
THEN WE'LL DIE KNOWING WE DID EVERYTHING WE COULD TO SAVE ONE OF OUR OWN.
WE'VE DECIDED TO RELEASE ANDROS TO YOU, BUT THERE ARE CONDITIONS.
PROCEED.
WE NEED TO WIPE ANDROS' NAVIGATION DATA HER ONBOARD OUR SHIP S IT DOESN'T LEAVE WIT SENSITIVE HUMAN EMPI DATA, SO IT WILL BE DISORIENTED.
GRANTED
AND WE'LL NEED TO HAVE IT CONTAINED IN A DAMPING FIELD SO YOU CAN'T REMOTELY ACCESS OUR SHIP FROM THE SHUTTLE.
THIS SEEMS UNNECESSAR BUT GRANTED
WE'LL SEND ANDROS OVER NOW.
MAKE SURE THE DAMPING FIELD IS STRONG. IT HAS TO STOP ALL OF THE LUMINID PROBES LONG ENOUGH FOR THEM TO TAKE THIS SHELL ONTO ONE OF THEIR SHIPS.
YES, SIR. THIS WILL DO THE TRICK.
TZZT
NOW!

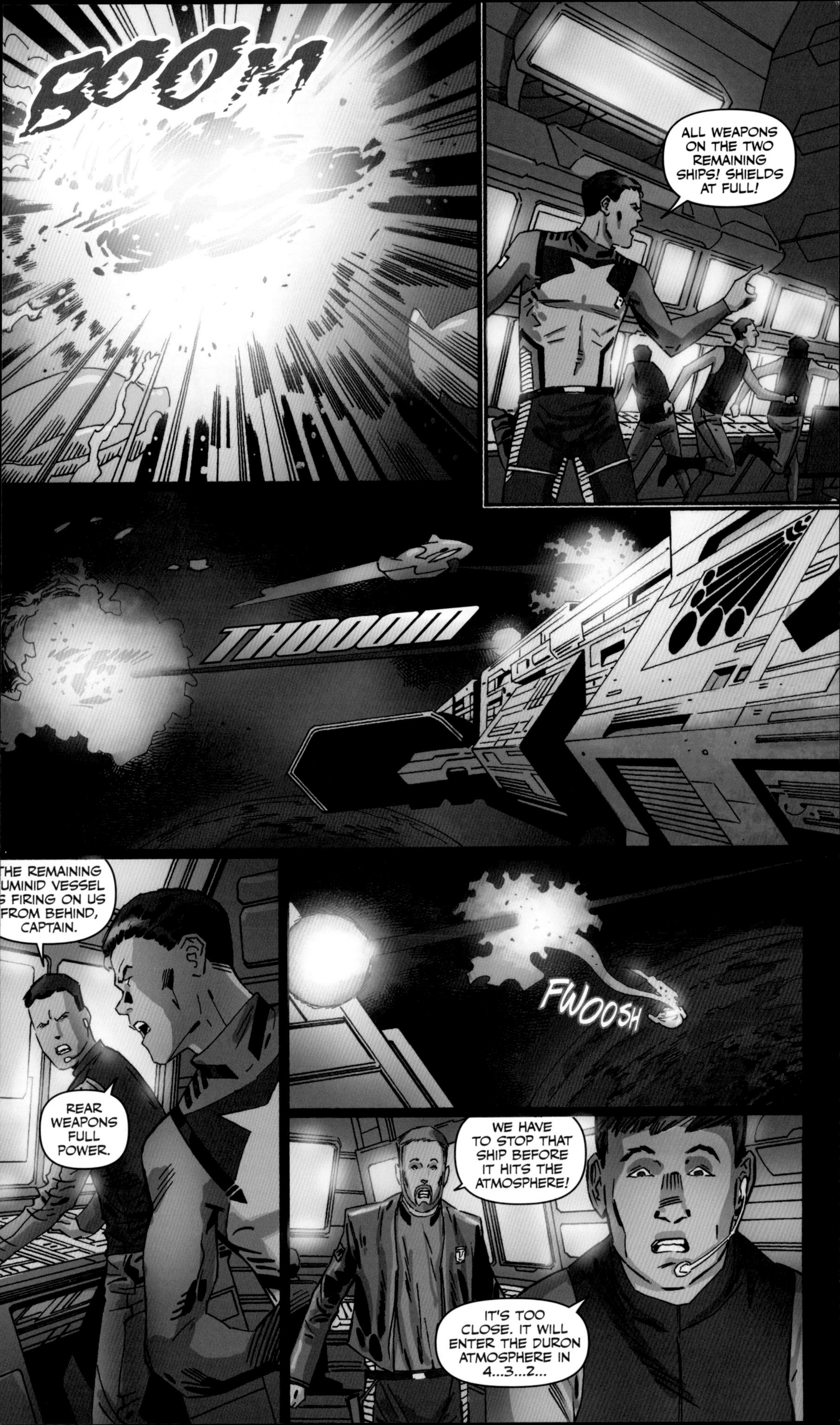
BOOM
ALL WEAPONS ON THE TWO REMAINING SHIPS! SHIELDS AT FULL!
THOOOM
THE REMAINING UMINID VESSEL S FIRING ON US FROM BEHIND, CAPTAIN.
REAR WEAPONS FULL POWER.
FWOOSH
WE HAVE TO STOP THAT SHIP BEFORE IT HITS THE ATMOSPHERE!
IT'S TOO CLOSE. IT WILL ENTER THE DURON ATMOSPHERE IN 4...3...2...

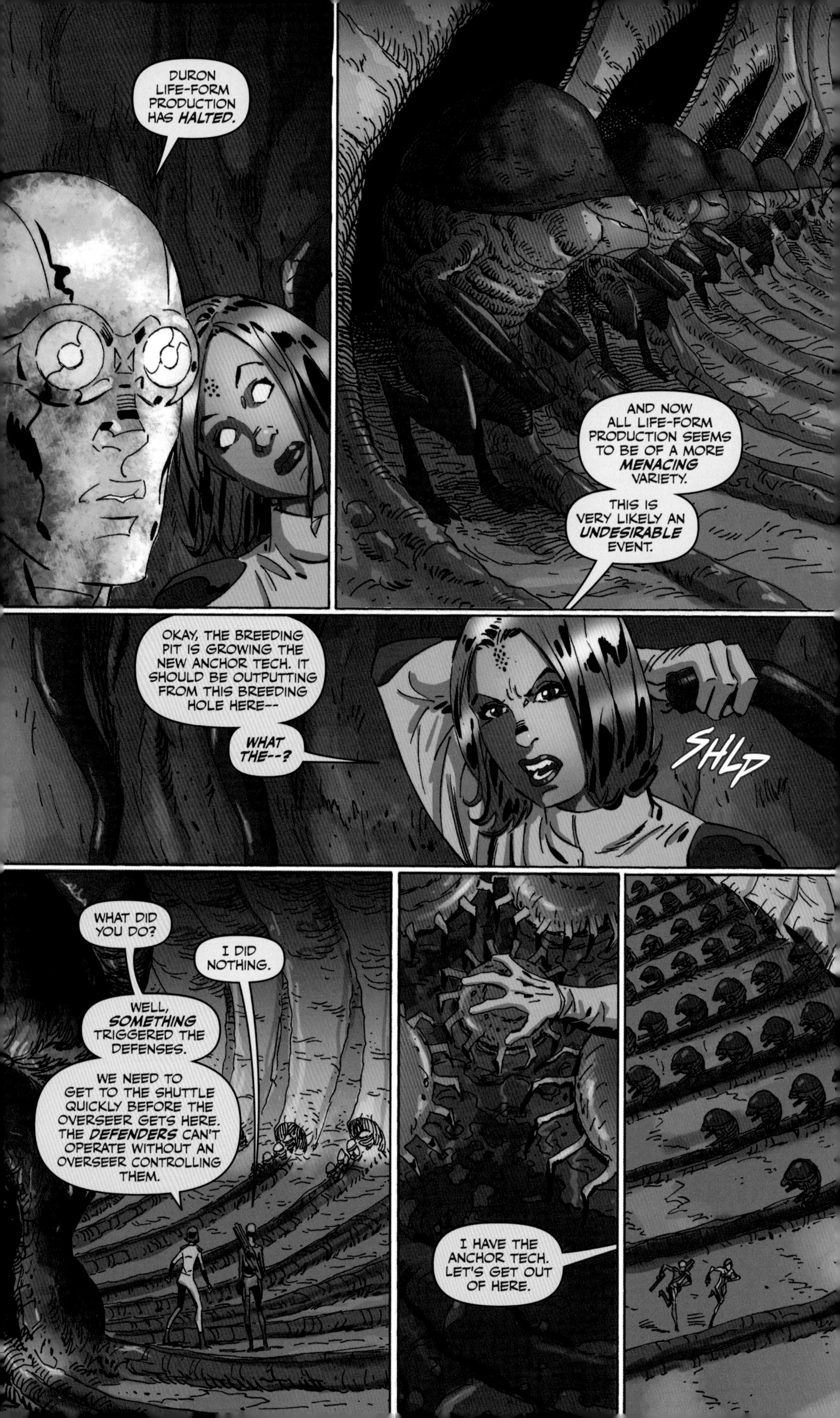
DURON LIFE-FORM PRODUCTION HAS *HALTED.*
AND NOW ALL LIFE-FORM PRODUCTION SEEMS TO BE OF A MORE *MENACING* VARIETY.
THIS IS VERY LIKELY AN *UNDESIRABLE* EVENT.
OKAY, THE BREEDING PIT IS GROWING THE NEW ANCHOR TECH. IT SHOULD BE OUTPUTTING FROM THIS BREEDING HOLE HERE--
WHAT THE--?
SHLP
WHAT DID YOU DO?
I DID NOTHING.
WELL, *SOMETHING* TRIGGERED THE DEFENSES.
WE NEED TO GET TO THE SHUTTLE QUICKLY BEFORE THE OVERSEER GETS HERE. THE *DEFENDERS* CAN'T OPERATE WITHOUT AN OVERSEER CONTROLLING THEM.
I HAVE THE ANCHOR TECH. LET'S GET OUT OF HERE.

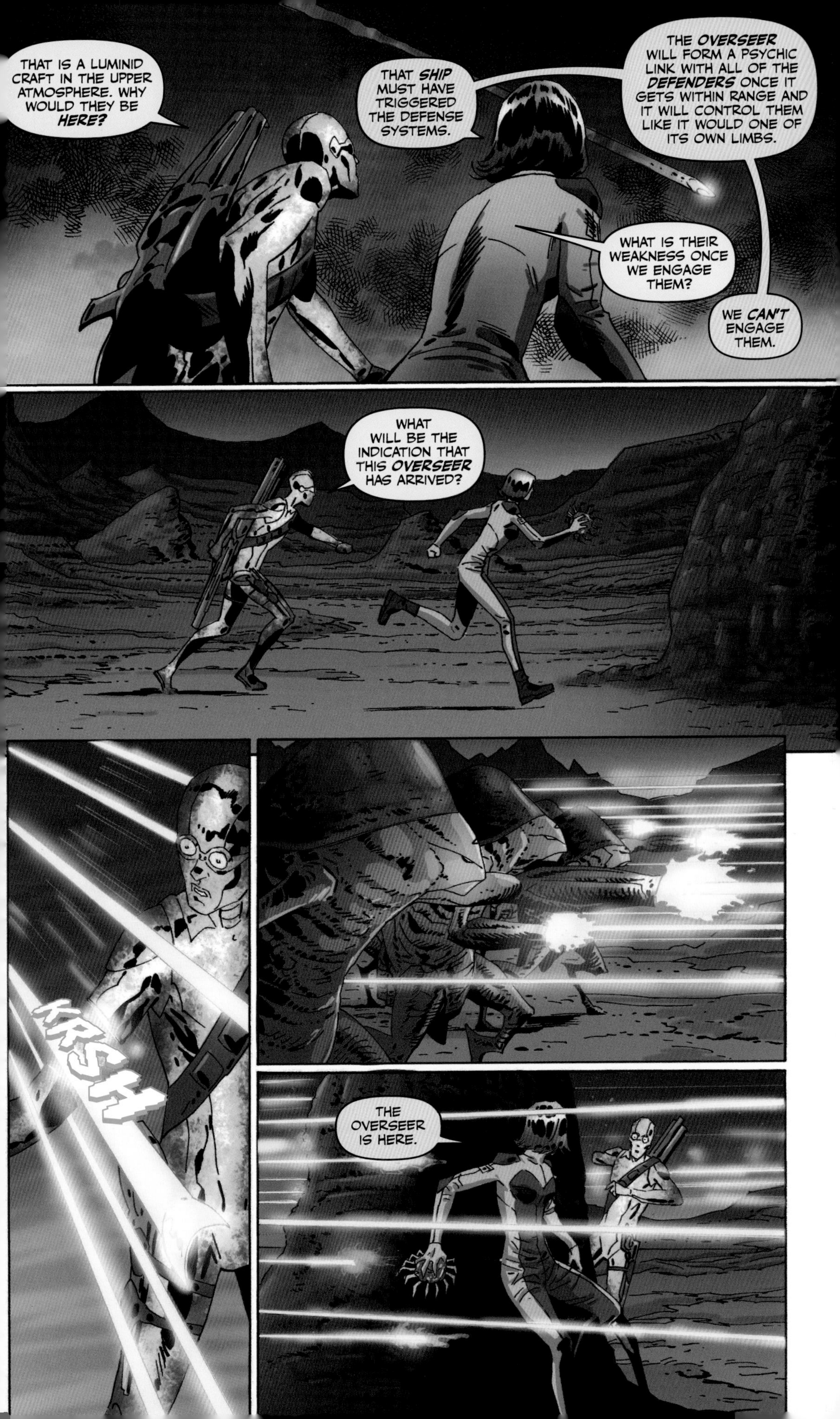
THAT IS A LUMINID CRAFT IN THE UPPER ATMOSPHERE. WHY WOULD THEY BE *HERE?*
THAT *SHIP* MUST HAVE TRIGGERED THE DEFENSE SYSTEMS.
THE *OVERSEER* WILL FORM A PSYCHIC LINK WITH ALL OF THE *DEFENDERS* ONCE IT GETS WITHIN RANGE AND IT WILL CONTROL THEM LIKE IT WOULD ONE OF ITS OWN LIMBS.
WHAT IS THEIR WEAKNESS ONCE WE ENGAGE THEM?
WE *CAN'T* ENGAGE THEM.
WHAT WILL BE THE INDICATION THAT THIS *OVERSEER* HAS ARRIVED?
KRSH
THE OVERSEER IS HERE.

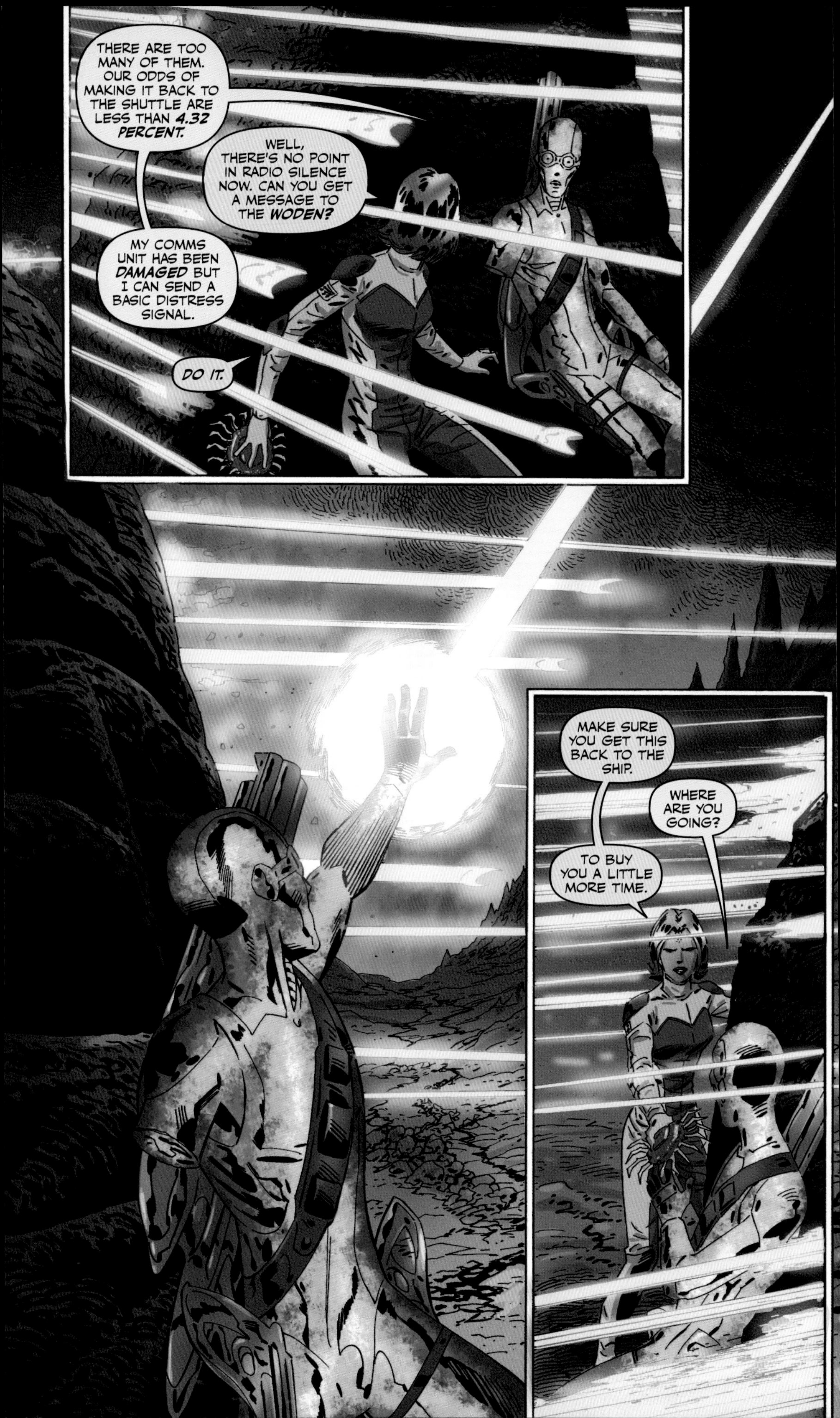
THERE ARE TOO MANY OF THEM. OUR ODDS OF MAKING IT BACK TO THE SHUTTLE ARE LESS THAN 4.32 PERCENT.
WELL, THERE'S NO POINT IN RADIO SILENCE NOW. CAN YOU GET A MESSAGE TO THE WODEN?
MY COMMS UNIT HAS BEEN DAMAGED BUT I CAN SEND A BASIC DISTRESS SIGNAL.
DO IT.
MAKE SURE YOU GET THIS BACK TO THE SHIP.
WHERE ARE YOU GOING?
TO BUY YOU A LITTLE MORE TIME.

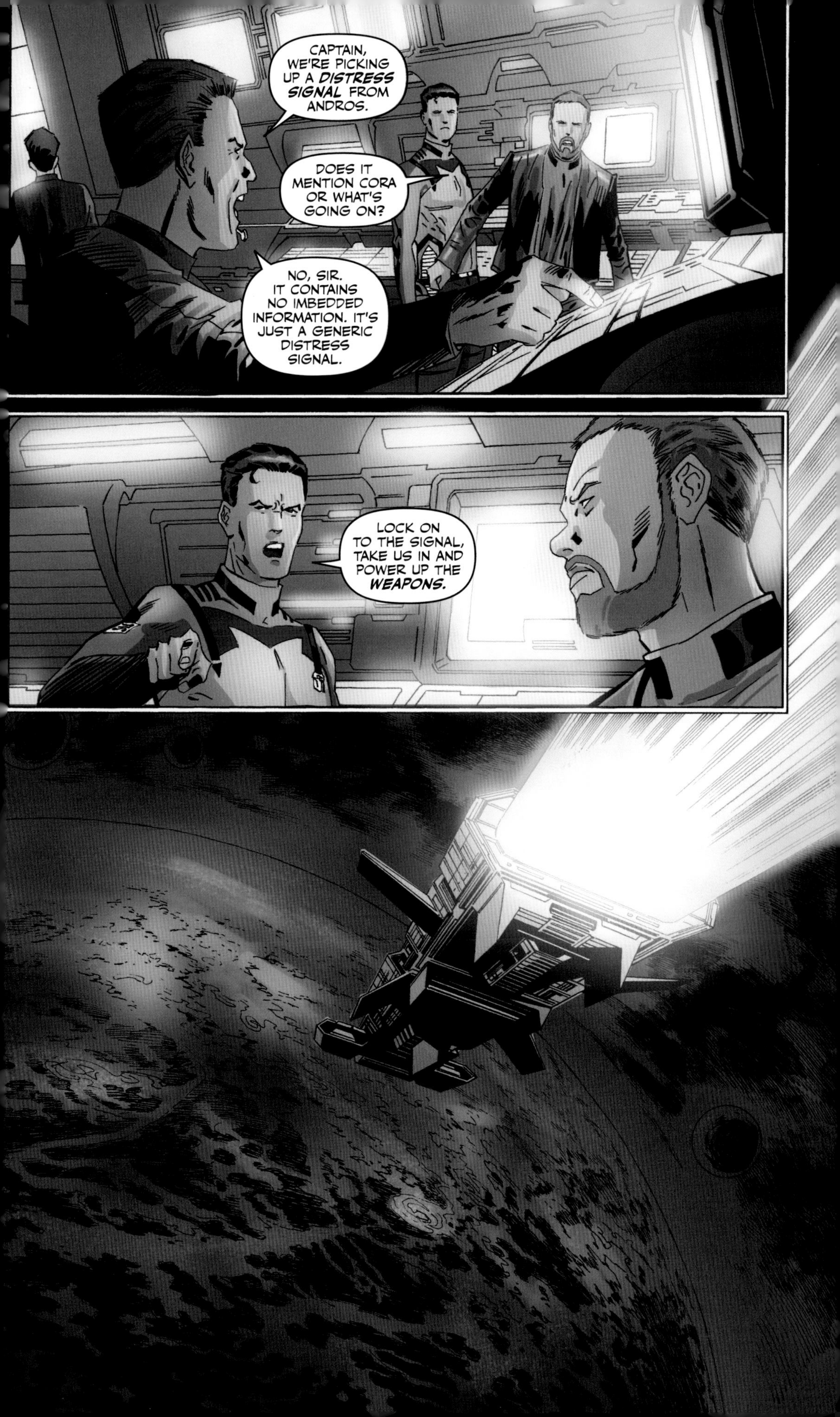
CAPTAIN, WE'RE PICKING UP A *DISTRESS SIGNAL* FROM ANDROS.
DOES IT MENTION CORA OR WHAT'S GOING ON?
NO, SIR. IT CONTAINS NO IMBEDDED INFORMATION. IT'S JUST A GENERIC DISTRESS SIGNAL.
LOCK ON TO THE SIGNAL, TAKE US IN AND POWER UP THE *WEAPONS.*

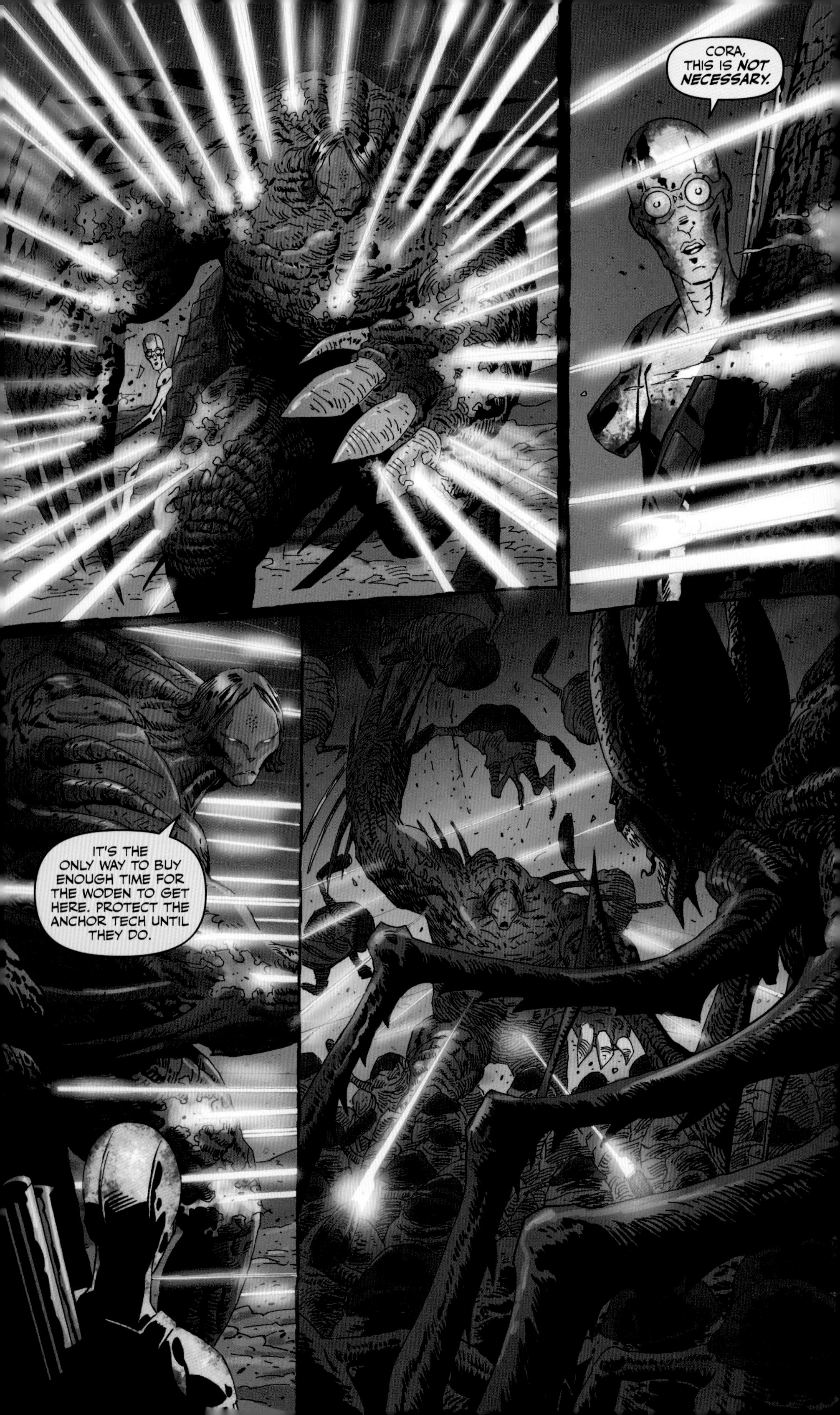
CORA, THIS IS NOT NECESSARY.
IT'S THE ONLY WAY TO BUY ENOUGH TIME FOR THE WODEN TO GET HERE. PROTECT THE ANCHOR TECH UNTIL THEY DO.

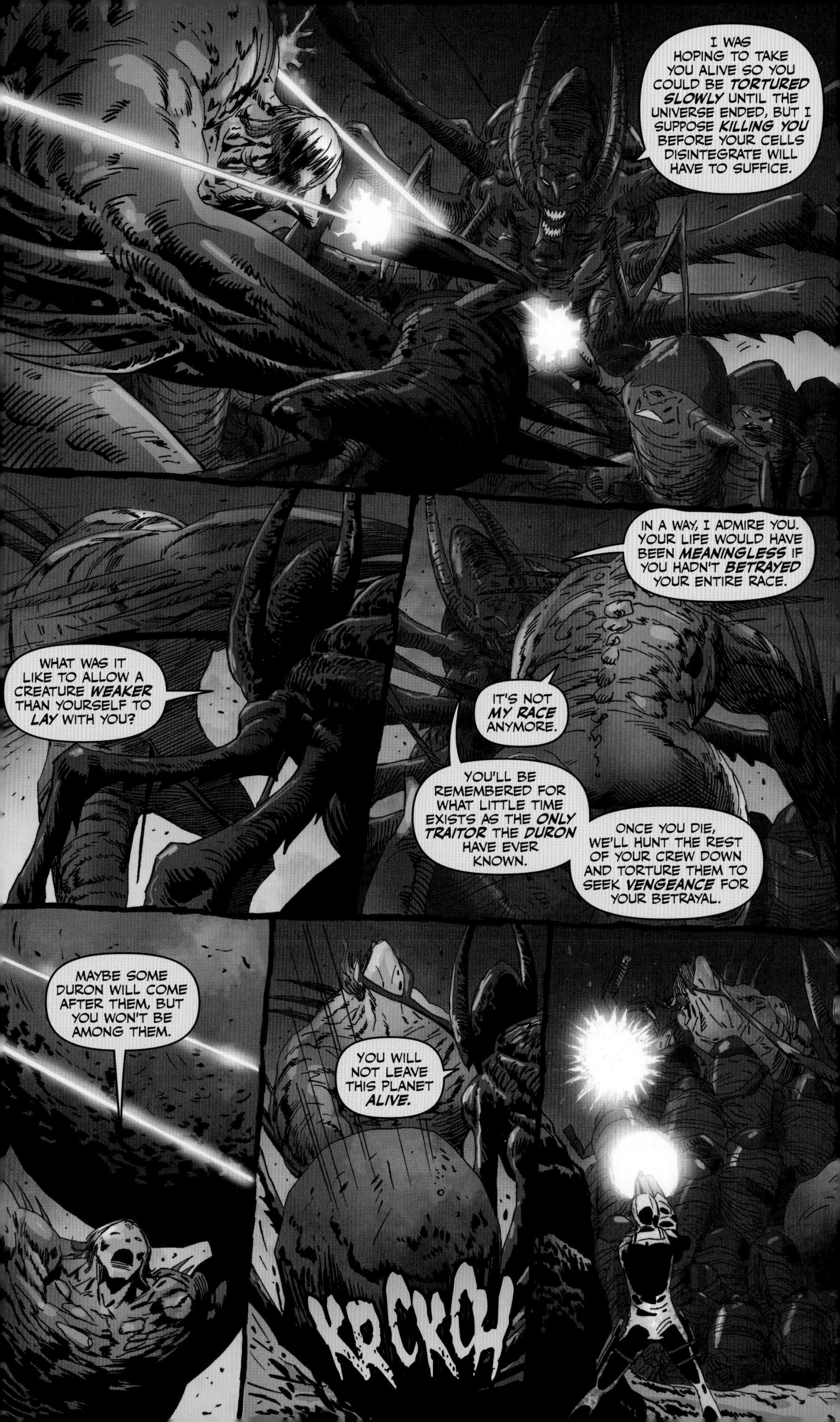
I WAS HOPING TO TAKE YOU ALIVE SO YOU COULD BE TORTURED SLOWLY UNTIL THE UNIVERSE ENDED, BUT I SUPPOSE KILLING YOU BEFORE YOUR CELLS DISINTEGRATE WILL HAVE TO SUFFICE.
IN A WAY, I ADMIRE YOU. YOUR LIFE WOULD HAVE BEEN MEANINGLESS IF YOU HADN'T BETRAYED YOUR ENTIRE RACE.
WHAT WAS IT LIKE TO ALLOW A CREATURE WEAKER THAN YOURSELF TO LAY WITH YOU?
IT'S NOT MY RACE ANYMORE.
YOU'LL BE REMEMBERED FOR WHAT LITTLE TIME EXISTS AS THE ONLY TRAITOR THE DURON HAVE EVER KNOWN.
ONCE YOU DIE, WE'LL HUNT THE REST OF YOUR CREW DOWN AND TORTURE THEM TO SEEK VENGEANCE FOR YOUR BETRAYAL.
MAYBE SOME DURON WILL COME AFTER THEM, BUT YOU WON'T BE AMONG THEM.
YOU WILL NOT LEAVE THIS PLANET ALIVE.
KRCKCH

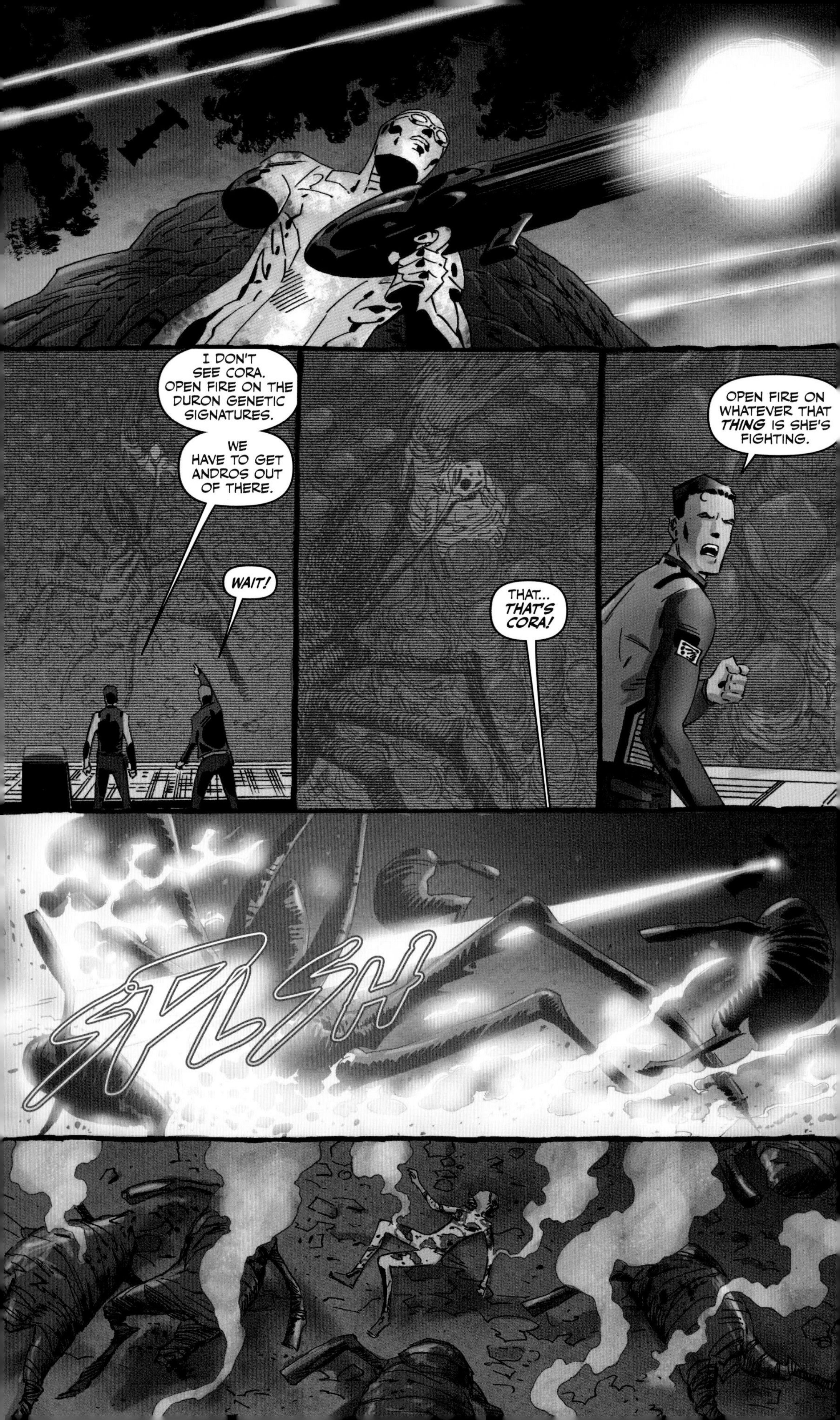
I DON'T SEE CORA. OPEN FIRE ON THE DURON GENETIC SIGNATURES.
WE HAVE TO GET ANDROS OUT OF THERE.
WAIT!
THAT... THAT'S CORA!
OPEN FIRE ON WHATEVER THAT THING IS SHE'S FIGHTING.
SPLSH

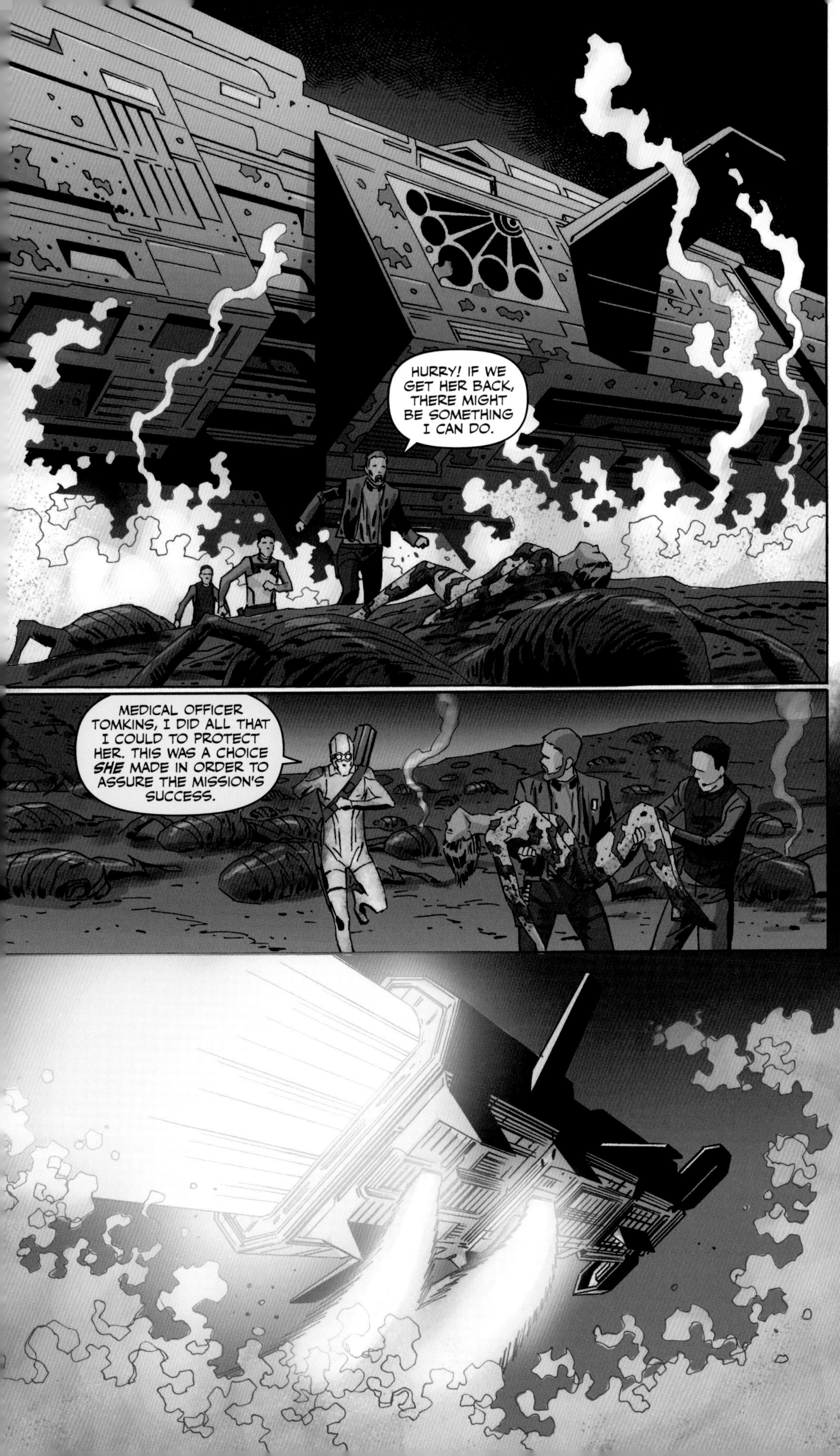
HURRY! IF WE GET HER BACK, THERE MIGHT BE SOMETHING I CAN DO.
MEDICAL OFFICER TOMKINS, I DID ALL THAT I COULD TO PROTECT HER. THIS WAS A CHOICE *SHE* MADE IN ORDER TO ASSURE THE MISSION'S SUCCESS.

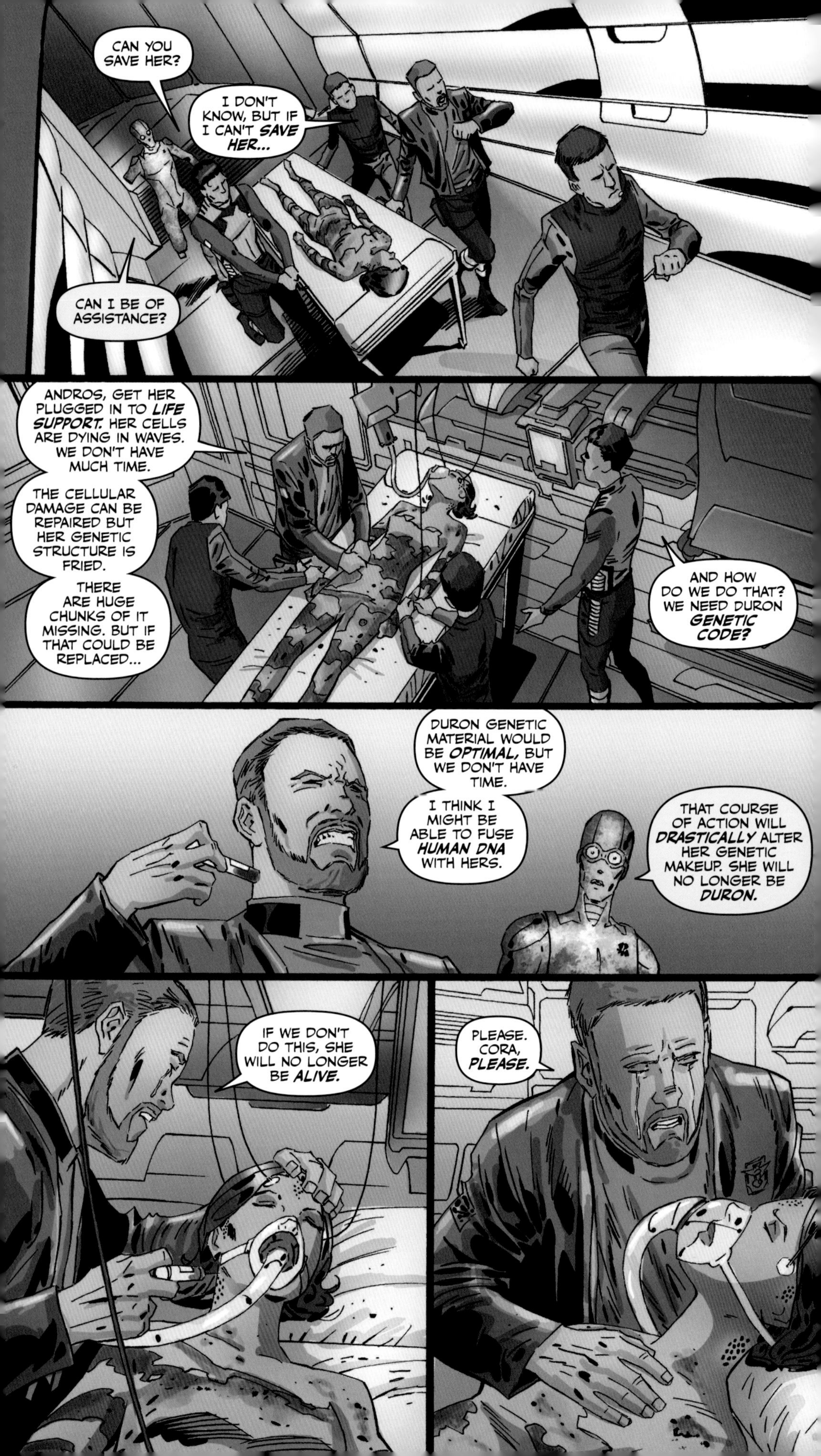
CAN YOU SAVE HER?
I DON'T KNOW, BUT IF I CAN'T SAVE HER...
CAN I BE OF ASSISTANCE?
ANDROS, GET HER PLUGGED IN TO LIFE SUPPORT. HER CELLS ARE DYING IN WAVES. WE DON'T HAVE MUCH TIME.
THE CELLULAR DAMAGE CAN BE REPAIRED BUT HER GENETIC STRUCTURE IS FRIED.
THERE ARE HUGE CHUNKS OF IT MISSING. BUT IF THAT COULD BE REPLACED...
AND HOW DO WE DO THAT? WE NEED DURON GENETIC CODE?
DURON GENETIC MATERIAL WOULD BE OPTIMAL, BUT WE DON'T HAVE TIME.
I THINK I MIGHT BE ABLE TO FUSE HUMAN DNA WITH HERS.
THAT COURSE OF ACTION WILL DRASTICALLY ALTER HER GENETIC MAKEUP. SHE WILL NO LONGER BE DURON.
IF WE DON'T DO THIS, SHE WILL NO LONGER BE ALIVE.
PLEASE. CORA, PLEASE.

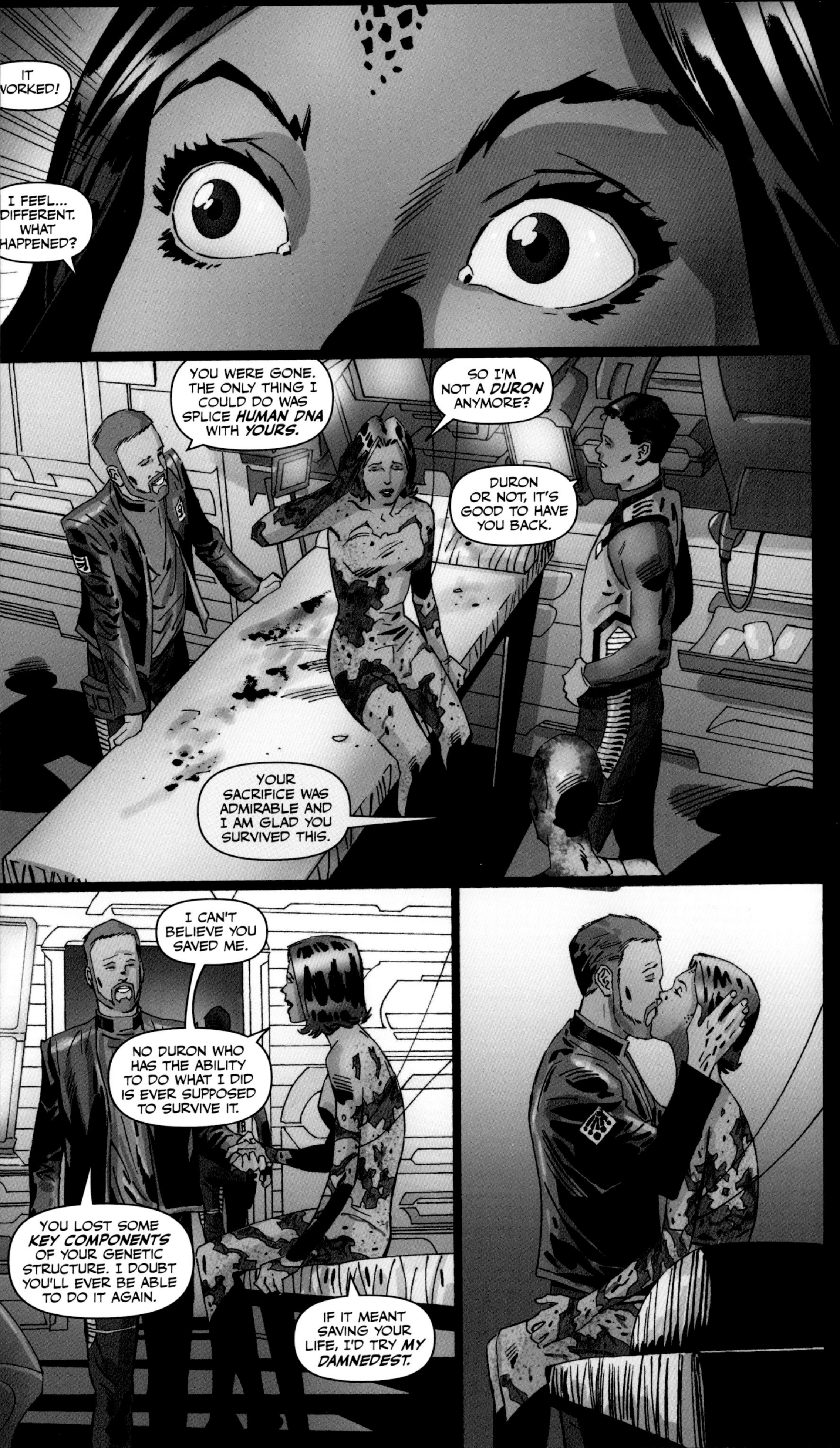
IT WORKED!
I FEEL... DIFFERENT. WHAT HAPPENED?
YOU WERE GONE. THE ONLY THING I COULD DO WAS SPLICE HUMAN DNA WITH YOURS.
SO I'M NOT A DURON ANYMORE?
DURON OR NOT, IT'S GOOD TO HAVE YOU BACK.
YOUR SACRIFICE WAS ADMIRABLE AND I AM GLAD YOU SURVIVED THIS.
I CAN'T BELIEVE YOU SAVED ME.
NO DURON WHO HAS THE ABILITY TO DO WHAT I DID IS EVER SUPPOSED TO SURVIVE IT.
YOU LOST SOME KEY COMPONENTS OF YOUR GENETIC STRUCTURE. I DOUBT YOU'LL EVER BE ABLE TO DO IT AGAIN.
IF IT MEANT SAVING YOUR LIFE, I'D TRY MY DAMNEDEST.

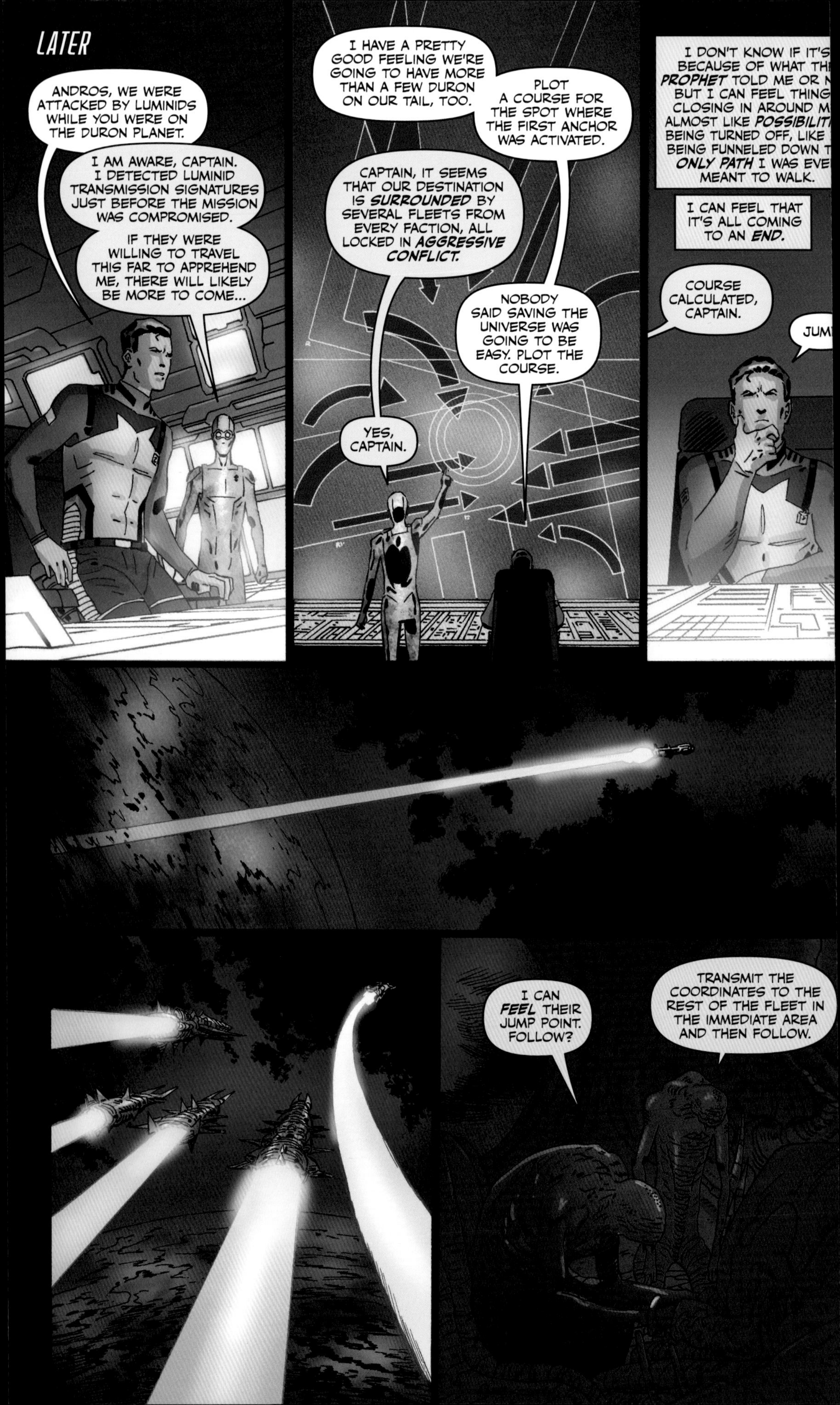
LATER
ANDROS, WE WERE ATTACKED BY LUMINIDS WHILE YOU WERE ON THE DURON PLANET.
I AM AWARE, CAPTAIN. I DETECTED LUMINID TRANSMISSION SIGNATURES JUST BEFORE THE MISSION WAS COMPROMISED.
IF THEY WERE WILLING TO TRAVEL THIS FAR TO APPREHEND ME, THERE WILL LIKELY BE MORE TO COME...
I HAVE A PRETTY GOOD FEELING WE'RE GOING TO HAVE MORE THAN A FEW DURON ON OUR TAIL, TOO.
PLOT A COURSE FOR THE SPOT WHERE THE FIRST ANCHOR WAS ACTIVATED.
CAPTAIN, IT SEEMS THAT OUR DESTINATION IS SURROUNDED BY SEVERAL FLEETS FROM EVERY FACTION, ALL LOCKED IN AGGRESSIVE CONFLICT.
NOBODY SAID SAVING THE UNIVERSE WAS GOING TO BE EASY. PLOT THE COURSE.
YES, CAPTAIN.
I CAN FEEL THAT IT'S ALL COMING TO AN END.
COURSE CALCULATED, CAPTAIN.
I CAN FEEL THEIR JUMP POINT. FOLLOW?
TRANSMIT THE COORDINATES TO THE REST OF THE FLEET IN THE IMMEDIATE AREA AND THEN FOLLOW.

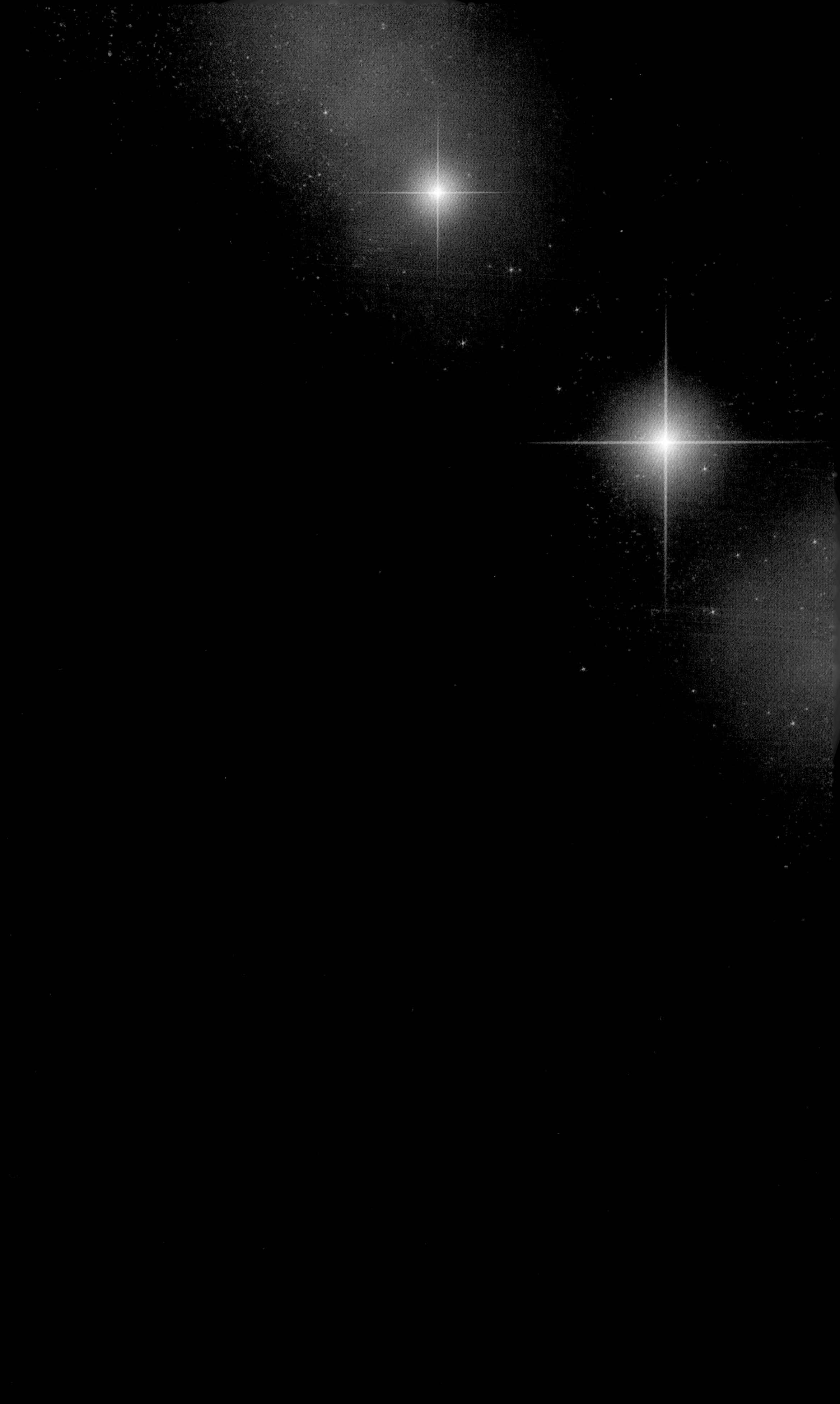

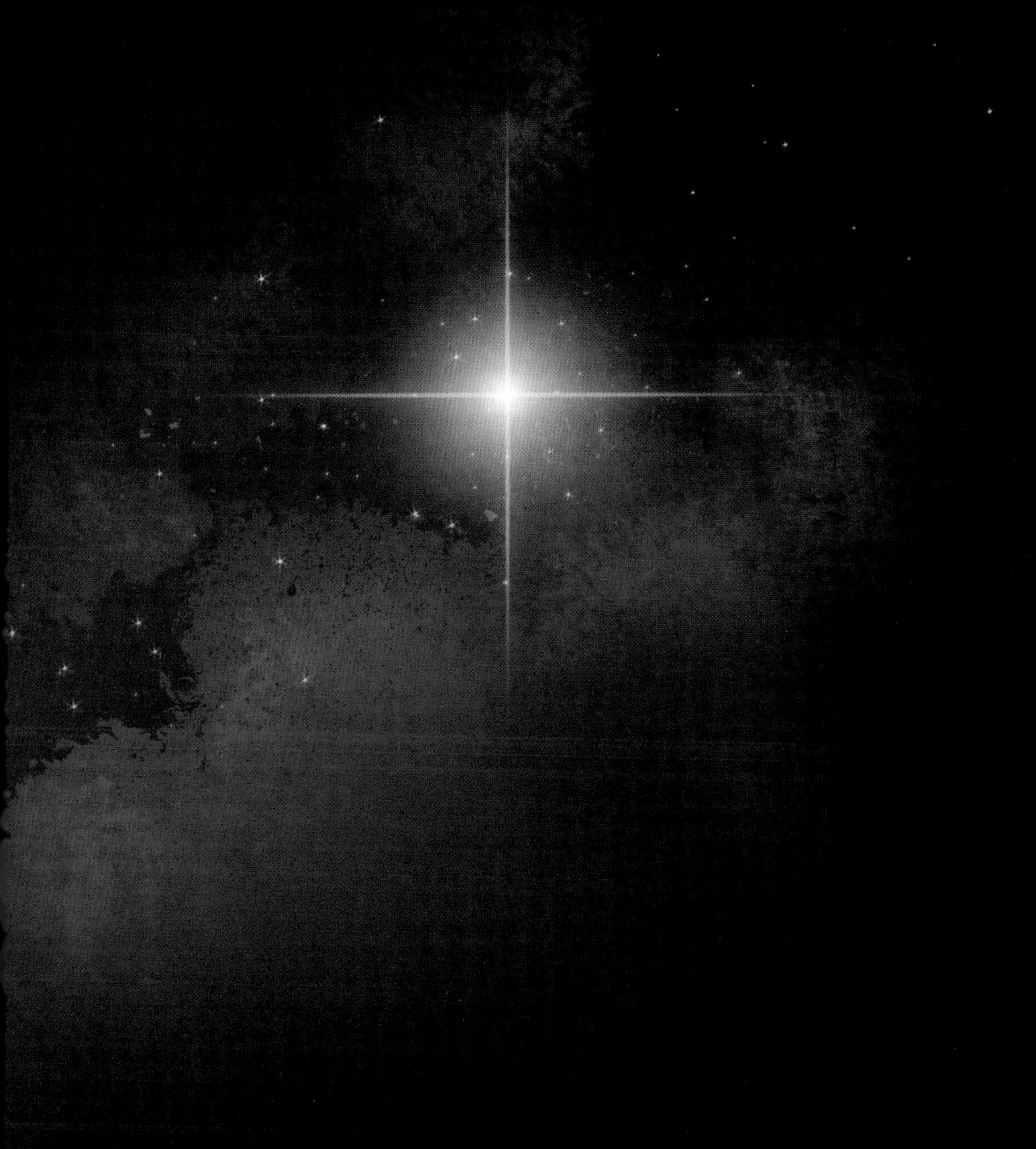

CHAPTER FOUR //

//THE ANCHOR

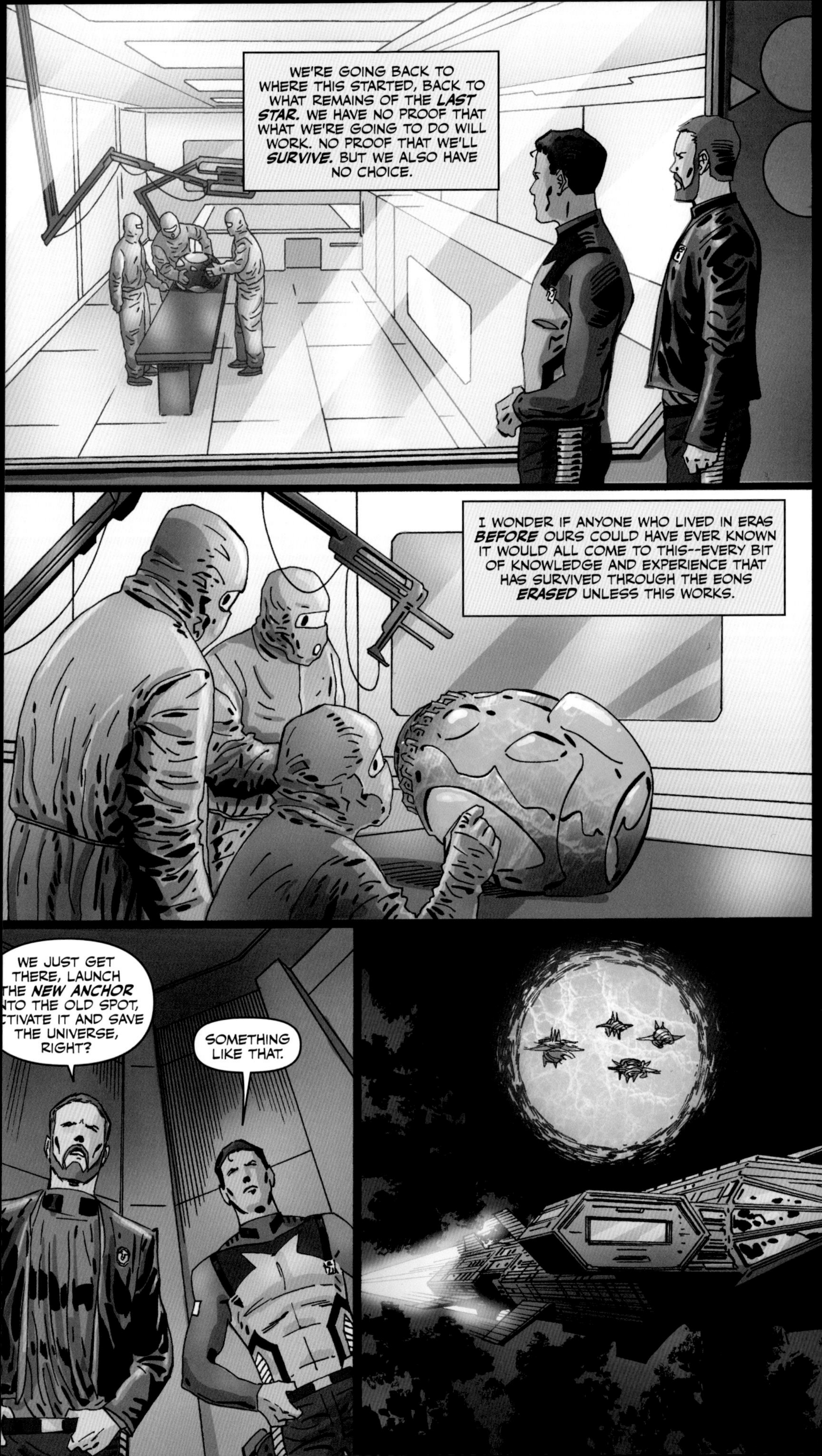
WE'RE GOING BACK TO WHERE THIS STARTED, BACK TO WHAT REMAINS OF THE *LAST STAR.* WE HAVE NO PROOF THAT WHAT WE'RE GOING TO DO WILL WORK. NO PROOF THAT WE'LL *SURVIVE.* BUT WE ALSO HAVE NO CHOICE.
I WONDER IF ANYONE WHO LIVED IN ERAS *BEFORE* OURS COULD HAVE EVER KNOWN IT WOULD ALL COME TO THIS--EVERY BIT OF KNOWLEDGE AND EXPERIENCE THAT HAS SURVIVED THROUGH THE EONS *ERASED* UNLESS THIS WORKS.
WE JUST GET THERE, LAUNCH THE *NEW ANCHOR* NTO THE OLD SPOT, CTIVATE IT AND SAVE THE UNIVERSE, RIGHT?
SOMETHING LIKE THAT.

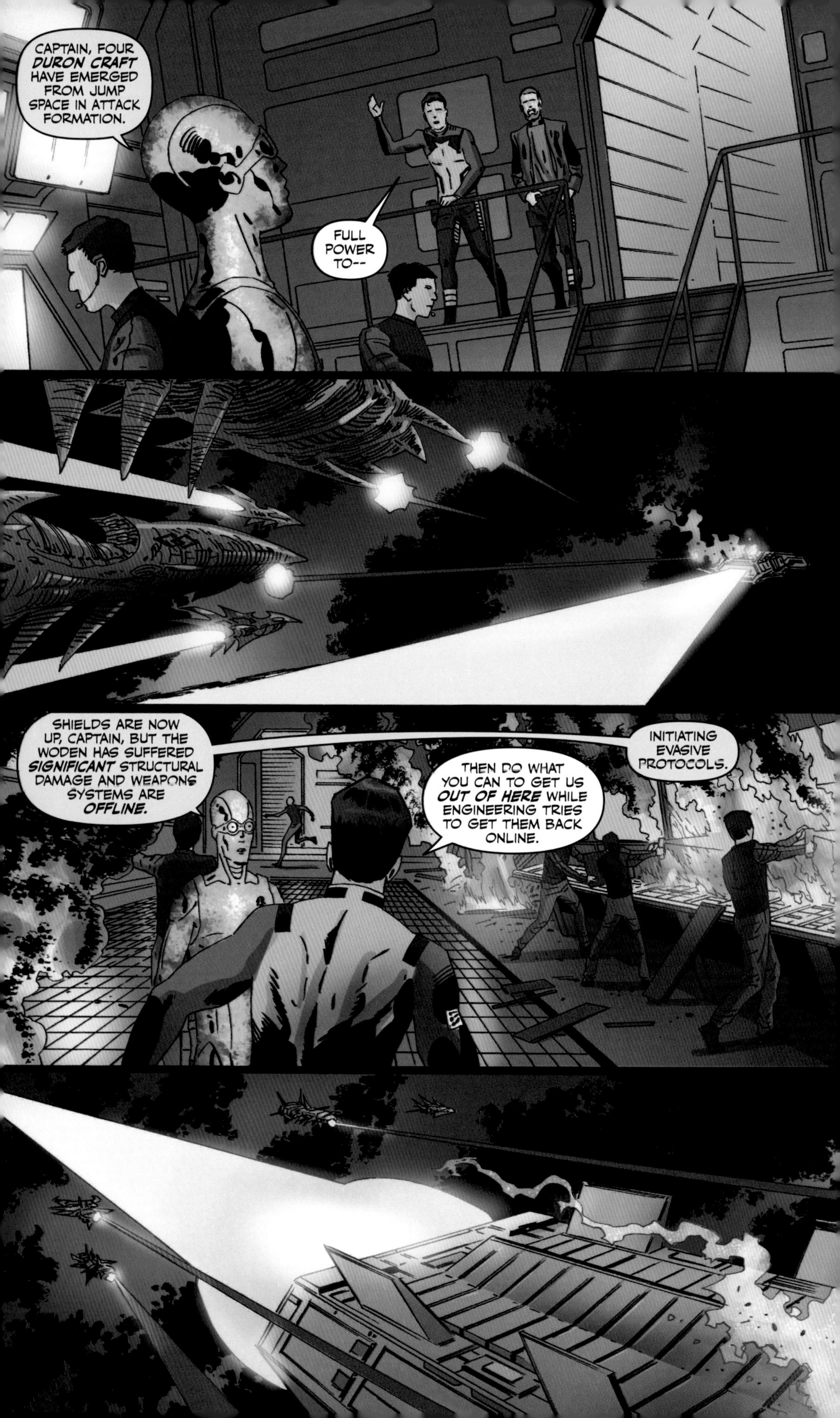
CAPTAIN, FOUR DURON CRAFT HAVE EMERGED FROM JUMP SPACE IN ATTACK FORMATION.
FULL POWER TO--
SHIELDS ARE NOW UP, CAPTAIN, BUT THE WODEN HAS SUFFERED SIGNIFICANT STRUCTURAL DAMAGE AND WEAPONS SYSTEMS ARE OFFLINE.
THEN DO WHAT YOU CAN TO GET US OUT OF HERE WHILE ENGINEERING TRIES TO GET THEM BACK ONLINE.
INITIATING EVASIVE PROTOCOLS.

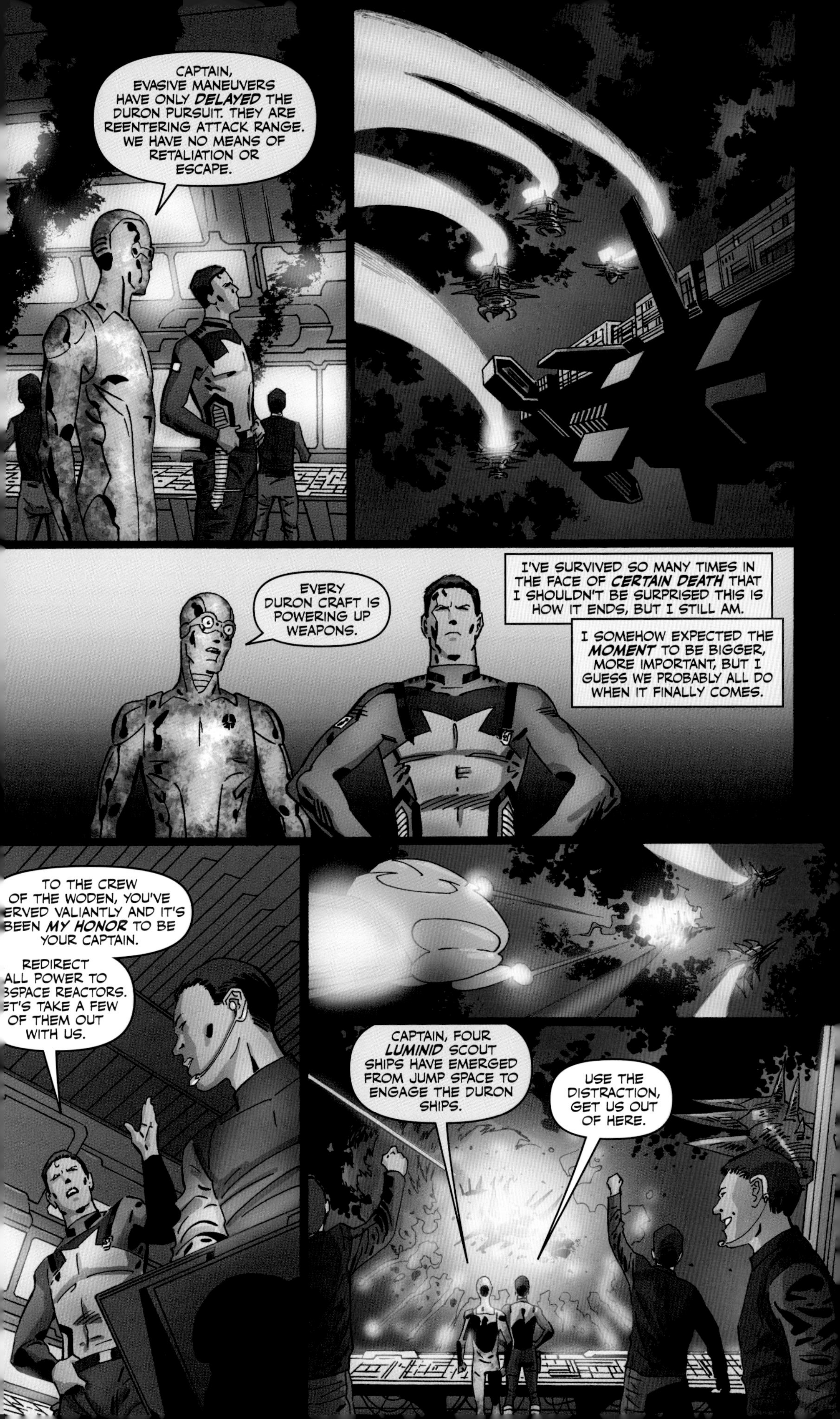
CAPTAIN, EVASIVE MANEUVERS HAVE ONLY DELAYED THE DURON PURSUIT. THEY ARE REENTERING ATTACK RANGE. WE HAVE NO MEANS OF RETALIATION OR ESCAPE.
EVERY DURON CRAFT IS POWERING UP WEAPONS.
I'VE SURVIVED SO MANY TIMES IN THE FACE OF CERTAIN DEATH THAT I SHOULDN'T BE SURPRISED THIS IS HOW IT ENDS, BUT I STILL AM.
I SOMEHOW EXPECTED THE MOMENT TO BE BIGGER, MORE IMPORTANT, BUT I GUESS WE PROBABLY ALL DO WHEN IT FINALLY COMES.
TO THE CREW OF THE WODEN, YOU'VE ERVED VALIANTLY AND IT'S BEEN MY HONOR TO BE YOUR CAPTAIN.
REDIRECT ALL POWER TO BSPACE REACTORS. ET'S TAKE A FEW OF THEM OUT WITH US.
CAPTAIN, FOUR LUMINID SCOUT SHIPS HAVE EMERGED FROM JUMP SPACE TO ENGAGE THE DURON SHIPS.
USE THE DISTRACTION, GET US OUT OF HERE.

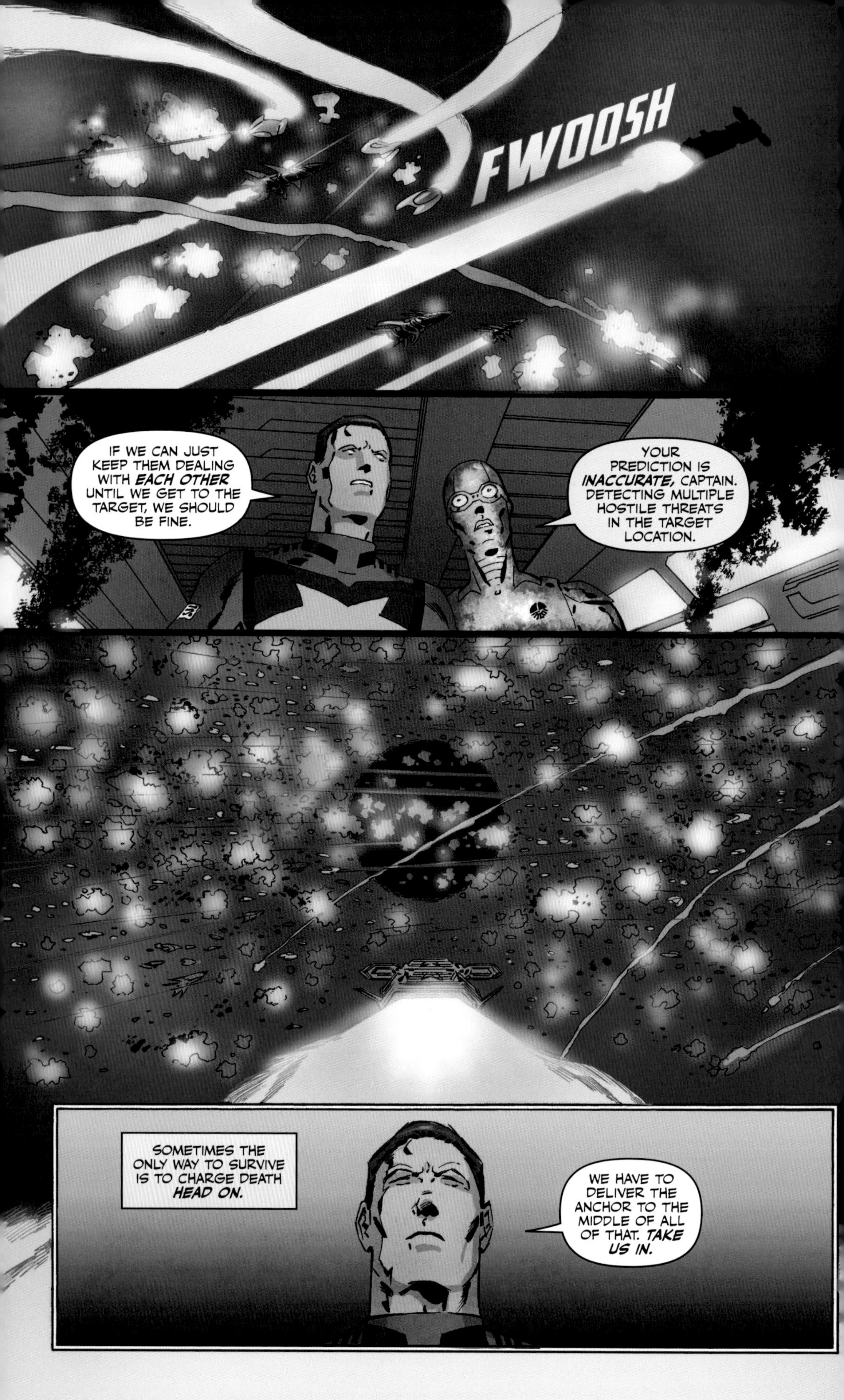
FWOOSH
IF WE CAN JUST KEEP THEM DEALING WITH EACH OTHER UNTIL WE GET TO THE TARGET, WE SHOULD BE FINE.
YOUR PREDICTION IS INACCURATE, CAPTAIN. DETECTING MULTIPLE HOSTILE THREATS IN THE TARGET LOCATION.
SOMETIMES THE ONLY WAY TO SURVIVE IS TO CHARGE DEATH HEAD ON.
WE HAVE TO DELIVER THE ANCHOR TO THE MIDDLE OF ALL OF THAT. TAKE US IN.

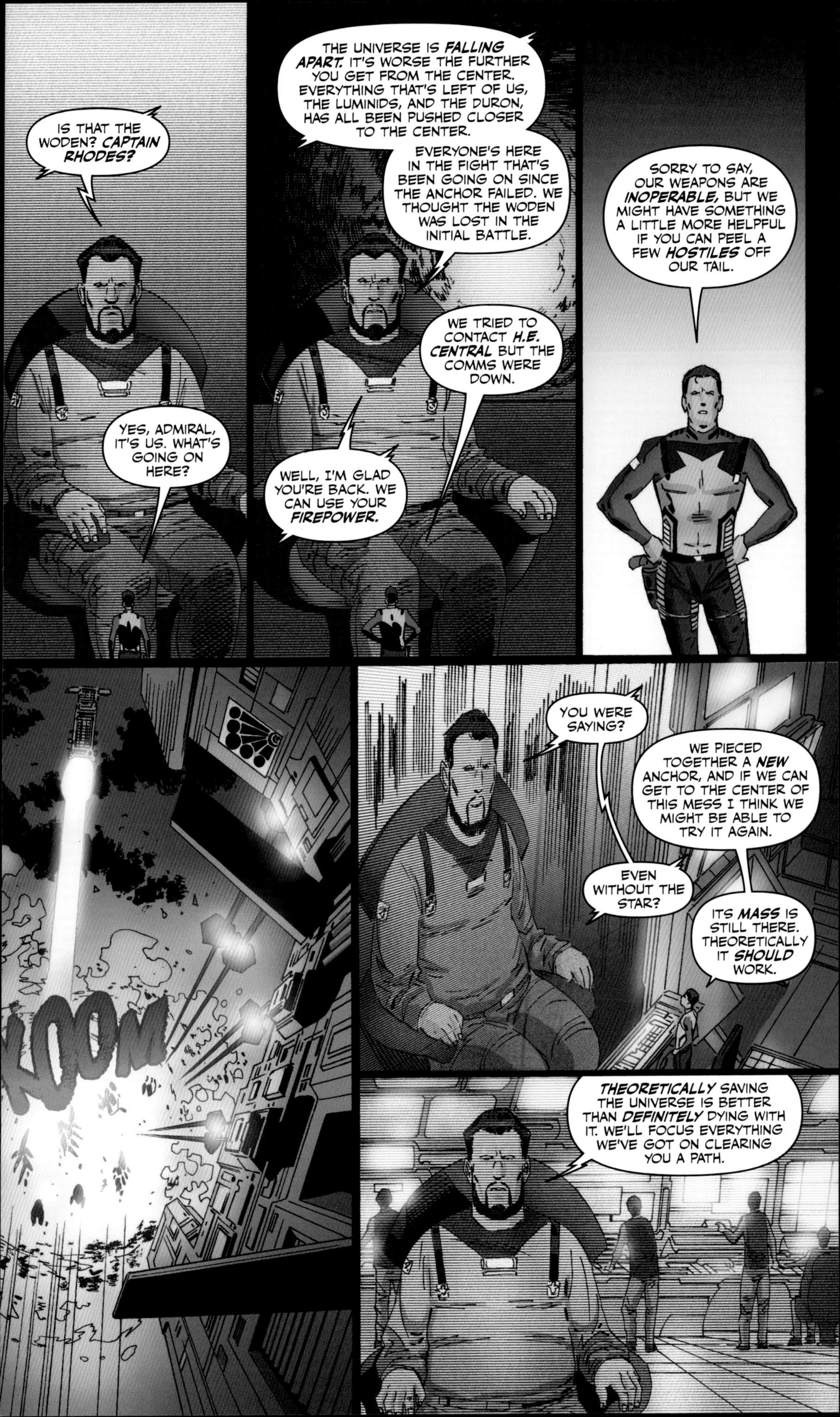

IS THAT THE WODEN? CAPTAIN RHODES?
YES, ADMIRAL, IT'S US. WHAT'S GOING ON HERE?
THE UNIVERSE IS FALLING APART. IT'S WORSE THE FURTHER YOU GET FROM THE CENTER. EVERYTHING THAT'S LEFT OF US, THE LUMINIDS, AND THE DURON, HAS ALL BEEN PUSHED CLOSER TO THE CENTER.
EVERYONE'S HERE IN THE FIGHT THAT'S BEEN GOING ON SINCE THE ANCHOR FAILED. WE THOUGHT THE WODEN WAS LOST IN THE INITIAL BATTLE.
WE TRIED TO CONTACT H.E. CENTRAL BUT THE COMMS WERE DOWN.
WELL, I'M GLAD YOU'RE BACK. WE CAN USE YOUR FIREPOWER.
SORRY TO SAY, OUR WEAPONS ARE INOPERABLE, BUT WE MIGHT HAVE SOMETHING A LITTLE MORE HELPFUL IF YOU CAN PEEL A FEW HOSTILES OFF OUR TAIL.
KOOM
YOU WERE SAYING?
WE PIECED TOGETHER A NEW ANCHOR, AND IF WE CAN GET TO THE CENTER OF THIS MESS I THINK WE MIGHT BE ABLE TO TRY IT AGAIN.
EVEN WITHOUT THE STAR?
ITS MASS IS STILL THERE. THEORETICALLY IT SHOULD WORK.
THEORETICALLY SAVING THE UNIVERSE IS BETTER THAN DEFINITELY DYING WITH IT. WE'LL FOCUS EVERYTHING WE'VE GOT ON CLEARING YOU A PATH.

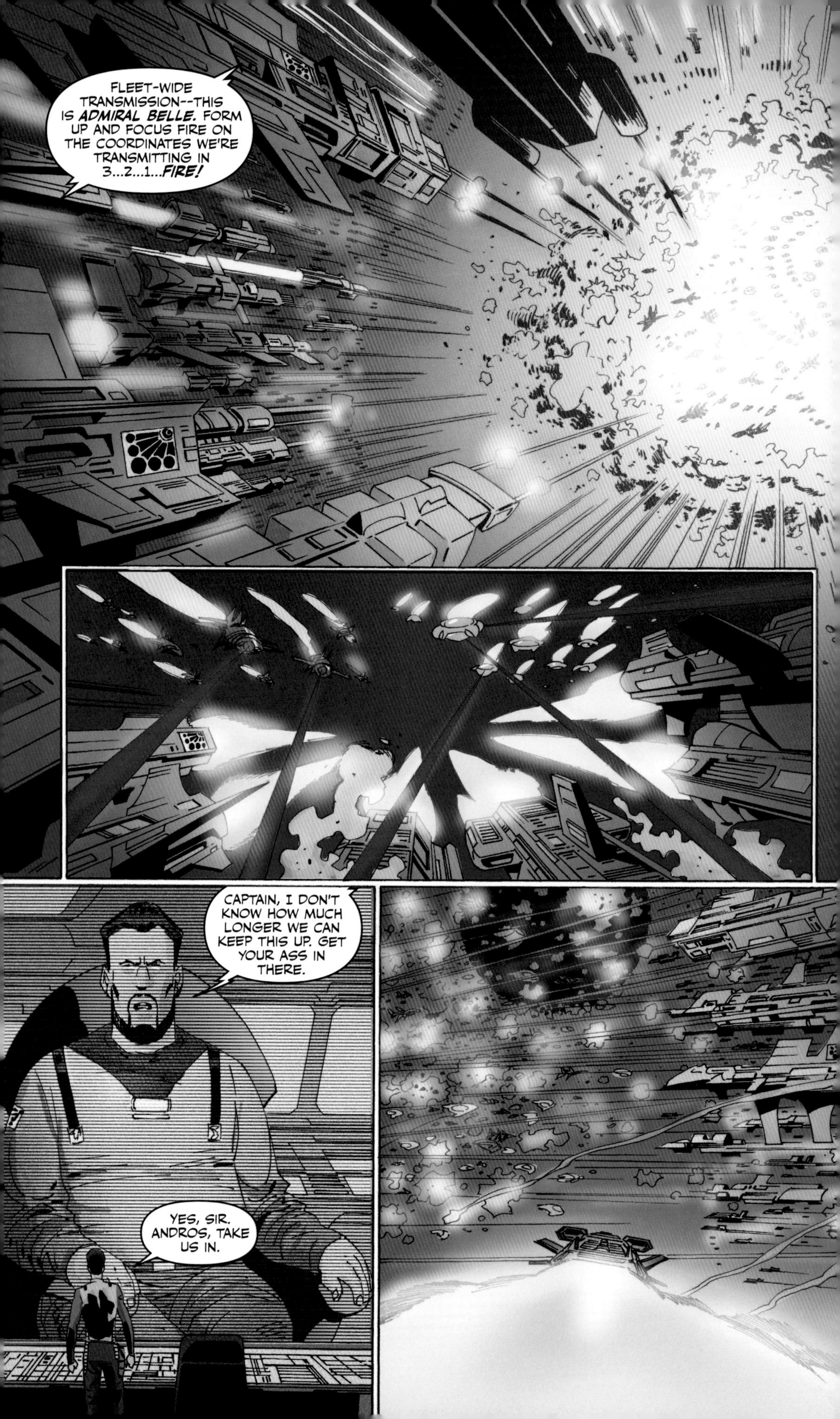
FLEET-WIDE TRANSMISSION--THIS IS ADMIRAL BELLE. FORM UP AND FOCUS FIRE ON THE COORDINATES WE'RE TRANSMITTING IN 3...2...1...FIRE!
CAPTAIN, I DON'T KNOW HOW MUCH LONGER WE CAN KEEP THIS UP. GET YOUR ASS IN THERE.
YES, SIR. ANDROS, TAKE US IN.

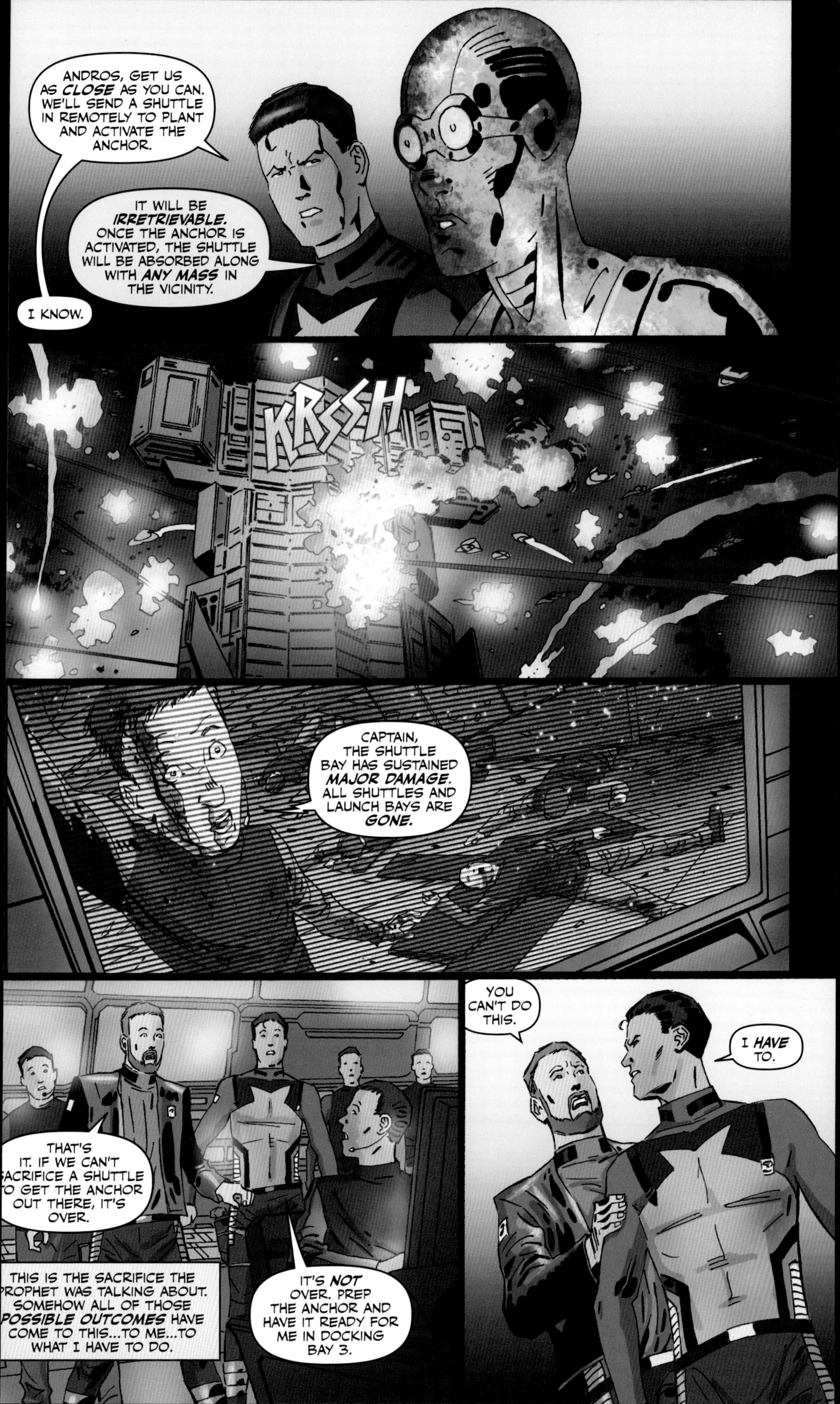
ANDROS, GET US AS CLOSE AS YOU CAN. WE'LL SEND A SHUTTLE IN REMOTELY TO PLANT AND ACTIVATE THE ANCHOR.
IT WILL BE IRRETRIEVABLE. ONCE THE ANCHOR IS ACTIVATED, THE SHUTTLE WILL BE ABSORBED ALONG WITH ANY MASS IN THE VICINITY.
I KNOW.
KRSSH
CAPTAIN, THE SHUTTLE BAY HAS SUSTAINED MAJOR DAMAGE. ALL SHUTTLES AND LAUNCH BAYS ARE GONE.
THAT'S IT. IF WE CAN'T SACRIFICE A SHUTTLE TO GET THE ANCHOR OUT THERE, IT'S OVER.
THIS IS THE SACRIFICE THE PROPHET WAS TALKING ABOUT. SOMEHOW ALL OF THOSE POSSIBLE OUTCOMES HAVE COME TO THIS...TO ME...TO WHAT I HAVE TO DO.
IT'S NOT OVER. PREP THE ANCHOR AND HAVE IT READY FOR ME IN DOCKING BAY 3.
YOU CAN'T DO THIS.
I HAVE TO.

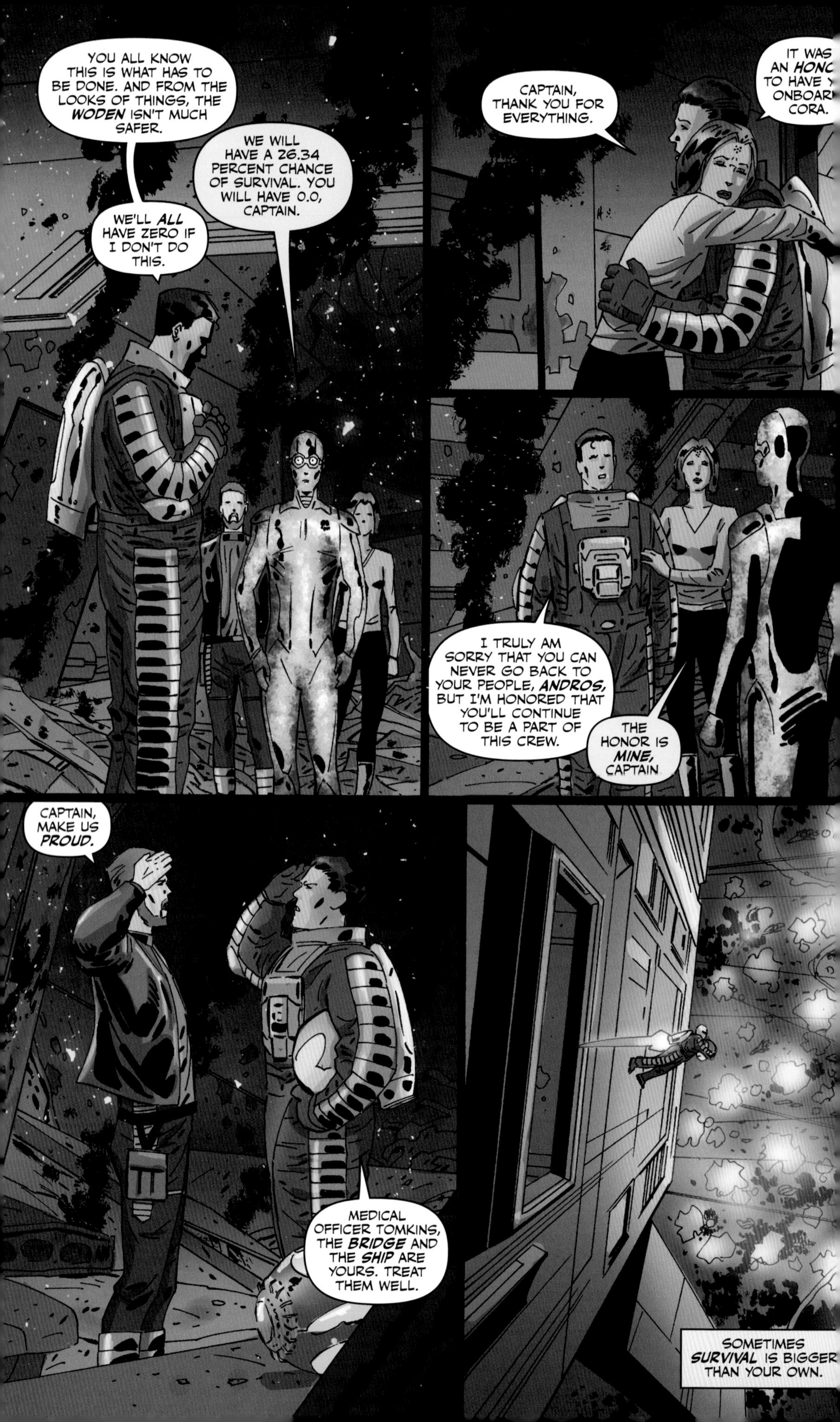
YOU ALL KNOW THIS IS WHAT HAS TO BE DONE. AND FROM THE LOOKS OF THINGS, THE *WODEN* ISN'T MUCH SAFER.
WE WILL HAVE A 26.34 PERCENT CHANCE OF SURVIVAL. YOU WILL HAVE 0.0, CAPTAIN.
WE'LL *ALL* HAVE ZERO IF I DON'T DO THIS.
CAPTAIN, THANK YOU FOR EVERYTHING.
I TRULY AM SORRY THAT YOU CAN NEVER GO BACK TO YOUR PEOPLE, *ANDROS,* BUT I'M HONORED THAT YOU'LL CONTINUE TO BE A PART OF THIS CREW.
THE HONOR IS *MINE,* CAPTAIN.
CAPTAIN, MAKE US *PROUD.*
MEDICAL OFFICER TOMKINS, THE *BRIDGE* AND THE *SHIP* ARE YOURS. TREAT THEM WELL.
SOMETIMES *SURVIVAL* IS BIGGER THAN YOUR OWN.

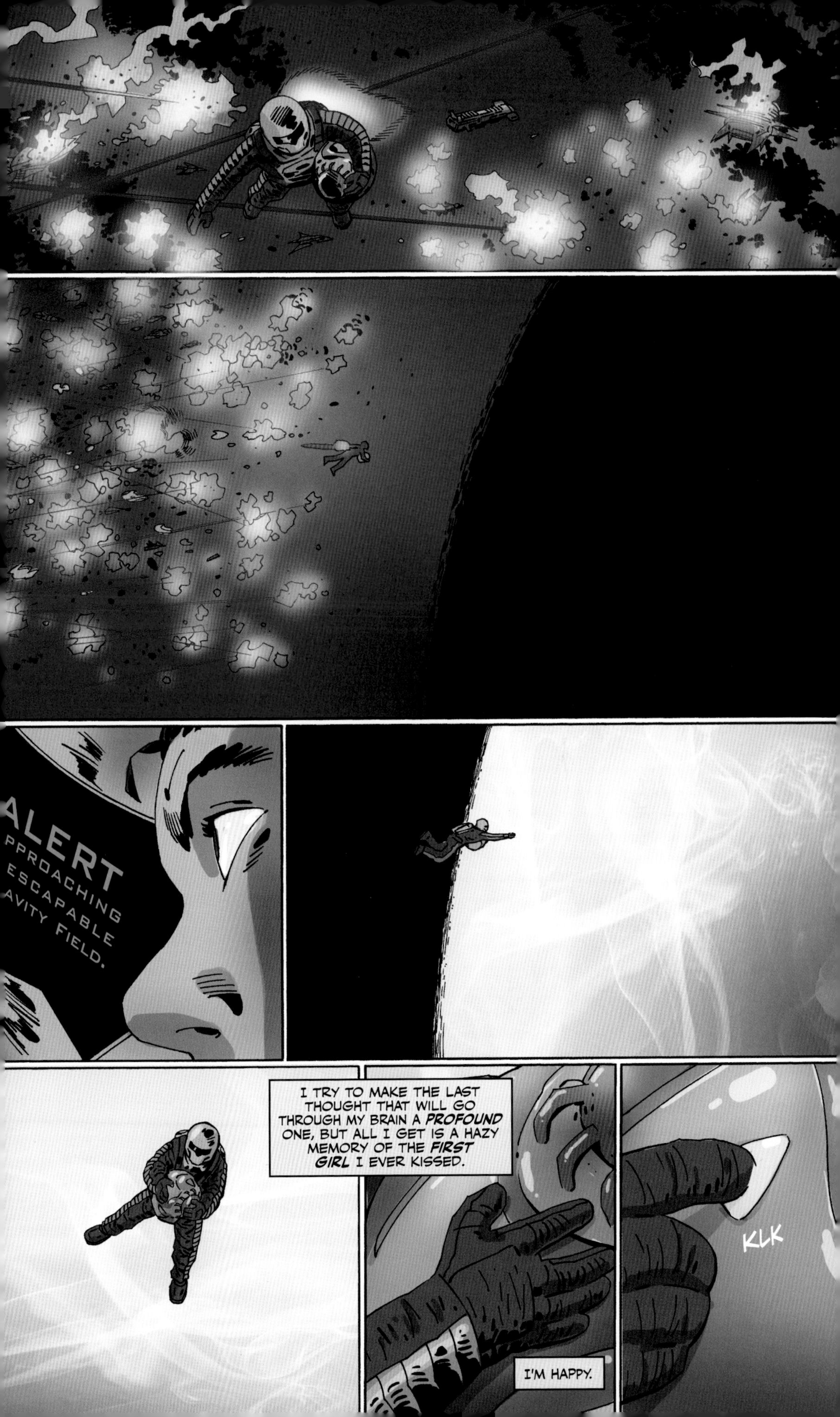
ALERT
PPROACHING
ESCAPABLE
AVITY FIELD.
I TRY TO MAKE THE LAST THOUGHT THAT WILL GO THROUGH MY BRAIN A *PROFOUND* ONE, BUT ALL I GET IS A HAZY MEMORY OF THE *FIRST GIRL* I EVER KISSED.
KLK
I'M HAPPY.

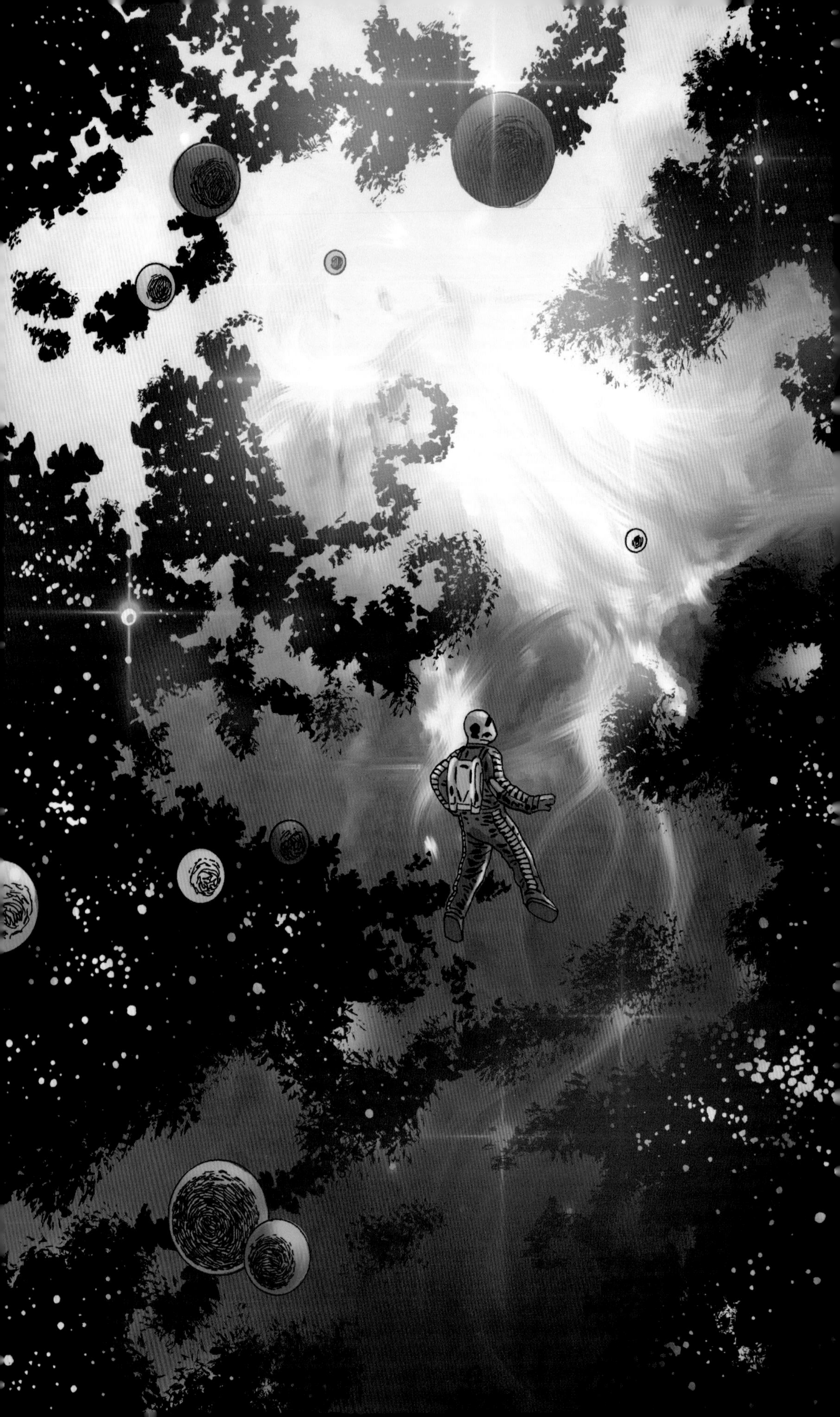

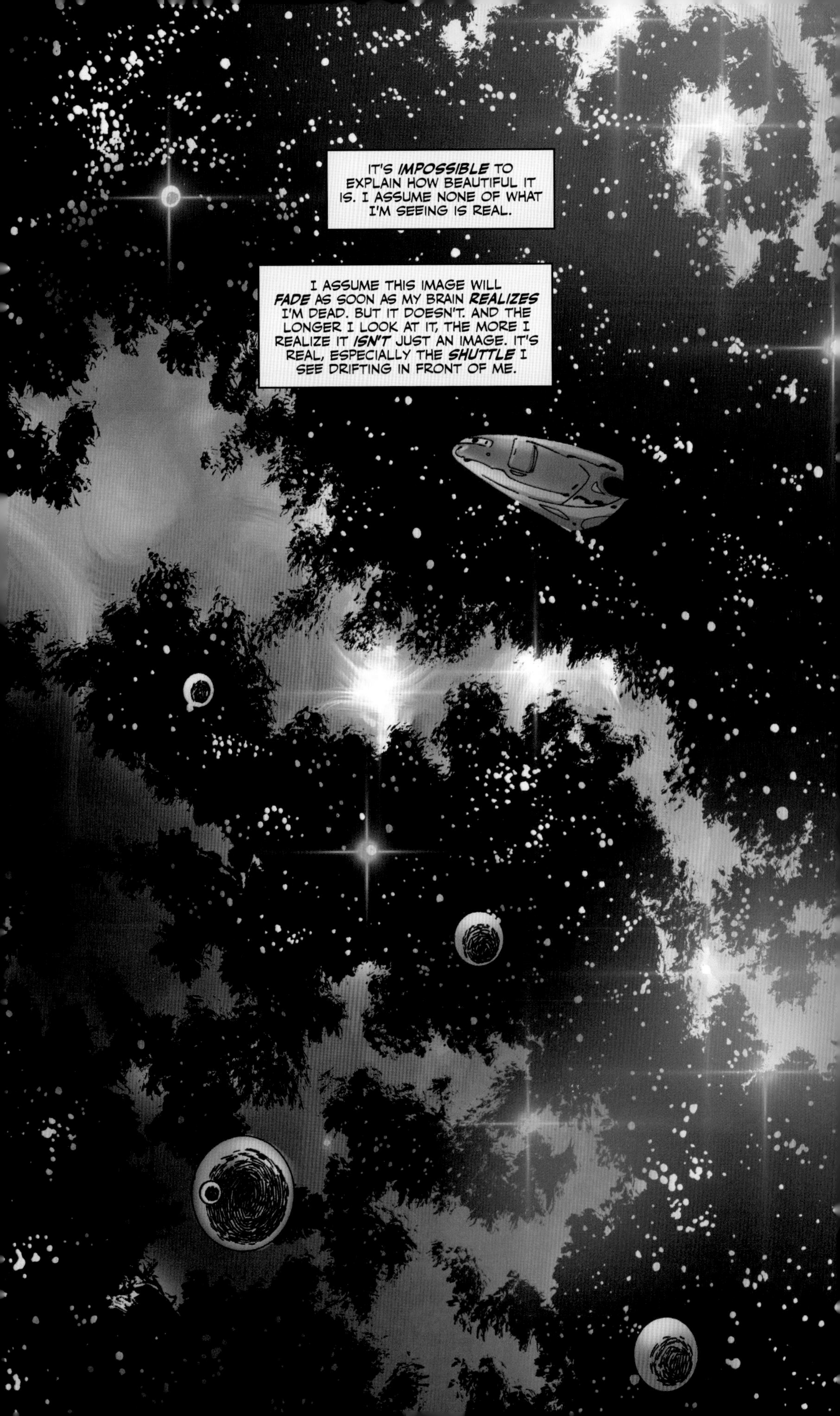
IT'S IMPOSSIBLE TO EXPLAIN HOW BEAUTIFUL IT IS. I ASSUME NONE OF WHAT I'M SEEING IS REAL.
I ASSUME THIS IMAGE WILL FADE AS SOON AS MY BRAIN REALIZES I'M DEAD. BUT IT DOESN'T. AND THE LONGER I LOOK AT IT, THE MORE I REALIZE IT ISN'T JUST AN IMAGE. IT'S REAL, ESPECIALLY THE SHUTTLE I SEE DRIFTING IN FRONT OF ME.

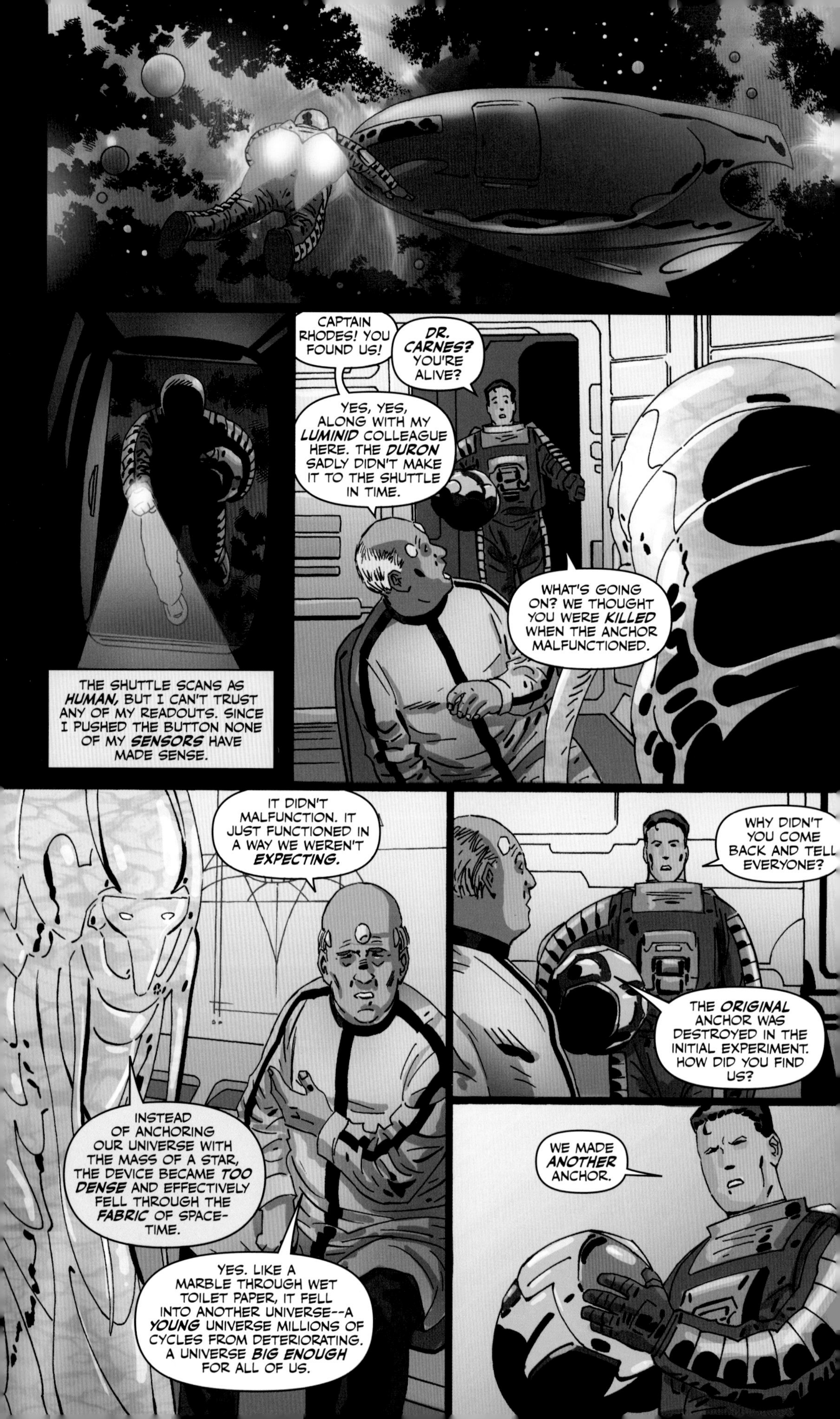
THE SHUTTLE SCANS AS *HUMAN,* BUT I CAN'T TRUST ANY OF MY READOUTS. SINCE I PUSHED THE BUTTON NONE OF MY *SENSORS* HAVE MADE SENSE.
CAPTAIN RHODES! YOU FOUND US!
DR. CARNES? YOU'RE ALIVE?
YES, YES, ALONG WITH MY *LUMINID* COLLEAGUE HERE. THE *DURON* SADLY DIDN'T MAKE IT TO THE SHUTTLE IN TIME.
WHAT'S GOING ON? WE THOUGHT YOU WERE *KILLED* WHEN THE ANCHOR MALFUNCTIONED.
IT DIDN'T MALFUNCTION. IT JUST FUNCTIONED IN A WAY WE WEREN'T *EXPECTING.*
INSTEAD OF ANCHORING OUR UNIVERSE WITH THE MASS OF A STAR, THE DEVICE BECAME *TOO DENSE* AND EFFECTIVELY FELL THROUGH THE *FABRIC* OF SPACE-TIME.
YES. LIKE A MARBLE THROUGH WET TOILET PAPER, IT FELL INTO ANOTHER UNIVERSE--A *YOUNG* UNIVERSE MILLIONS OF CYCLES FROM DETERIORATING. A UNIVERSE *BIG ENOUGH* FOR ALL OF US.
WHY DIDN'T YOU COME BACK AND TELL EVERYONE?
THE *ORIGINAL* ANCHOR WAS DESTROYED IN THE INITIAL EXPERIMENT. HOW DID YOU FIND US?
WE MADE *ANOTHER* ANCHOR.

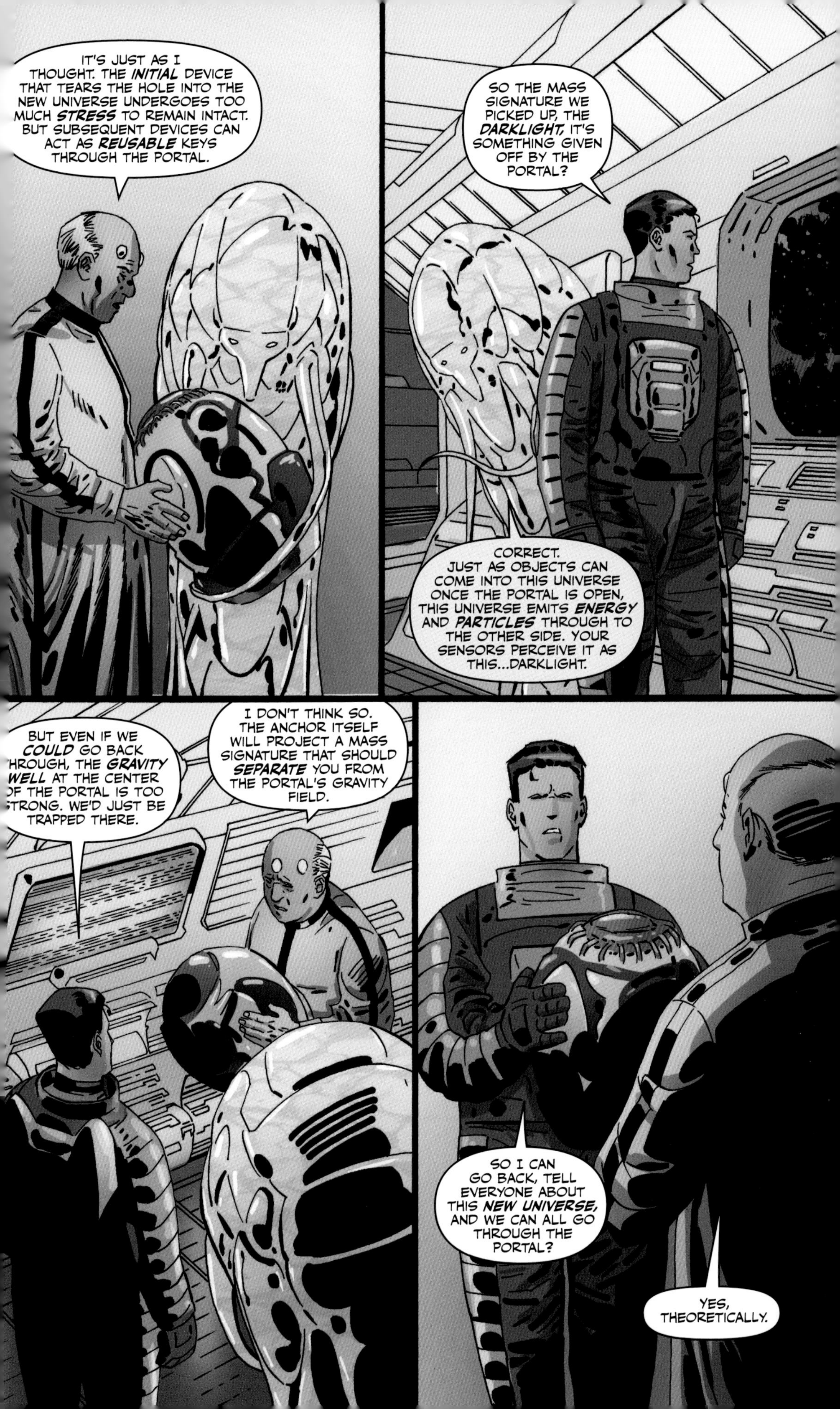
IT'S JUST AS I THOUGHT. THE INITIAL DEVICE THAT TEARS THE HOLE INTO THE NEW UNIVERSE UNDERGOES TOO MUCH STRESS TO REMAIN INTACT. BUT SUBSEQUENT DEVICES CAN ACT AS REUSABLE KEYS THROUGH THE PORTAL.
SO THE MASS SIGNATURE WE PICKED UP, THE DARKLIGHT, IT'S SOMETHING GIVEN OFF BY THE PORTAL?
CORRECT. JUST AS OBJECTS CAN COME INTO THIS UNIVERSE ONCE THE PORTAL IS OPEN, THIS UNIVERSE EMITS ENERGY AND PARTICLES THROUGH TO THE OTHER SIDE. YOUR SENSORS PERCEIVE IT AS THIS...DARKLIGHT.
BUT EVEN IF WE COULD GO BACK THROUGH, THE GRAVITY WELL AT THE CENTER OF THE PORTAL IS TOO STRONG. WE'D JUST BE TRAPPED THERE.
I DON'T THINK SO. THE ANCHOR ITSELF WILL PROJECT A MASS SIGNATURE THAT SHOULD SEPARATE YOU FROM THE PORTAL'S GRAVITY FIELD.
SO I CAN GO BACK, TELL EVERYONE ABOUT THIS NEW UNIVERSE, AND WE CAN ALL GO THROUGH THE PORTAL?
YES, THEORETICALLY.

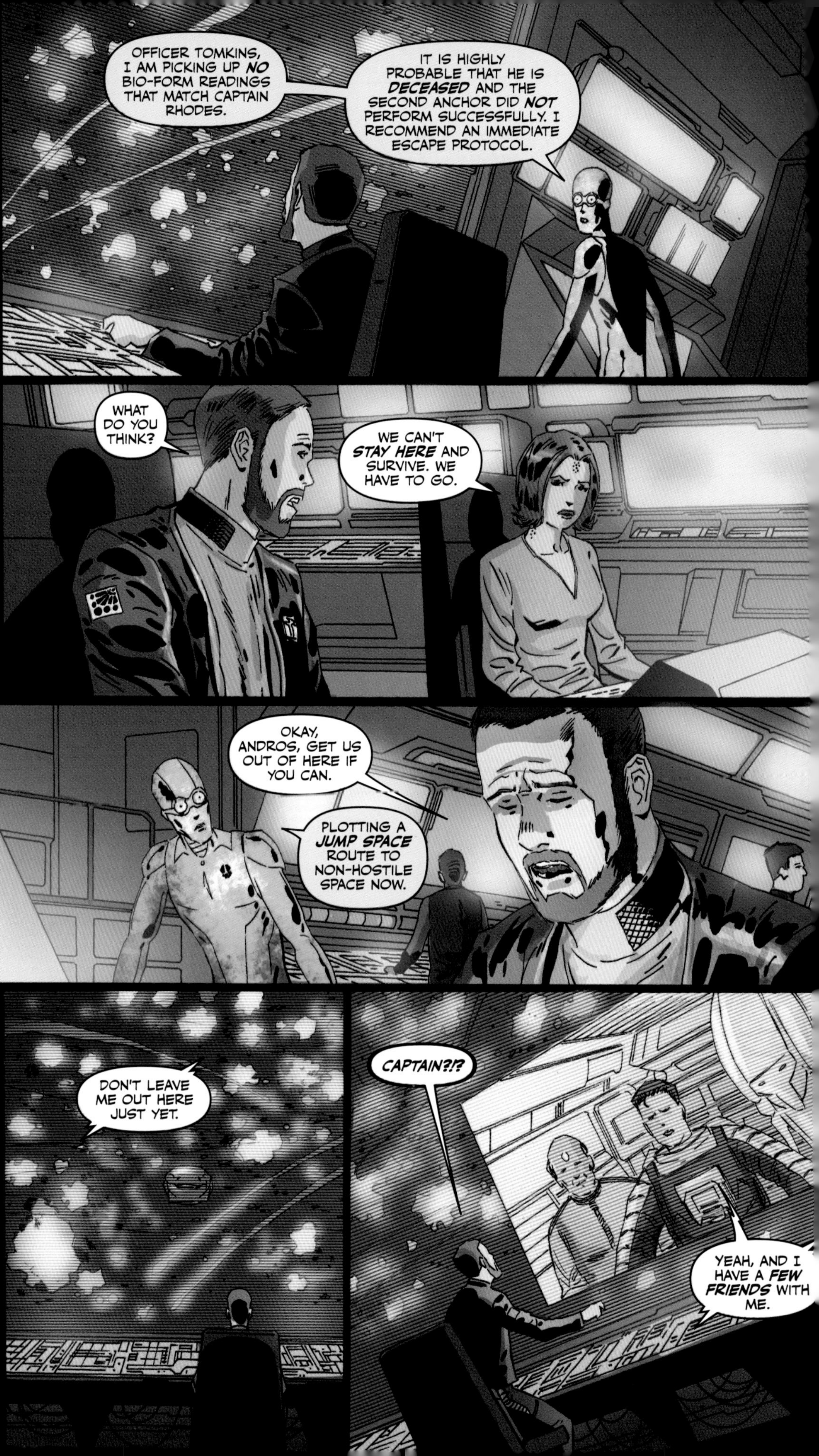

OFFICER TOMKINS, I AM PICKING UP NO BIO-FORM READINGS THAT MATCH CAPTAIN RHODES.
IT IS HIGHLY PROBABLE THAT HE IS DECEASED AND THE SECOND ANCHOR DID NOT PERFORM SUCCESSFULLY. I RECOMMEND AN IMMEDIATE ESCAPE PROTOCOL.
WHAT DO YOU THINK?
WE CAN'T STAY HERE AND SURVIVE. WE HAVE TO GO.
OKAY, ANDROS, GET US OUT OF HERE IF YOU CAN.
PLOTTING A JUMP SPACE ROUTE TO NON-HOSTILE SPACE NOW.
DON'T LEAVE ME OUT HERE JUST YET.
CAPTAIN?!?
YEAH, AND I HAVE A FEW FRIENDS WITH ME.

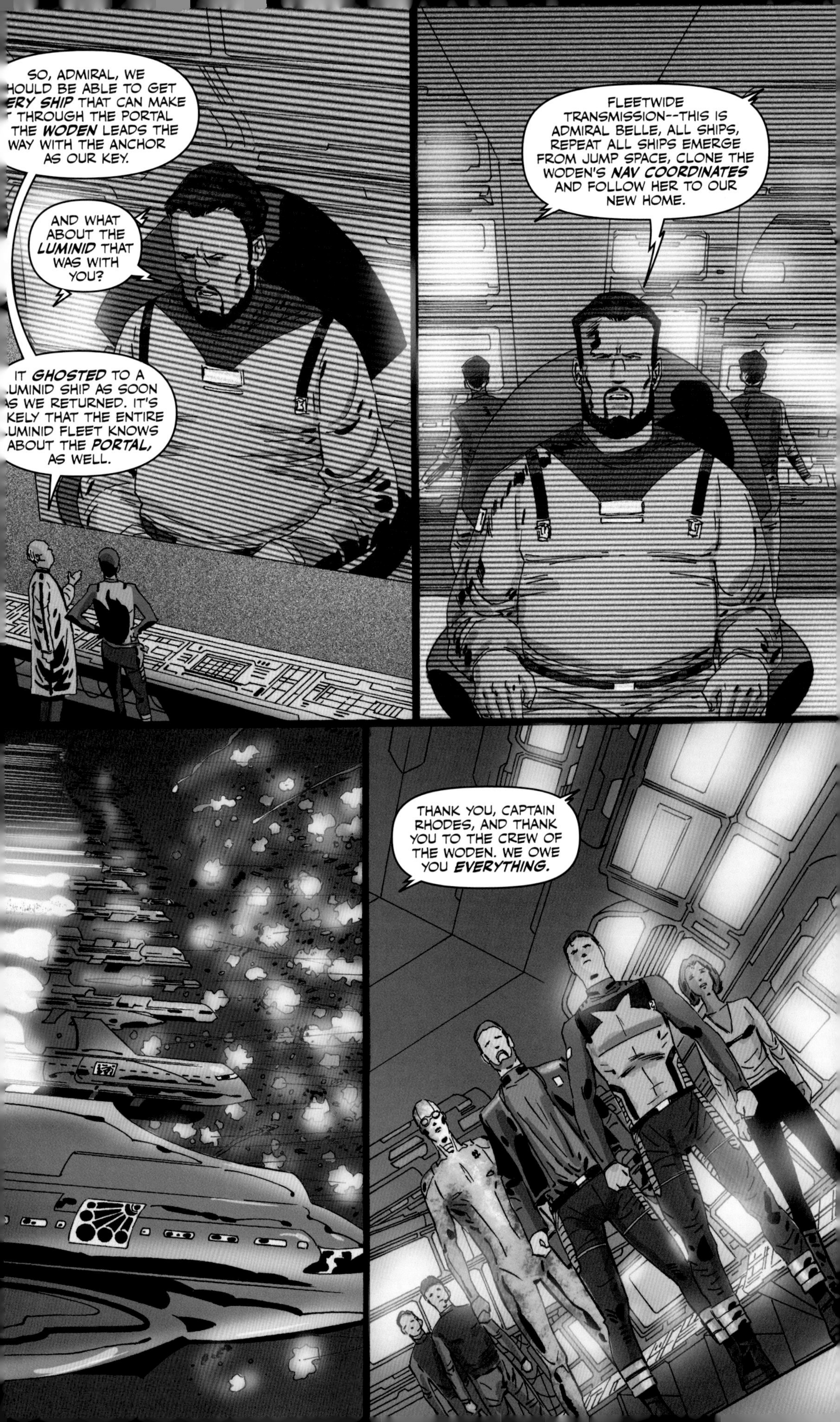
SO, ADMIRAL, WE HOULD BE ABLE TO GET ERY SHIP THAT CAN MAKE T THROUGH THE PORTAL THE WODEN LEADS THE WAY WITH THE ANCHOR AS OUR KEY.
AND WHAT ABOUT THE LUMINID THAT WAS WITH YOU?
IT GHOSTED TO A UMINID SHIP AS SOON AS WE RETURNED. IT'S KELY THAT THE ENTIRE UMINID FLEET KNOWS ABOUT THE PORTAL, AS WELL.
FLEETWIDE TRANSMISSION--THIS IS ADMIRAL BELLE, ALL SHIPS, REPEAT ALL SHIPS EMERGE FROM JUMP SPACE, CLONE THE WODEN'S NAV COORDINATES AND FOLLOW HER TO OUR NEW HOME.
THANK YOU, CAPTAIN RHODES, AND THANK YOU TO THE CREW OF THE WODEN. WE OWE YOU EVERYTHING.

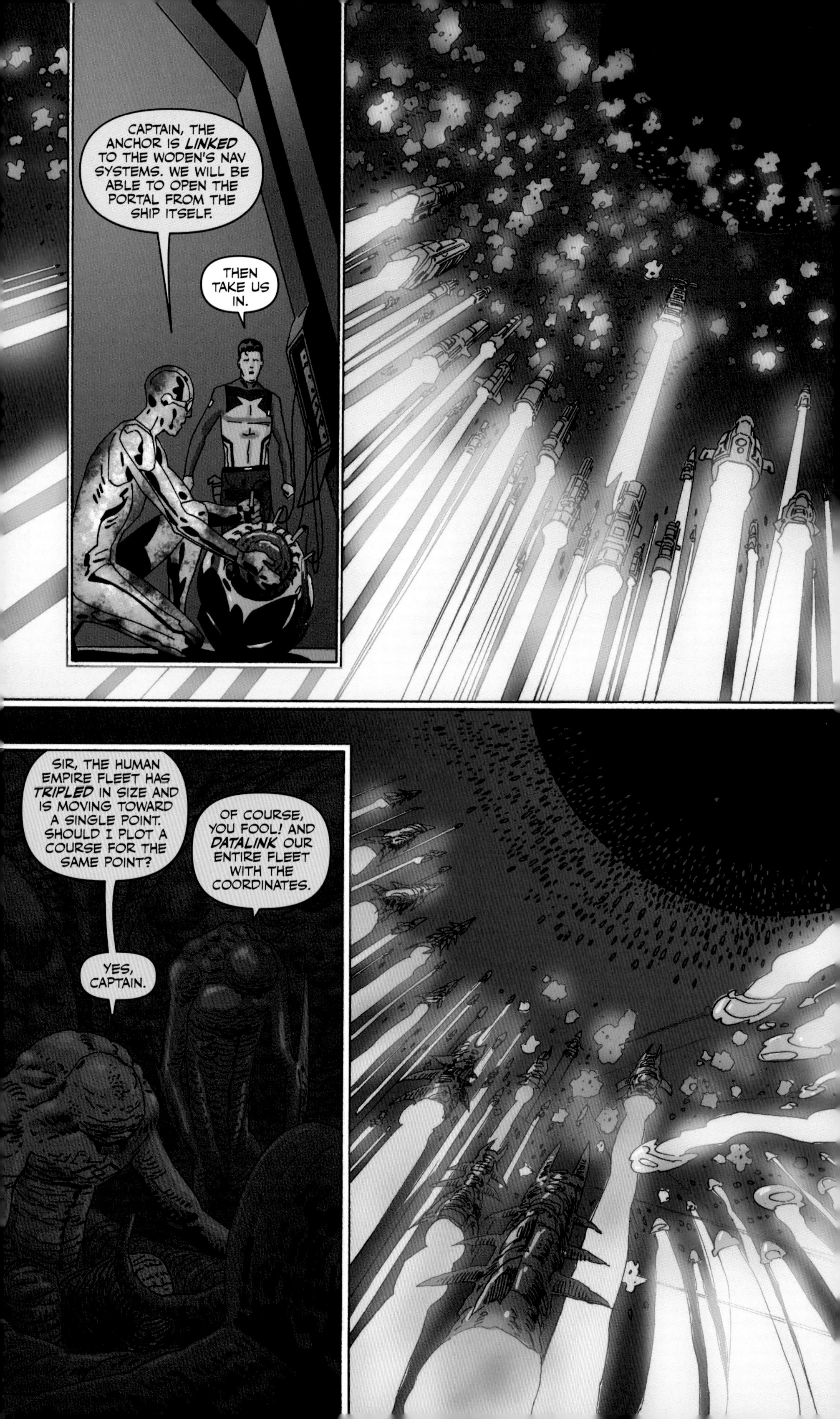
CAPTAIN, THE ANCHOR IS LINKED TO THE WODEN'S NAV SYSTEMS. WE WILL BE ABLE TO OPEN THE PORTAL FROM THE SHIP ITSELF.
THEN TAKE US IN.
SIR, THE HUMAN EMPIRE FLEET HAS TRIPLED IN SIZE AND IS MOVING TOWARD A SINGLE POINT. SHOULD I PLOT A COURSE FOR THE SAME POINT?
OF COURSE, YOU FOOL! AND DATALINK OUR ENTIRE FLEET WITH THE COORDINATES.
YES, CAPTAIN.

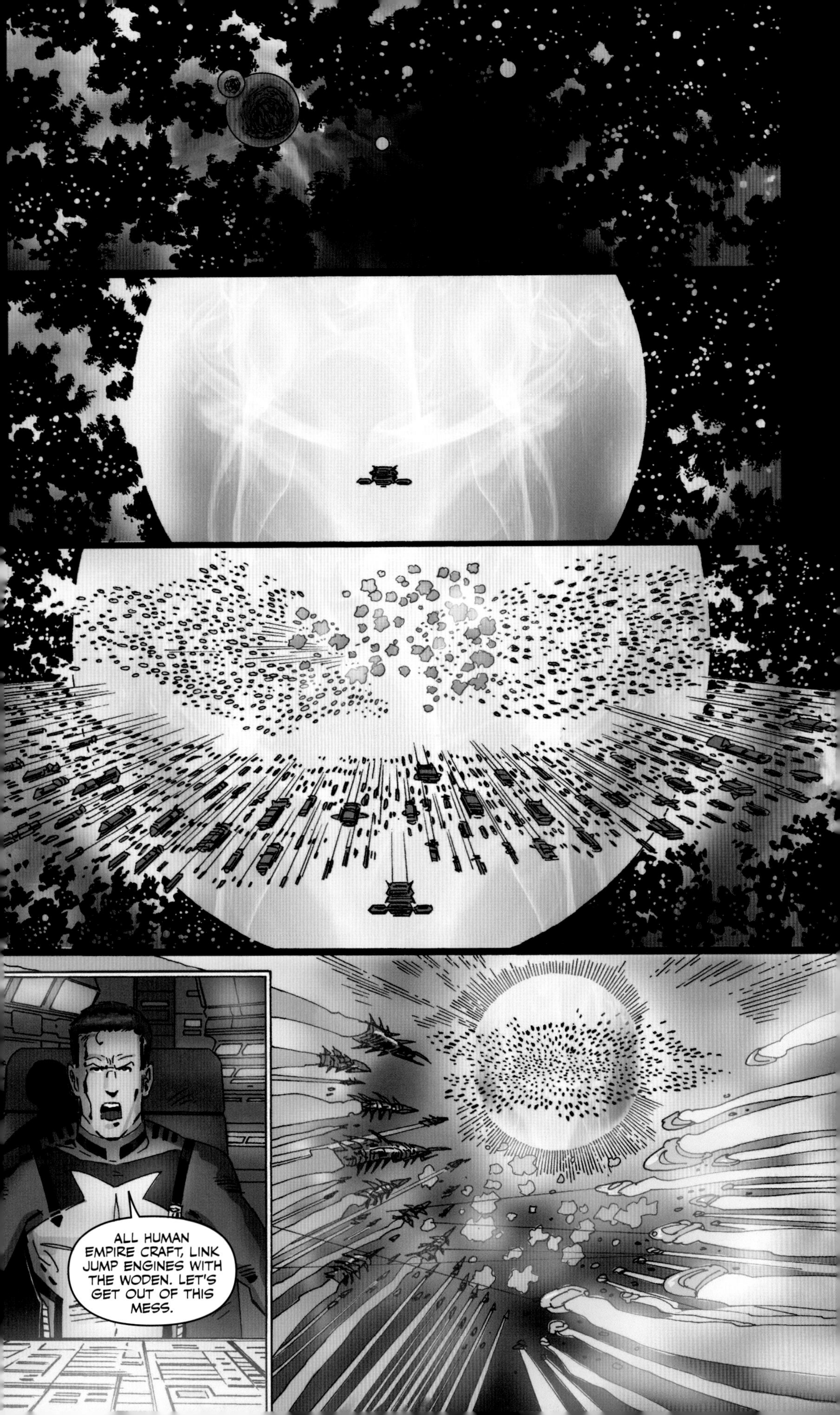
ALL HUMAN EMPIRE CRAFT, LINK JUMP ENGINES WITH THE WODEN. LET'S GET OUT OF THIS MESS.

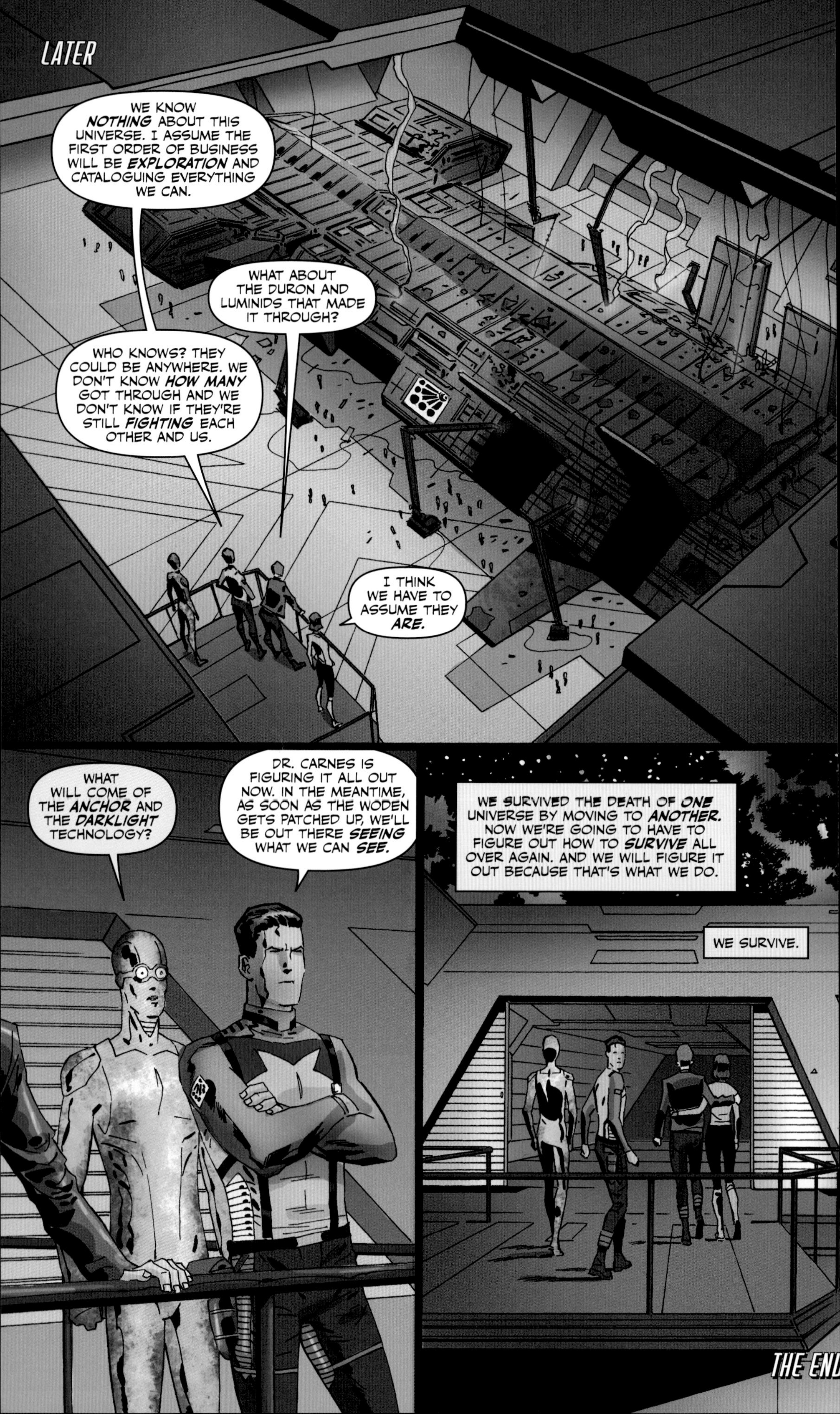
LATER
WE KNOW NOTHING ABOUT THIS UNIVERSE. I ASSUME THE FIRST ORDER OF BUSINESS WILL BE EXPLORATION AND CATALOGUING EVERYTHING WE CAN.
WHAT ABOUT THE DURON AND LUMINIDS THAT MADE IT THROUGH?
WHO KNOWS? THEY COULD BE ANYWHERE. WE DON'T KNOW HOW MANY GOT THROUGH AND WE DON'T KNOW IF THEY'RE STILL FIGHTING EACH OTHER AND US.
I THINK WE HAVE TO ASSUME THEY ARE.
WHAT WILL COME OF THE ANCHOR AND THE DARKLIGHT TECHNOLOGY?
DR. CARNES IS FIGURING IT ALL OUT NOW. IN THE MEANTIME, AS SOON AS THE WODEN GETS PATCHED UP, WE'LL BE OUT THERE SEEING WHAT WE CAN SEE.
WE SURVIVED THE DEATH OF ONE UNIVERSE BY MOVING TO ANOTHER. NOW WE'RE GOING TO HAVE TO FIGURE OUT HOW TO SURVIVE ALL OVER AGAIN. AND WE WILL FIGURE IT OUT BECAUSE THAT'S WHAT WE DO.
WE SURVIVE.

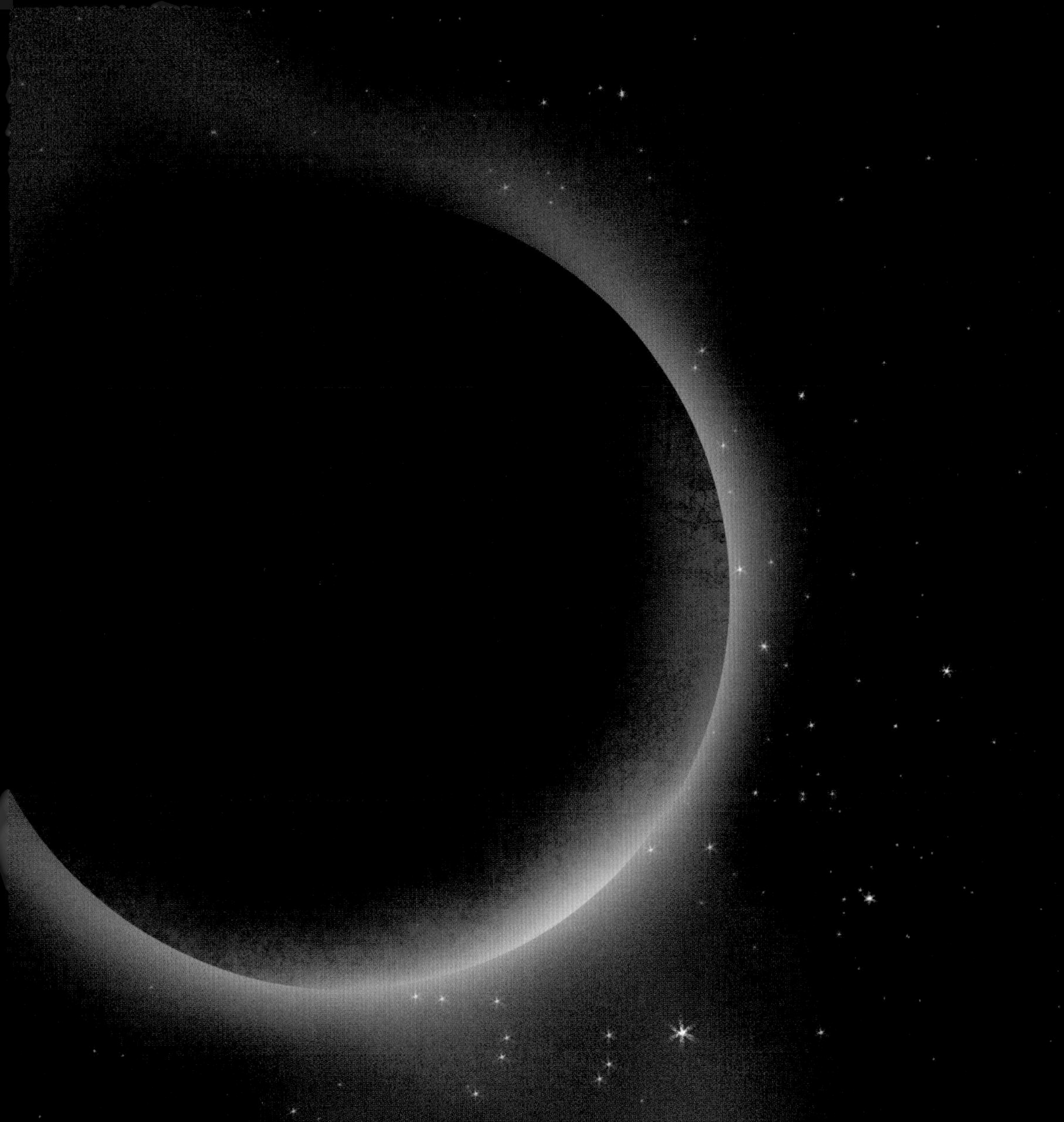

BONUS MATERIAL //

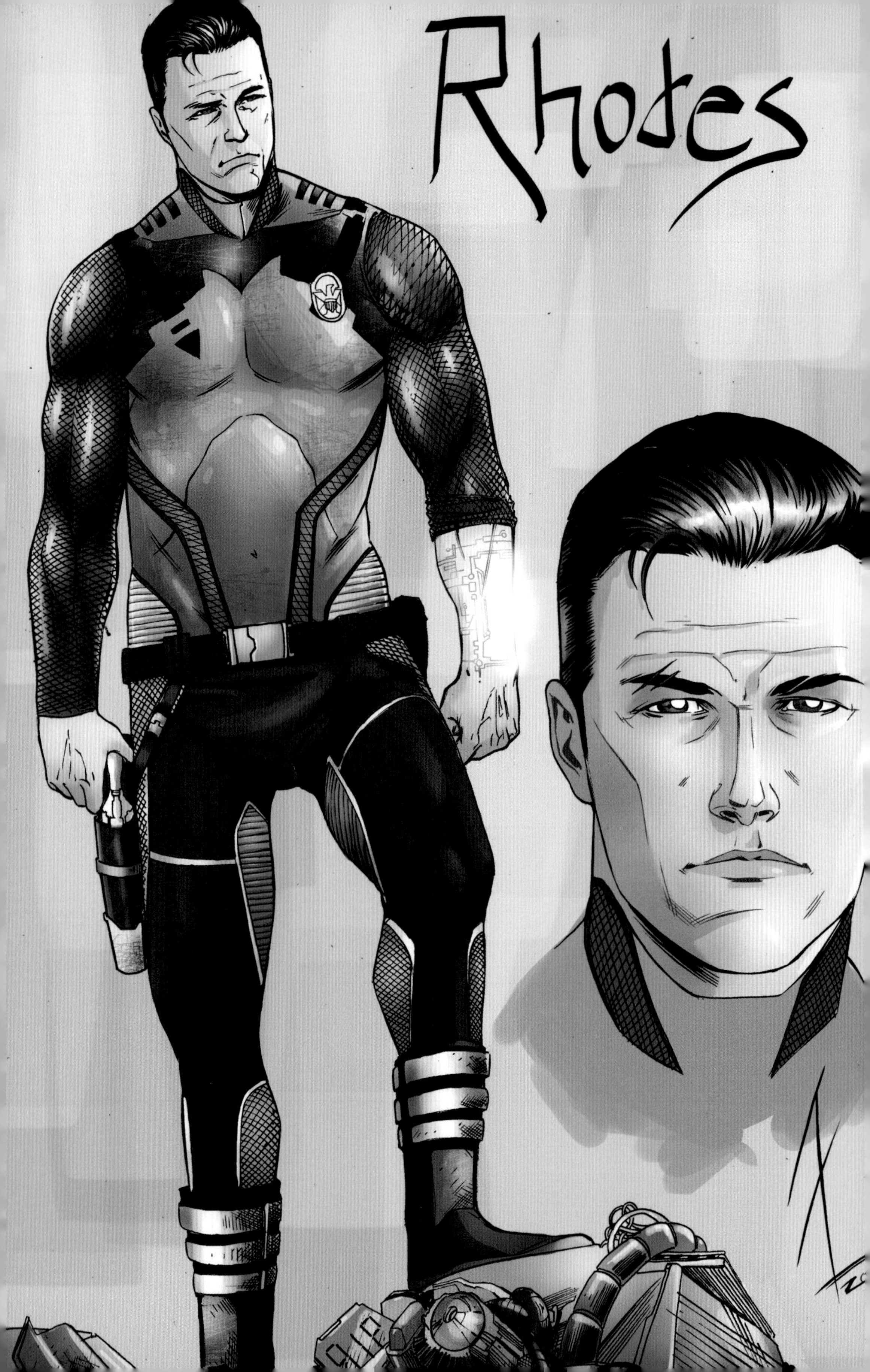
Rhodes

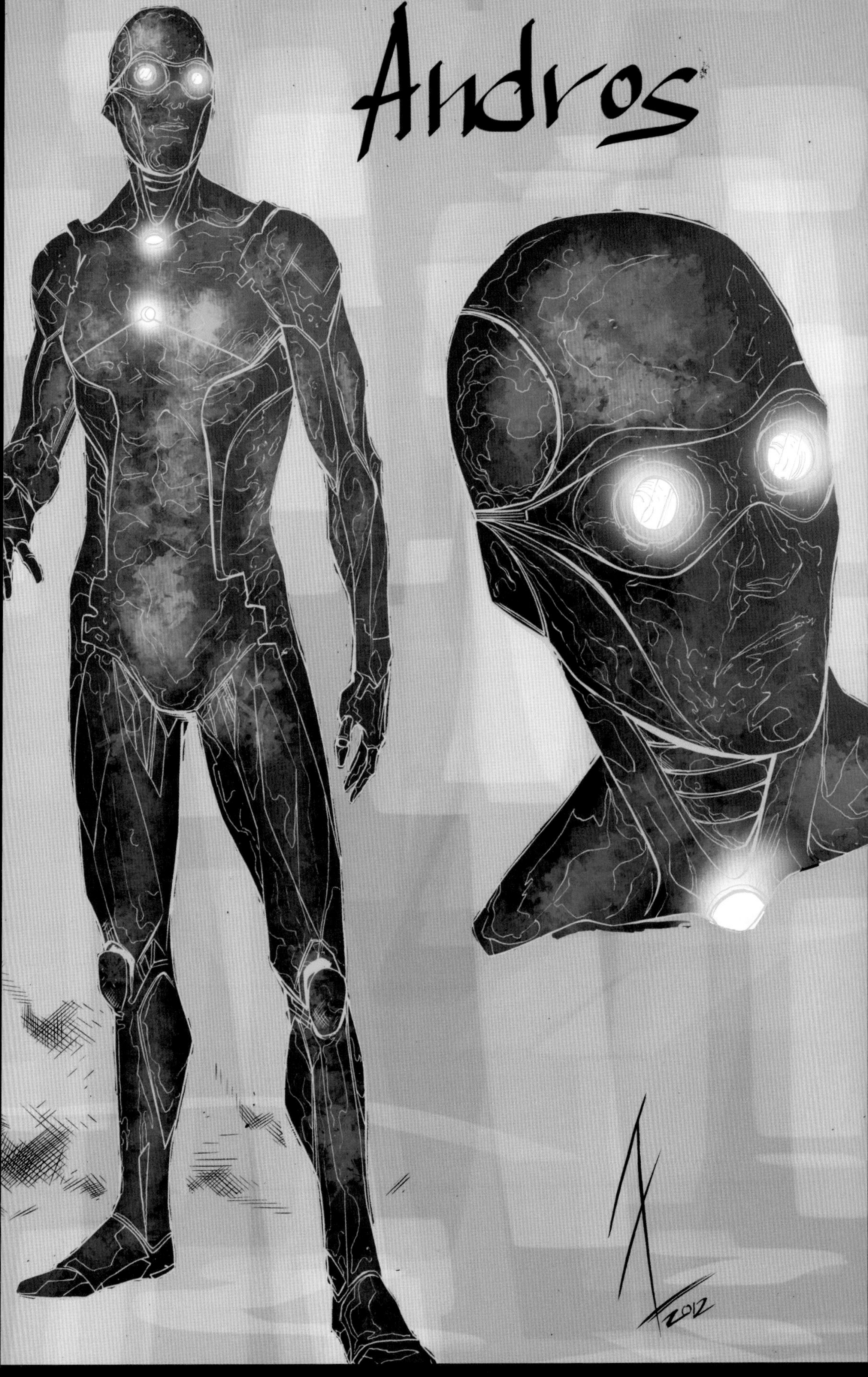
Andros
2012

CHARACTER DESIGNS BY **ALEX MASSACCI**

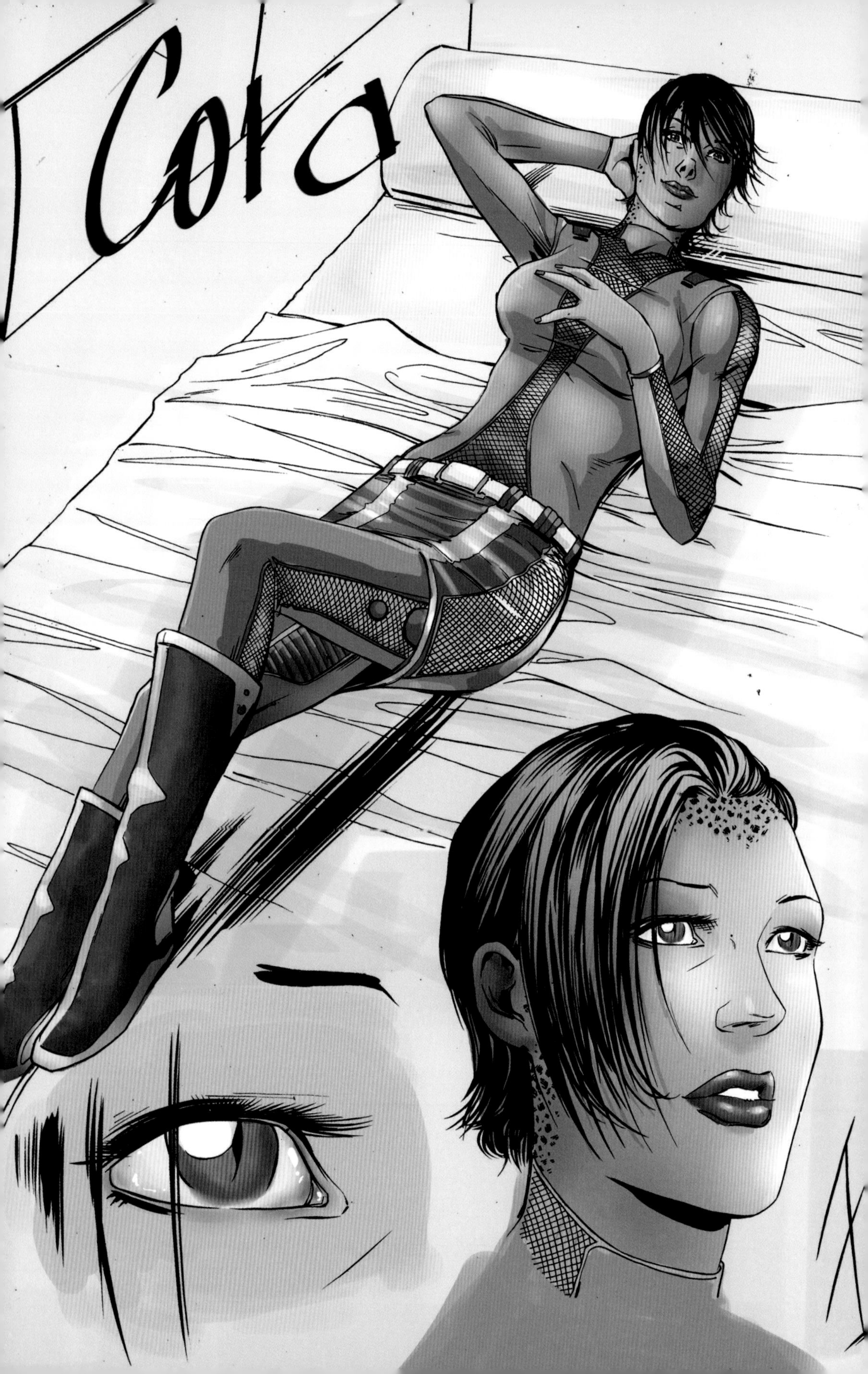
Cora

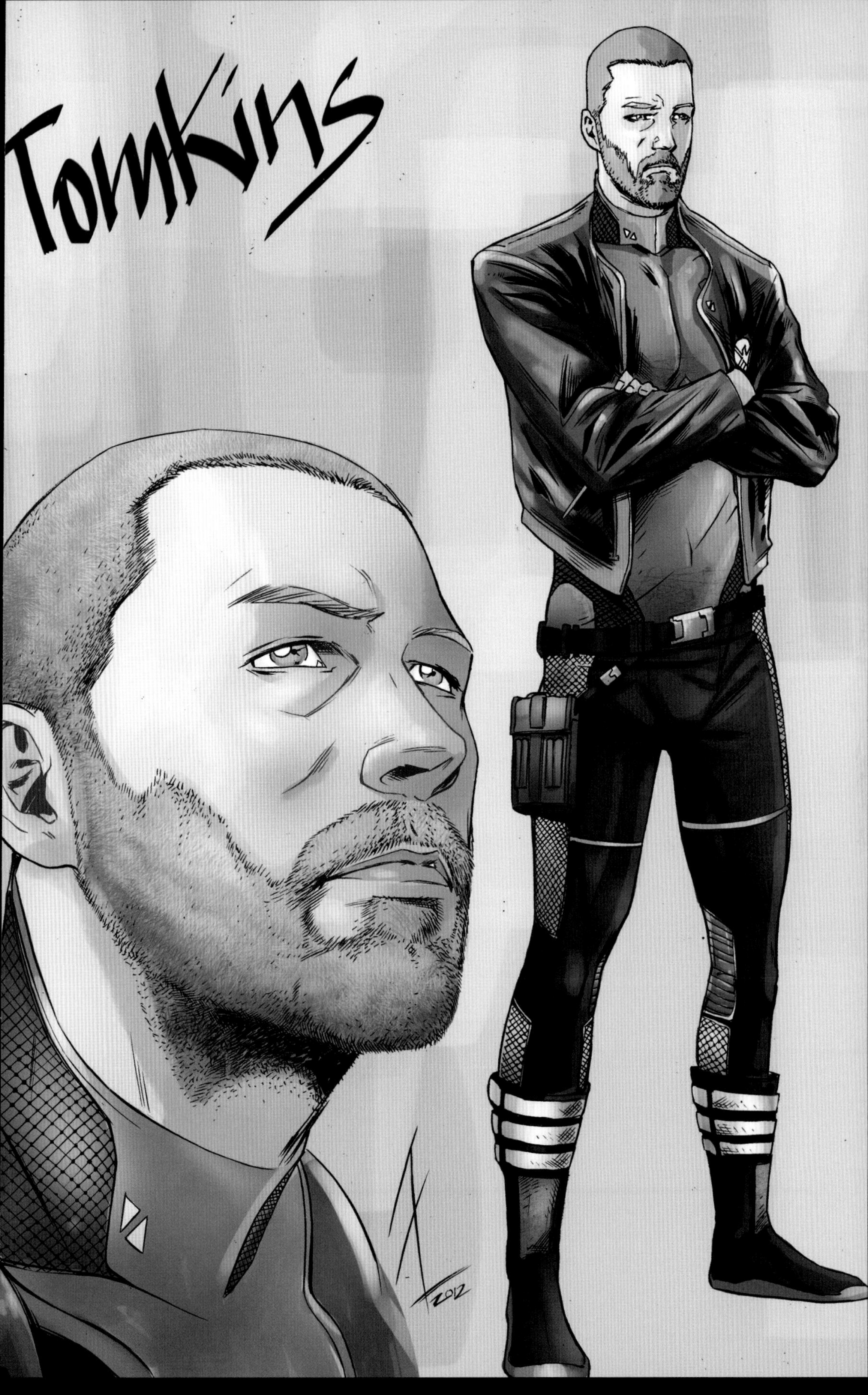
Tomkins
2012

CHARACTER DESIGNS BY **ALEX MASSACCI**

BERSERKER DESIGNS

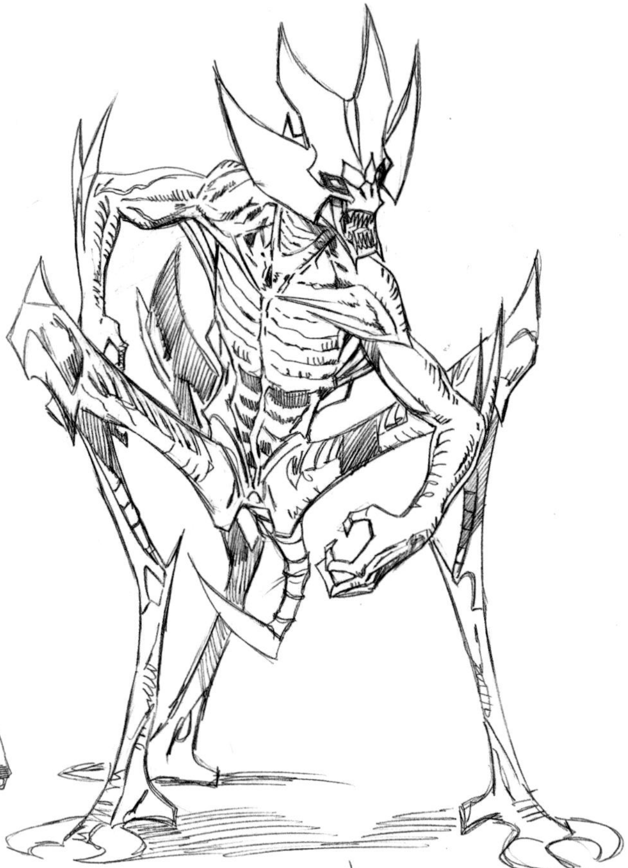

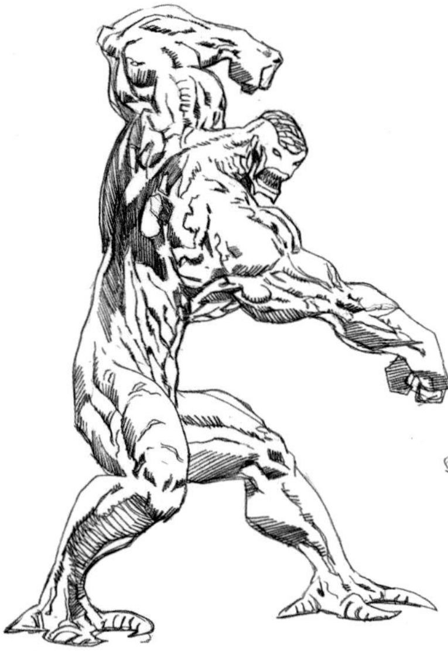

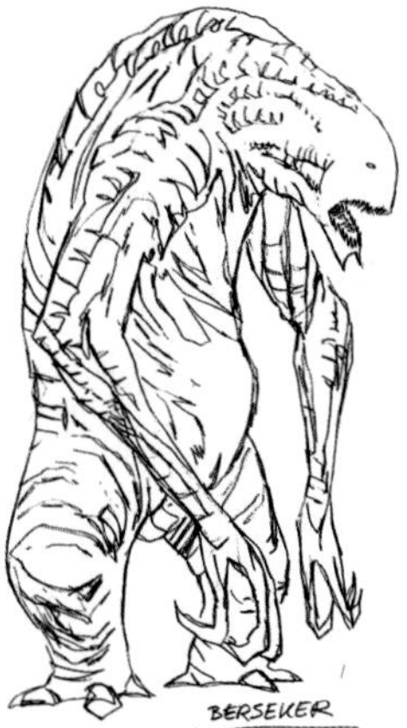
BERSEKER

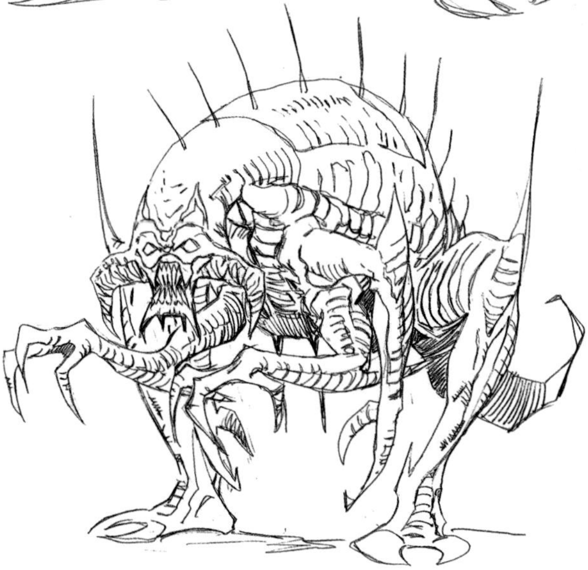

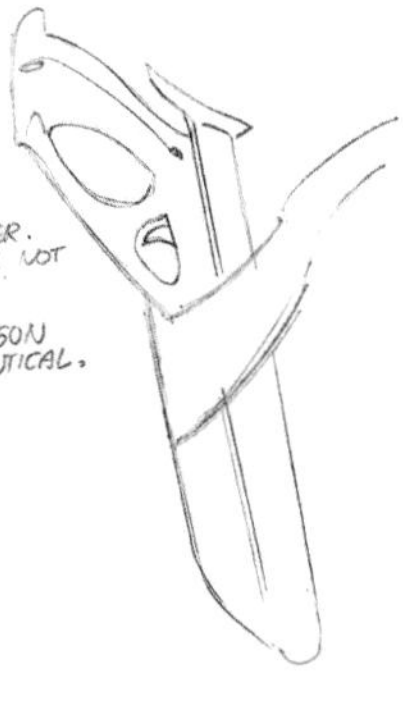
THE „GUN"
IN THE HOLSTER.
ANDROS WILL NOT
PULL IT OUT
ANYWAY.
THE SECOND GUN
CAN BE IDENTICAL.

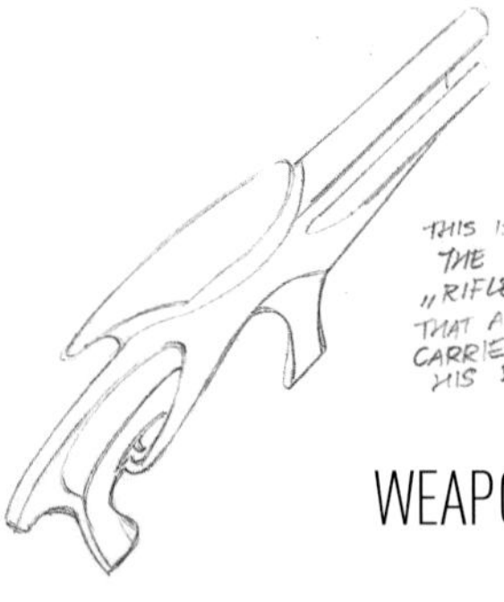
THIS IS
THE
„RIFLE"
THAT ANDROS
CARRIES ON
HIS BACK

WEAPON DESIGNS

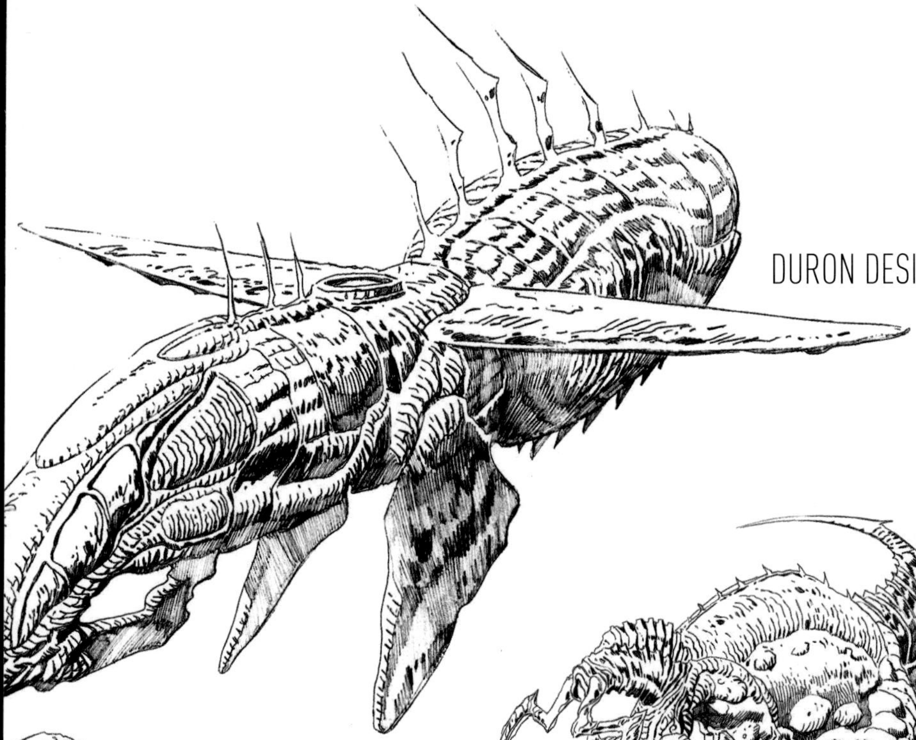

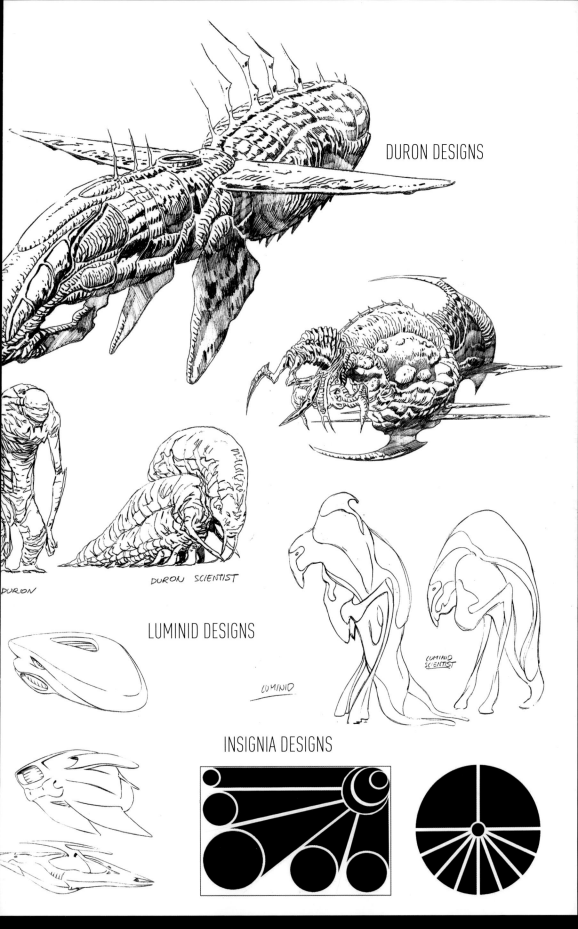

DURON DESIGNS

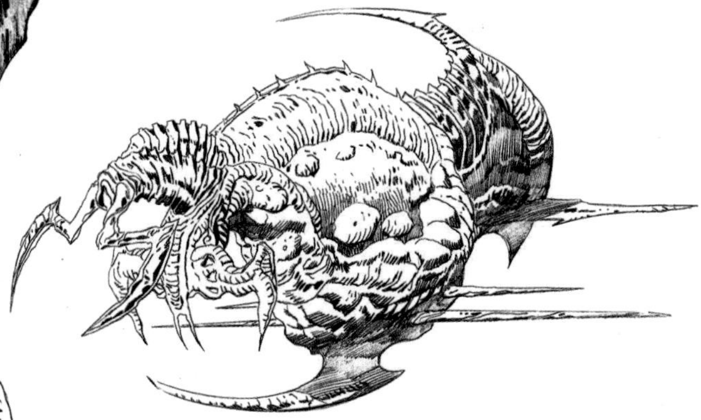

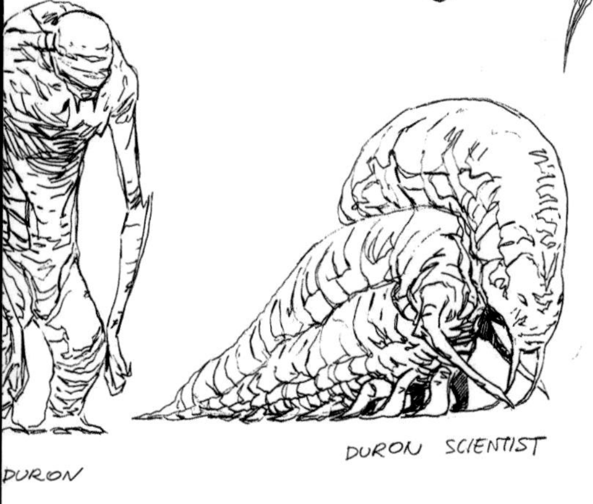
DURON SCIENTIST
DURON

LUMINID DESIGNS

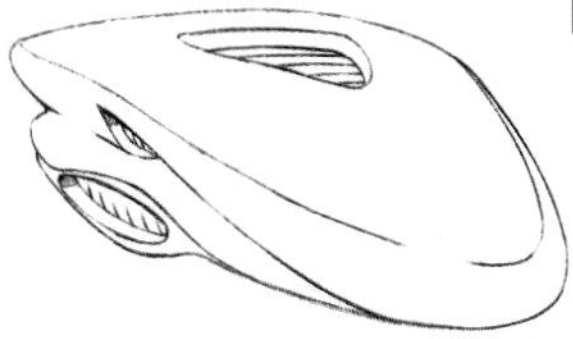

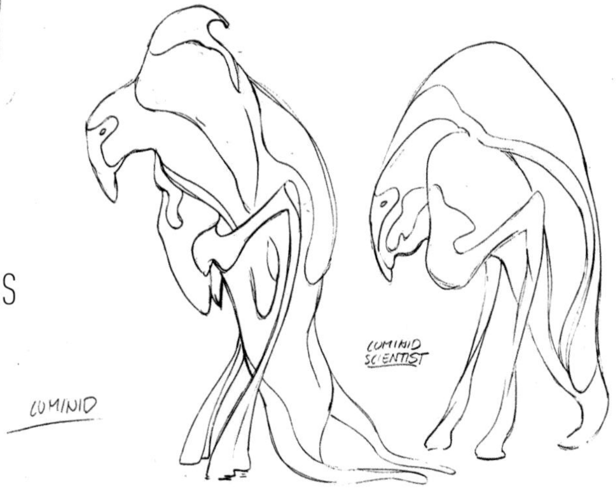
LUMINID SCIENTIST
LUMINID

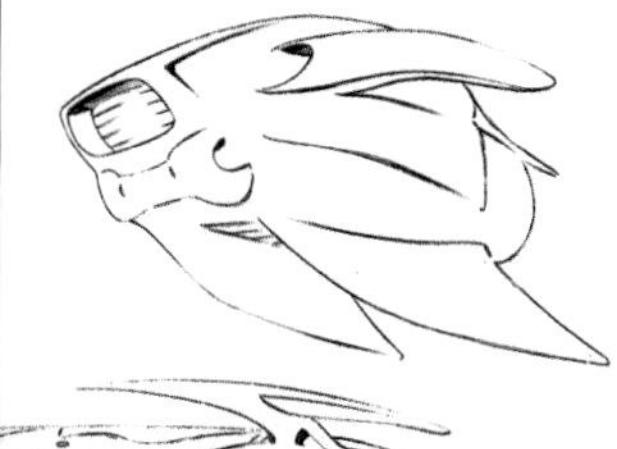

INSIGNIA DESIGNS

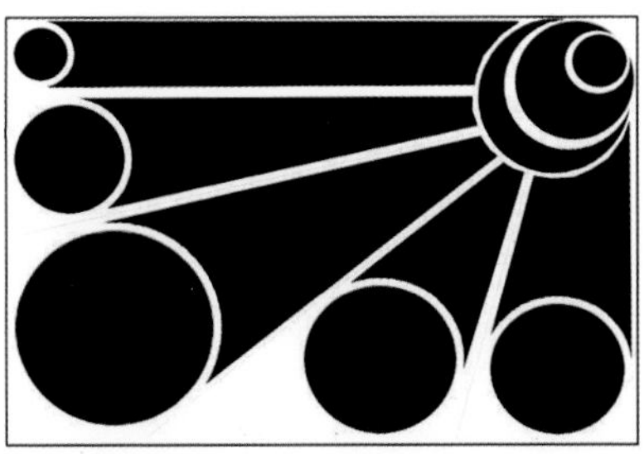

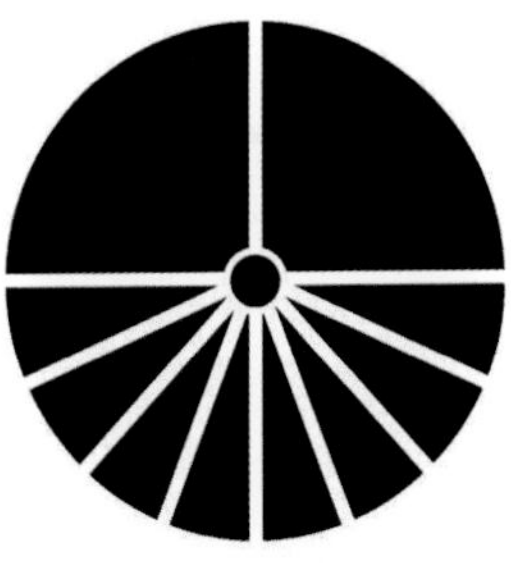

CONCEPT DESIGNS BY **PIOTR KOWALSKI**

//ABOUT THE CREATORS

Chad Kultgen is the author of four novels: *The Average American Male*; *The Lie*; *Men, Women, and Children*; and *The Average American Marriage*. He is also the greatest squirrel photographer in the world: www.instagram.com/chadkultgen.

Piotr Kowalski came from Europe where he had worked on the series *Urban Vampires*, *La Branche Lincoln*, *Dracula L'Immortel*, and many other comic books. For the American comic market, he worked on *Malignant Man*, *Sex*, and *Marvel Knights: Hulk*. He is also a big death metal fan and an amazing bass guitar player.

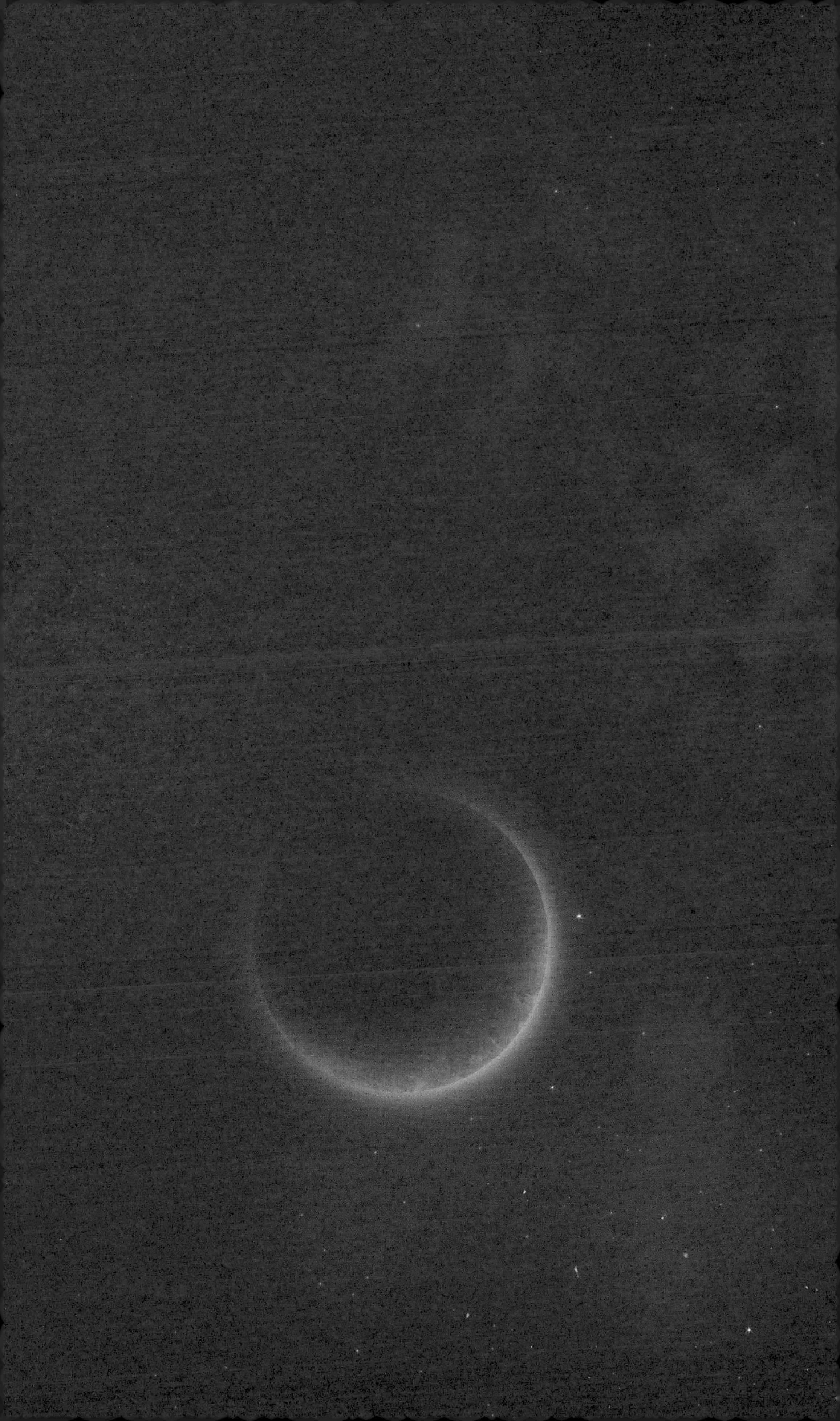